The American Journey Document Set Volume I

DERIVED FROM
RETRIEVING THE AMERICAN PAST

SIMON & SCHUSTER
CUSTOM PUBLISHING

Printed in the United States of America

10 9 8 7 6 5 4 3 2 1

ISBN 0–13–079853–3
BA 5567

SIMON & SCHUSTER CUSTOM PUBLISHING
160 Gould Street/Needham Heights, MA 02194
Simon & Schuster Education Group

CONTRIBUTORS

Senior Editors
Michael Les Benedict
Mark Grimsley
Susan M. Hartmann
Michael J. Hogan
Carla Gardina Pestana
David Stebenne
Warren R. Van Tine

Current Managing Editor
John Day Tully

Copy Editor
Ann Heiss

Contributing Editors

Kenneth J. Andrien
Michael Les Benedict
Mansel Blackford
Paul C. Bowers
Rowland Brucken
John C. Burnham
Joan E. Cashin
William R. Childs
Steven Conn
Saul Cornell
Jeanette Davis
Merton L. Dillon
Charles Coleman Finlay
Mark Grimsley
Bernard N. Grindel
Peter L. Hahn
Susan M. Hartmann
Michael J. Hogan

Bruce Karhoff
Terence Kehoe
K. Austin Kerr
Allan R. Millet
Pamela J. Mills
Margaret E. Newell
Josef Ostyn
Carla Gardina Pestana
Randolph A. Roth
John A. M. Rothney
Leila J. Rupp
Richard D. Shiels
David Sicilia
Amy L. S. Staples
David L. Stebenne
David Steigerwald
Marshall F. Stevenson, Jr.
Warren R. Van Tine

Contents

Chapter 8

A New Republic and the Rise of Parties, 1789–1800

Chapter 9

The Triumph and Collapse of Jeffersonian Republicanism, 1800–1824

Chapter 10

The Jacksonian Era, 1824–1845

Chapter 11

Industrial Change and Urbanization, 1820–1850

Worlds Apart

INTRODUCTION

Few historical figures have generated as much controversy over the last five hundred years as Christopher Columbus. For some he remains a heroic figure, advancing the frontiers of western civilization. For others his voyages are responsible for the ultimate deaths of millions of indigenous peoples and the destruction of the landscape that prevailed in the Americas before 1492. Despite the controversies surrounding his historical place in American and world history, Christopher Columbus remains an enigmatic figure. He left few documents for historians to analyze; even his journal of the first voyage was lost in the sixteenth century. From the scanty historical record, however, it seems clear that Columbus never really comprehended the consequences of his historic voyages, maintaining stubbornly to his death that he had reached Asia, not "discovered" a New World. From his return to Europe in 1493, his contemporaries also expressed widely divergent views about the man and his importance. These divisions have endured over time, so that modern historians most often speak of the multiple historical legacies of Christopher Columbus. Regardless of whether he is viewed as a hero or a villain, it is clear that his voyages began the process of global interdependency that characterizes our own modern world.

MODERN ASSESSMENTS OF CHRISTOPHER COLUMBUS

Modern scholarly works have expressed fundamental disagreements about the historical role and importance of Christopher Columbus. In most cases these differing interpretations of Columbus do not reflect new documentary discoveries about the life and times of the explorer. Instead, they tend to be influenced by the way the historical figure of Columbus fits into the scholarly and political currents of the historians' own times. This was particularly apparent in the quincentennary of the Columbian voyages in 1992, when various groups within the United States—such as Amerindians, environmentalists, Latinos, Italian Americans, and members of the scholarly community—all expressed widely divergent views about the historical legacies of the man. This has also proven true of virtually every historical period since the results of the first voyage of Columbus became public. For students of history, the "simple" construction and interpretation of the past is a very complex and difficult problem.

Christopher Columbus and the Spread of Western Civilization

Samuel Eliot Morison's biography of Christopher Columbus, published in 1942, emphasized the explorer's heroic efforts to advance western civilization. For Morison, Columbus was a daring mariner and a visionary, who served as an inspiration to a beleaguered United States during World War II and provided hope for the future. The following excerpt is taken from Samuel Eliot Morison, Admiral of the Ocean Sea: A Life of Christopher Columbus *(reprint edition, Philadelphia, 1978), 673–75.*

America would eventually have been discovered if the Great Enterprise of Columbus had been rejected; yet who can predict what would have been the outcome? The voyage that took him to "The Indies" and home was no blind chance, but the creation of his own brain and soul, long studied, carefully planned, repeatedly urged on indifferent princes, and carried through by virtue of his courage, sea-knowledge and indomitable will. No later voyage could ever have such spectacular results, and Columbus's fame would have been secure had he retired from the sea in 1493. Yet a lofty ambition to explore further, to organize the territories won for Castile, and to complete the circuit of the globe, sent him thrice more to America. These voyages, even more than the first, proved him to be the greatest navigator of his age, and enabled him to train the captains and pilots who were to display the banners of Spain off every American cape and island between Fifty North and Fifty South. The ease with which he dissipated the unknown terrors of the Ocean, the skill with which he found his way out and home, again and again, led thousands of men from every Western European nation into maritime adventure and exploration. And if Columbus was a failure as a colonial administrator, it was partly because his conception of a colony transcended the desire of his followers to impart, and the capacity of natives to receive, the institutions and culture of Renaissance Europe.

Columbus had a proud, passionate and sensitive nature that suffered deeply from the contempt to which he was early subjected, and the envy, disloyalty, ingratitude and injustice which he met as a discoverer. He wrote so freely out of the abundance of his complaint, as to give the impression that his life was more full of woe than of weal. That impression is false. As with other mariners, a month at sea healed the wounds of a year ashore, and a fair wind blew away the memory of foul weather. Command of a tall and gallant ship speeding over blue water before a fresh trade wind, shaping her course for some new and marvelous land where gold is abundant and the women are kind, is a mariner's dream of the good life. Columbus had a Hellenic sense of wonder at the new and strange, combined with an artist's appreciation of natural beauty; and his voyages to this strange new world brought him to some of the most gorgeous coastlines on the earth's surface. Moreover, Columbus had a deep conviction of the immanence, the sovereignty and the infinite wisdom of God, which transcended all his suffering, and enhanced all his triumphs. Waste no pity on the Admiral of the Ocean Sea! He enjoyed long stretches of pure delight such as only a seaman may know, and moments of high, proud exultation that only a discoverer can experience.

One only wishes that the Admiral might have been afforded the sense of fulfillment that would have come from foreseeing all that flowed from his discoveries; that would have turned all the sorrows of his last years to joy. The whole history of the Americas stems from the Four Voyages of Columbus; and as the Greek city-states looked back to the deathless gods as their founders, so today a score of independent nations and dominions unite in homage to Christopher the stout-hearted son of Genoa, who carried Christian civilization across the Ocean Sea.

What, according to Morison, are the greatest virtues of Columbus? What might explain this view?

Christopher Columbus and the Legacy of Colonial Brutality

In his classic study of the Spanish Caribbean, Carl Ortwin Sauer presents a very different image of Christopher Columbus than Morison's. For Sauer, Columbus was a romantic self-promoter, who never truly understood the significance of his discoveries. Moreover, he proved a poor leader and a ruthless administrator; his lust for profits led him to promote a legacy of exploitation and brutality that characterized much of the early European expansion into the New World. The following passage is taken from Carl Ortwin Sauer, The Early Spanish Main *(Berkeley, 1966), 290–91, 104, 291.*

Columbus had a genius for words, not as to their proper meaning but to cast a spell and to persuade. Soon after getting to Haiti he decided to name it "the Spanish Isle." One of its valleys earliest seen became the Valle del Paraiso. Other parts were likened to the fairest parts of Andalusia in spring. The silvery cloud-capped crest of a northern ridge gave name to Puerto Plata. The outlet of the Gulf of Paria was the Dragon's Mouth. Carib islands took the name of the shrines of Guadelupe and Montserrat. The romantic publicity he gave to the new lands above all was to portray them as lands of infinite gold. All the fabled gold lands of antiquity were relocated in his discoveries or in parts he was about to discover. Columbus was looking for gold mines from the first landing on a coral island to his last days in Veragua. It did not matter that his success was slight. Always and everywhere there was vast promise of gold. The sovereigns and people of Spain became imbued by his obsession, picturesquely and fantastically presented. The course of Spanish empire was first turned to its fateful search for gold by the *idée fixe* that dominated Columbus. . . .

The seven years of Columbus' government were a continuing and growing series of disappointments and deficits. The extravagant prospectuses of promised wealth went on but revenues did not materialize. When gold was not forthcoming, Columbus attributed it to a temporary withholding of divine favor and would bridge the interval by the easy and sure profits of dyewood and slaves, for which he presented wholly imaginary figures. As he continued to hold to an illusory geography undisturbed by every evidence that he was wrong, so he invented riches that did not exist. It was well apparent that he was a chronic, compulsive romancer who lived in a world of wishful thinking.

Nor did Columbus know how to govern men. He failed signally in getting men to follow him faithfully. . . . There had been no time of peace and goodwill. . . . Columbus lacked ability and inclination to adapt himself and to learn from changing circumstances. He had secured an excessive title to which he clung. These were his Indies over which his rule would be absolute and which he would pass on to his heirs. . . .

What could explain the dramatic difference between the views of Morison and Sauer concerning the character and achievement of Columbus?

COLUMBUS'S LEGACY IN THE DOCUMENTARY RECORD

The only original documentary record of the first voyage is the 1493 letter of Columbus, but this document has its limitations. It reads like an advertising brochure designed to encourage future investments in a second voyage of Columbus to the New World.

The remaining documents in this collection deal with the wide impact of the Columbian voyages on the course of world history. Nevertheless, they too contain exaggerations, reflecting the biases of their authors and the limited abilities of contemporaries to understand the magnitude of the changes affecting their lives.

The Letter of Columbus to Ferdinand and Isabel

The following excerpt from the letter of Christopher Columbus to King Ferdinand and Queen Isabel was undoubtedly intended to publicize the successes of the first voyage. The size and potential richness of the islands are apparently exaggerated to impress the monarchs (and any other potential investors) and generate support for any future voyages by

7

Columbus. Although he scarcely refers to the Caribs, Columbus does emphasize the exotic qualities of the newly discovered lands, particularly the nudity of the inhabitants. Apart from illustrating the "primitive" social system of the native peoples, these references were probably also meant to evoke (in the reading audience) an image of the biblical Garden of Eden. This copy of the letter may be found in The Journal of Christopher Columbus, *191, 194, 196–98, 200–201.*

SIR: Since I know that you will be pleased at the great victory with which Our Lord has crowned my voyage, I write this to you, from which you will learn how in thirty-three days I passed from the Canary Islands to the Indies, with the fleet which the most illustrious King and Queen, our Sovereigns, gave to me. There I found very many islands, filled with innumerable people, and I have taken possession of them all for their Highnesses, done by proclamation and with the royal standard unfurled, and no opposition was offered to me.

To the first island which I found I gave the name "San Salvador," in remembrance of the Divine Majesty, Who had marvellously bestowed all this; the Indians call it "Guanahani." To the second, I gave the name the island of "Santa Maria de Concepcion," to the third, "Fernandina," to the fourth, "Isabella," to the fifth island, "Juana," and so each received from me a new name. . . .

Española is a marvel. The sierras and the mountains, the plains, the champaigns, are so lovely and so rich for planting and sowing, for breeding cattle of every kind, for building towns and villages. The harbours of the sea here are such as cannot be believed to exist unless they have been seen, and so with the rivers, many and great, and of good water, the majority of which contain gold. In the trees, fruits and plants, there is a great difference from those of Juana. In this island, there are many spices and great mines of gold and of other metals.

The people of this island and of all the other islands which I have found and of which I have information, all go naked, men and women, as their mothers bore them, although some of the women cover a single place with the leaf of a plant or with a net of cotton which they make for the purpose. They have no iron or steel or weapons, nor are they fitted to use them. This is not because they are not well built and of handsome stature, but because they are very marvellously timorous. They have no other arms than spears made of canes, cut in seeding time, to the ends of which they fix a small sharpened stick. Of these they do not dare to make use, for many times it has happened that I have sent ashore two or three men to some town to have speech with them, and countless people have come out to them, and as soon as they have seen my men approaching, they have fled, a father not even waiting for his son. This is not because ill has been done to any one of them; on the contrary, at every place where I have been and have been able to have speech with them, I have given to them of that which I had, such as cloth and many other things, receiving nothing in exchange. But so they are, incurably timid. It is true that, after they have been reassured and have lost this fear, they are so guileless and so generous with all that they possess, that no one would believe it who has not seen it. They refuse nothing that they possess, if it be asked of them; on the contrary, they invite any one to share it and display as much love as if they would give their hearts. They are content with whatever trifle of whatever kind that may be given to them, whether it be of value or valueless. I forbade that they should be given things so worthless as fragments of broken crockery, scraps of broken glass and lace tips, although when they were able to get them, they fancied that they possessed the best jewel in the world. So it was found that for a thong a sailor received gold to the weight of two and a half castellanos, and others received much more for other things which were worth less. As for new blancas, for them they would give everything which they had, although it might be two or three castellanos' [gold coins] weight of gold or an arroba or two of spun cotton. They took even the pieces of the broken hoops of the wine barrels and, like savages, gave what they had, so that it seemed to me to be wrong and I forbade it. I gave them a thousand handsome good things, which I had brought, in order that they might conceive affection for us and, more than that, might become Christians and be inclined to the love and service of Your Highnesses and of the whole Castilian nation, and strive to collect and give us of the things which they have in abundance and which are necessary to us.

They do not hold any creed nor are they idolaters; but they all believe that power and good are in the heavens and were very firmly convinced that I, with these ships and men, came from the heavens, and in this belief they everywhere received me after they had mastered their fear. This belief is not the result of ignorance, for they are, on the contrary, of a very acute intelligence and they are men who navigate all those seas, so that it is amazing how good an account they give of everything. It is because they have never seen people clothed or ships of such a kind.

As soon as I arrived in the Indies, in the first island which I found, I took some of the natives by force, in order that they might learn and might give me information of whatever there is in these parts. And so it was that they soon understood us, and we them, either by speech or signs, and they have been very serviceable. At present, those I bring with me are still of the opinion that I come from Heaven, for all the intercourse which they have had with me. They were the first to announce this wherever I went, and the others went running from house to house, and to the neighbouring towns, with loud cries of, "Come! Come! See the men from Heaven!" So all came, men and women alike, when their minds were set at rest concerning us, not one, small or great, remaining behind, and they all brought something to eat and drink, which they gave with extraordinary affection. . . .

In all these islands, I saw no great diversity in the appearance of the people or in their manners and language. On the contrary, they all understand one another, which is a very curious thing, on account of which I hope that their Highnesses will determine upon their conversion to our holy faith, towards which they are very inclined.

I have already said how I went one hundred and seven leagues in a straight line from west to east along the seashore of the island of Juana, and as a result of this voyage I can say that this island is larger than England and Scotland together, for, beyond these one hundred and seven leagues, there remain to the west-ward two provinces to which I have not gone. One of these provinces they call "Avan," and there people are born with tails. These provinces cannot have a length of less than fifty or sixty leagues, as I could understand from those Indians whom I have and who know all the islands.

The other island, Española, has a circumference greater than all Spain from Collioure by the seacoast to Fuenterabia in Vizcaya, for I voyaged along one side for one hundred and eighty-eight great leagues in a straight line from west to east. It is a land to be desired and, when seen, never to be left. I have taken possession of all for their Highnesses, and all are more richly endowed than I know how or am able to say, and I hold all for their Highnesses, so that they may dispose of them as they do of the kingdoms of Castile and as absolutely. But especially, in this Española, in the situation most convenient and in the best position for the mines of gold and for all trade as well with the mainland here as with that there, belonging to the Grand Khan, where will be great trade and profit, I have taken possession of a large town, to which I gave the name "Villa de Navidad," and in it I have made fortifications and a fort, which will now by this time be entirely completed. In it I have left enough men for such a purpose with arms and artillery and provisions for more than a year, and a fusta, and one, a master of all seacraft, to build others, and I have established great friendship with the king of that land, so much so, that he was proud to call me "brother" and to treat me as such. . . .

In conclusion, to speak only of what has been accomplished on this voyage, which was so hasty, their Highnesses can see that I will give them as much gold as they may need, if their Highnesses will render me very slight assistance; presently, I will give them spices and cotton, as much as their Highnesses shall command; and mastic, as much as they shall order to be shipped and which, up to now, has been found only in Greece, in the island of Chios, and the Seignory sells it for what it pleases; and aloe, as much as they shall order to be shipped; and slaves, as many as they shall order, and who will be from the idolaters. I believe also that I have found rhubarb and cinnamon, and I shall find a thousand other things of value, which the people whom I have left there will have discovered, for I have not delayed at any point, so far as the wind allowed me to sail, except in the town of Navidad, in order to leave it secured and well established, and in truth I should have done much more if the ships had served me as reason demanded. . . .

This is an account of the facts, thus abridged.

Done in the caravel, off the Canary Islands, on the fifteenth day of February, in the year one thousand four hundred and ninety-three.

How could Columbus reconcile his view of the native peoples with his stated intention of taking their gold and enslaving them?

11

The Amerindians and the "Garden of Eden"

The attempt to picture the Amerindians as an innocent and childlike race, so apparent in the Columbus letter, was a common theme in the sixteenth century. Members of the clergy often used this image to prove that the indigenous peoples were "real" human beings (rather than some form of savage animals), to protect them from exploitation from the settlers, and also to gain control over their conversion to Christianity from rival clerical or lay organizations. The following passage is filled with language meant to evoke an image of the Garden of Eden, not the realities of Amerindian life in the Americas. The passage is taken from Bartolomé de las Casas, Very Brief Account of the Destruction of the Indies, *trans. Francis Augustus MacNutt in* Bartholomew De Las Casas: His Life, His Apostolate, and His Writings *(New York, 1909), 314–15.*

God has created all these numberless people to be quite the simplest, without malice or duplicity, most obedient, most faithful to their natural Lords, and to the Christians, whom they serve; the most humble, most patient, most peaceful, and calm, without strife nor tumults; not wrangling, nor querulous, as free from uproar, hate and desire of revenge, as any in the world.

They are likewise the most delicate people, weak and of feeble constitution, and less than any other can they bear fatigue, and they very easily die of whatsoever infirmity; so much so, that not even the sons of our Princes and of nobles, brought up in royal and gentle life, are more delicate than they; although there are among them such as are of the peasant class. They are also a very poor people, who of worldly goods possess little, nor wish to possess: and they are therefore neither proud, nor ambitious, nor avaricious. . . .

They are likewise of a clean, unspoiled, and vivacious intellect, very capable, and receptive to every good doctrine; most prompt to accept our Holy Catholic Faith, to be endowed with virtuous customs; and they have as little difficulty with such things as any people created by God in the world.

Once they have begun to learn of matters pertaining to faith, they are so importunate to know them, and in frequenting the sacraments and divine service of the Church, that to tell the truth, the clergy have need to be endowed of God with the gift of pre-eminent patience to bear with them: and finally, I have heard many lay Spaniards frequently say many years ago, (unable to deny the goodness of those they saw) certainly these people were the most blessed of the earth, had they only knowledge of God.

The "Sins" of the Spanish Invasion

Militant friars like Las Casas and many of his fellow Dominicans also tried to picture the Spanish conquistadors and settlers as vicious and cruel exploiters. These tales had some basis in reality, but they were also aimed at convincing a European audience that the excesses of the conquest had to be curbed and the powers of the crown and the clergy expanded in the New World. Along with the images of the indigenous peoples as innocents reminiscent of the Garden of Eden, they created a powerful picture of European excesses. According to many friars, these abuses undermined the chances for salvation of all Christians who tolerated such "sins" against humanity. The selection below is taken from Bartolomé de las Casas, Very Brief Account of the Destruction of the Indies, *trans. Francis Augustus MacNutt in* Bartholomew De Las Casas, 319–20.

The Christians, with their horses and swords and lances, began to slaughter and practise strange cruelty among them. They penetrated into the country and spared neither children nor the aged, nor pregnant women, nor those in child labour, all of whom they ran through the body and lacerated, as though they were assaulting so many lambs herded in their sheepfold.

They made bets as to who would slit a man in two, or cut off his head at one blow: or they opened up his bowels. They tore the babes from their mothers' breast by the feet, and dashed their heads against the rocks. Others they seized by the shoulders and threw into the rivers, laughing and joking, and when they fell into the water they exclaimed: "boil body of so and so!" They spitted the bodies of other babes, together with their mothers and all who were before them, on their swords.

They made a gallows just high enough for the feet to nearly touch the ground, and by thirteens, in honour and reverence of our Redeemer and the twelve Apostles, they put wood underneath and, with fire, they burned the Indians alive. . . .

And because all the people who could flee, hid among the mountains and climbed the crags to escape from men so deprived of humanity, so wicked, such wild beasts, exterminators and capital enemies of all the human race, the Spaniards taught and trained the fiercest boar-hounds to tear an Indian to pieces as soon as they saw him, so that they more willingly attacked and ate one, than if he had been a boar. These hounds made great havoc and slaughter.

What are the similarities between Columbus's view of the natives and that of Las Casas? What explains the dramatic difference in how they then sought to treat the natives?

The Columbian Exchange

The first European explorers and settlers were often astounded by the rich and diverse plant and animal life, much of it unknown to them. Indeed, the concept of the Americas as a "New World" stemmed in part from the very different natural environment. As the passage below catalogs, the Americas had rich supplies of plant and animal life, which enriched the food supply of many parts of the world after 1492. Before the Columbian voyages, for example, Ireland had no potatoes, and commodities like corn or chocolate were unknown outside of the Western Hemisphere. Even the coca leaf was a traditional Andean crop. This passage is taken from José de Acosta, Historia natural y moral de las Indias *(Mexico City, 1940), in* Latin American Civilization: History and Society, 1492 to the Present, *ed. Benjamin Keen, 4th ed. (Boulder, 1986), 76–79.*

The Indians have their own words to signify bread, which in Peru is called *tanta* and in other parts is given other names. But the quality and substance of the bread the Indians use is very different from ours, for they have no kind of wheat, barley, millet, panic grass, or any grain such as is used in Europe to make bread. Instead they have other kinds of grains and roots, among which maize, called Indian wheat in Castile and Turkey grain in Italy, holds the first place. . . .

Maize is the Indian bread, and they commonly eat it boiled in the grain, hot, when it is called *mote* . . . ; sometimes they eat it toasted. There is a large and round maize, like that of the Lucanas, which the Spaniards eat as a delicacy; it has better flavor than toasted chickpeas. There is another and more pleasing way of preparing it, which consists in grinding the maize and making the flour into pancakes, which are put on the fire and later placed on the table and eaten piping hot; in some places they call them *arepas*. . . .

Maize is used by the Indians to make not only their bread but also their wine; from it they make beverages which produce drunkenness more quickly than wine made of grapes. They make this maize wine in various ways, calling it *azua* in Peru and more generally throughout the Indies *chicha*. The strongest sort is made like beer, steeping the grains of maize until they begin to break, after which they boil the juice in a certain way, which makes it so strong that a few drinks will produce intoxication. . . .

The cacao tree is most esteemed in Mexico and coca is favored in Peru; both trees are surrounded with considerable superstition. Cacao is a bean smaller and fattier than the almond, and when roasted has not a bad flavor. It is so much esteemed by the Indians, and even by the Spaniards, that it is the object of one of the richest and largest lines of trade of New Spain; since it is a dry fruit, and one that keeps a long time without spoiling, they send whole ships loaded with it from the province of Guatemala. Last year an English corsair burned in the port of Guatulco, in New Spain, more than one hundred thousand *cargas* of cacao. They also use it as money, for five cacao beans will buy one thing, thirty another, and one hundred still another, and no objections are made to its use. They also use it as alms to give to the poor.

The chief use of this cacao is to make a drink that they call chocolate, which they greatly cherish in that country. But those who have not formed a taste for it dislike it, for it has a froth at the

Selections by José de Acosta, reprinted from *Latin American Civilization: History and Society, 1492 to the Present,* Fourth Edition, Benjamin Keen, editor, translator. Copyright © 1986 by WestviewPress. Reprinted by permission of WestviewPress.

top and an effervescence like that formed in wine by dregs, so that one must really have great faith in it to tolerate it. In fine, it is the favorite drink of Indians and Spaniards alike, and they regale visitors to their country with it; the Spanish women of that land are particularly fond of the dark chocolate. They prepare it in various ways: hot, cold, and lukewarm. They usually put spices and much chili in it; they also make a paste of it, and they say that it is good for the chest and the stomach, and also for colds. Be that as it may, those who have not formed a taste for it do not like it. . . .

The cacao does not grow in Peru; instead they have the coca, which is surrounded with even greater superstition and really seems fabulous. In Potosí alone the commerce in coca amounts to more than 5,000,000 pesos, with a consumption of from 90 to 100,000 hampers, and in the year 1583 it was 100,000. . . . This coca that they so greatly cherish is a little green leaf which grows upon shrubs about one *estado* high. . . . It is commonly brought from the Andes, from valleys of insufferable heat, where it rains the greater part of the year, and it costs the Indians much labor and takes many lives, for they must leave their highlands and cold climates in order to cultivate it and carry it away. . . .

The Indians prize it beyond measure, and in the time of the Inca kings plebeians were forbidden to use coca without the permission of the Inca or his governor. Their custom is to hold it in their mouths, chewing and sucking it; they do not swallow it; they say that it gives them great strength and is a great comfort to them. Many serious men say that this is pure superstition and imagination. To tell the truth, I do not think so; I believe that it really does lend strength and endurance to the Indians, for one sees effects that cannot be attributed to imagination, such as their ability to journey two whole days on a handful of coca, eating nothing else, and similar feats.

What similarities between European and native cultures are revealed in this reading?

Transplantation, 1600–1685

INTRODUCTION

Puritans suffer from a bad reputation. Since the early twentieth century when American social critic H. L. Mencken ridiculed the first English settlers in New England, the word "puritan" conjures up images of sexual prudery, censoriousness, and hypocrisy. Although American school children are told that the Puritans came to America to establish religious freedom, as adults we learn that they in fact repressed dissent. Not only that, they limited political participation to (adult male) church members, even though admission to the church was by no means automatic. Many college students learning anew about early New England history wonder: Why would anyone be a Puritan?

The English men and women who migrated to New England between 1630 and 1642 to settle the Massachusetts Bay Colony would probably not be surprised that they have an unflattering image. By the time they left England they were accustomed to being ridiculed. In part they departed because they were committed to a religious movement that was increasingly coming under attack. In their view, the Church of England (established by Henry VIII in 1534) ought to participate more fully in the Protestant Reformation that had converted many on the European continent. Their criticisms of religious practices and social mores had ceased to be tolerated in the years leading up to their exodus, and Archbishop William Laud was intent on suppressing their movement. Financial hardships and religious woes combined to persuade over thirteen thousand people to leave the island of their birth to travel to northern North America in the dozen years after 1629.

They carried on—in spite of the travails they experienced— because they believed that God required it of them. To understand

18

the Puritans, we must think about that conviction and the meaning that it gave to their lives. Many women and men braved first the displeasure of the English authorities and then the dangers of colonization because of their belief that they were fulfilling God's will. Early New England residents embraced the faith that we call "Puritan" out of the sense of personal commitment to reformed Protestantism. Theologically, they generally followed the teachings of John Calvin, a leading Protestant reformer of the previous century. The Puritans' church organization has been described as "non-separating congregationalism." Congregationalists rejected the ecclesiastical hierarchy of the Church of England (with its bishops, like their old nemesis Archbishop Laud, and its system of courts); they believed that the individual congregation should be autonomous, with the power to call a minister and to admit and discipline members. They earned the appellation "non-separating" because—unlike the separatists ("Pilgrims") who settled Plymouth—they refused to renounce their affiliation with the Anglican church, claiming that they wished to work for its reformation from within. Although we may find it difficult to comprehend their beliefs and the depth of their convictions, we must understand the Puritans as people dedicated to a cause. This cause guided them to New England in the first place and led them to create a unique society once they arrived. Their commitment to their cause was their reason for being Puritans.

RELIGION IN EARLY NEW ENGLAND:
FROM PERSONAL PIETY TO
SOCIAL FORCE

The selections that follow have been drawn from a massive literature on early New England. They attempt to convey something of the appeal that this religious faith held for the men and women who embraced it. Like all religions, Puritanism provided meaning and offered comfort, as some of these readings suggest. In addition, Puritanism shaped basic social attitudes and, hence, colonial New England society. As you read, you may conclude that a number of the accusations against the Puritans had some grounding in reality—for instance, they did police one another's behavior; but notice, too, how they thought about what they were doing. Do you consider them hypocritical and repressed after reading these selections?

Lay Puritans Form a Police Force

No scholar has done more to make the Puritans comprehensible to the modern reader than Edmund S. Morgan. In his biography of early Massachusetts governor John Winthrop (1588–1649), Morgan discusses sin and temptation as social problems for Puritans like Winthrop. This selection gives a sense of how the community viewed its obligation to monitor the activities of its members. Think about the charge of hypocrisy as you read Morgan's sympathetic account. Excerpted from Edmund S. Morgan, The Puritan Dilemma: The Story of John Winthrop, (New York, 1958), 69, 71.

To PLEASE God the Puritans demanded of themselves a standard of behavior not far different from that required by most modern codes of morality. They did not think it necessary to be either prudes or prohibitionists. They did not dress in drab clothes or live in drab houses or speak in drab words. The people who appear in the pages of Winthrop's journal, the good men and women who showered him with venison and partridges and fat hogs to celebrate Margaret's arrival [i.e., Margaret Tyndal Winthrop, John's third wife], the boys and girls who skipped rope on the decks of the *Arbella*, the men who built ships and caught fish and planted corn were all human enough.

Nevertheless, the Puritans did make strong demands on human nature, for they were engaged in a mission that required great exertion. They had undertaken to establish a society where the will of God would be observed in every detail, a kingdom of God on earth. While still aboard the *Arbella*, Winthrop had explained to his fellow emigrants their solemn commitment to this task. Every nation, they all knew, existed by virtue of a covenant with God in which it promised to obey His commands. They had left England because England was failing in its promise. In high hope that God was guiding them and would find their efforts acceptable, they had proposed to form a new society. Now God had demonstrated His approval. He had made way for them by a "special overruling providence." By staying His wrath so long and allowing them to depart in peace, by delivering them safe across the water, He had sealed a covenant with them and given them a special responsibility to carry out the good intentions that had brought them into the wilderness. . . .

Winthrop was determined that Massachusetts should not deal falsely with God. Before arriving in New England, he and the other leaders of the exodus had thought long and hard about the articles of God's special commission, and they were confident that they knew what was required of them. They knew, in the most elementary terms, that they must punish every sin committed in Massachusetts. And punish they did, with the eager cooperation of the whole community, who knew that sin unpunished might expose them all to the wrath of God. Families became little cells of

Reprinted from *The Puritan Dilemma: The Story of John Winthrop* by Edmund S. Morgan, edited by Oscar Handlin. Published by HarperCollins Publishers, 1958. Copyright © 1958 by Edmund S. Morgan.

righteousness where the mother and father disciplined not only their children but also their servants and any boarders they might take in. In order that no one should escape this wholesome control, it was forbidden for anyone to live alone: unmarried men and maids were required to place themselves in some family if their own had been left behind. Parents were obliged to take care that all their children and apprentices learned to read, so that everyone would be able to see for himself in the Bible what opportunities for salvation God offered to man and what sins He forbade. The churches were thronged every Sunday with willing and unwilling worshipers—everyone was required to attend—and church members guarded each other's morals by censuring or excommunicating those who strayed from the straight path.

With virtually the whole population for a police force Winthrop found it no problem to punish sin.

Why were the Puritans willing to make such "strong demands on human nature"? Why do you think Morgan is sympathetic to this effort?

Puritanism as a Source of Social Stability

In an important essay on the social stability that characterized early New England society, Timothy H. Breen and Stephen Foster suggest that Puritanism played an important role in creating that stability. If most New Englanders approved of the society that Breen and Foster describe, they would have appreciated their faith all the more for the kind of community that it helped them to erect. Abridged from "The Puritans' Greatest Achievement: A Study of Social Cohesion in Seventeenth-Century Massachusetts," Journal of American History *60 (June 1973): 10–13.*

Left to themselves, however, the Massachusetts colonists found Congregationalism a source of stability. Flexible enough to accommodate moderate differences of opinion, the orthodox faith still served as a useful test for detecting and expelling extremists, thereby precluding any prolonged clash over religious fundamentals. Irreconcilables quickly discovered the charms of Rhode Island and left the Bay Colony in relative peace. Nathaniel Ward, the colony's most exuberant propagandist, explained this phenomenon in his *Simple Cobler of Aggawam:* "True Religion is *Ignis probationis* [a testing fire] which doth *congregare homogenea & segregare heterogenia* [bring together the alike and drive away the different]."

Ward was correct to emphasize the homogenizing effect of "true religion," any true religion, providing it could be widely and exclusively inculcated as in Massachusetts. The Bay Colony fortunately possessed an official priestly caste supported at public expense and periodically replenished by the graduates of Harvard College. Unhampered by anything but the most futile and sporadic opposition, the authorized interpreters of the exclusive faith provided the citizens of the Bay Colony with meaning for their present, a mission for their future, and, what was more, and perhaps most of all, a synthetic but compelling past. . . .

Puritanism gave to Massachusetts the same kind of provincial identity that was supplied by local tradition in the counties of seventeenth-century England. Indeed, in its physical situation no less than in its mental set the Bay Colony would have made a typical county community. The colony was small in extent, its population was about the right size and relatively compact in distribution, it possessed a coherent intellectual and gentry class, and it was ready to offer fierce resistance to central power emanating from London. . . .

By contributing a common ideology to the Bay Colony, Puritanism did much to create in America the kind of community capable of maintaining order within its borders. If anything, the artificiality of Massachusetts "countyness" assisted its function. Conflicting loyalties to patrons, family, or guilds, which could tear apart even the most traditional European community, were all comparatively weak or absent in New England. In this sense the social utility of Puritanism lay in its position as the monopoly faith rather than in its particular tenets. Hinduism might have served equally well if Harvard could have turned out genuine Brahmins trained in the learned exposition of the *Bhagavad-gita*

"The Puritans' Greatest Achievements: A Study of Social Cohesion in Seventeenth-Century Massachusetts," by Timothy H. Breen and Stephen Foster, as it appeared in *The Journal of American History* (formerly *The Mississippi Valley Historical Review*), Vol. 60, No. 1, June 1973. Copyright © 1973 by the Organization of American Historians.

and the printing press, pulpit, and schools been adapted to the inculcation of the Word in Sanskrit. But the specific preachings of the Puritan Word also had a contribution to make. From the very first the leaders of New England spoke of love as the foundation of their society. While still aboard the *Arbella*, John Winthrop set the tone for life in the Bay Colony, urging the settlers to be "knitt together in this worke as one man" and warning that their failure to do so would make them "a story and a by-word through the world." Winthrop and the other Puritans who moved to Massachusetts assumed that the Lord had made a covenant with them as He had once done for the people of England. This initial "national Covenant" was followed by a proliferation of other covenants on every level of life in New England. The Massachusetts Puritans organized churches, towns, indeed, the entire commonwealth upon the contractual model. The essential ingredient in this contract was free will: the individual voluntarily promised to obey civil and scriptural law, for the seventeenth-century Puritans believed that meaningful obedience could only grow out of voluntary consent, never out of coercion. With this principle in mind, Thomas Hooker insisted that the man who desired to enter a social convenant had to "*willingly* binde and ingage himself to each member of that society . . . or else a member actually he is not." The strong sense of communal responsibility that developed out of this voluntary commitment influenced the character of conflict within the Bay Colony. It was incumbent upon all men to work out their disputes as peacefully as possible, thinking always of their greater obligation to the commonwealth as a whole and ultimately to God himself. Thus, when the future townsmen of Dedham drew up their covenant, they pledged to practice "everlasting love," and should that bond ever be strained by local differences "then, such party or parties shall presently refer all such differences unto some one, two or three others of our said society to be fully accorded and determined without any further delay."

The logic of the covenant determined that the towns and churches of New England would be homogeneous units. Puritan villagers excluded anyone from their midst whom they believed endangered their way of life, and unwanted strangers were frequently "warned out" when they failed to meet the community's standards. In Winthrop's time the concern for social purity was so great that colonial authorities sometimes asked newcomers to present evidence of good character before allowing them to settle. Such conscious self-selection strengthened social cohesion within Massachusetts by forcing potential troublemakers to find homes in other parts of America. Historians have often criticized the leaders of the Bay Colony for their intolerance of other men's opinions, but when one considers Catholics fighting Protestants in colonial Maryland or the Dutch quarreling with the English in New York, one begins to understand why the Puritan fathers acted as they did.

Morgan, Breen and Foster discuss the importance of the covenant idea in Puritan society. How did the idea of a covenant contribute to social order? How could the Puritan covenant be seen as a forerunner to the American Constitution?

PURITAN FAITH:
THE PERSONAL AND THE POLITICAL

Since the popular negative image of Puritanism is a fairly recent development, the Puritans themselves did not respond systematically to the various charges that have been levelled against them. Thus, the written records they left—a sampling of which is reprinted below—do not necessarily address our issues. For the Puritans, the compelling question— Am I saved or damned?—was unanswerable in this life. Unable to know their fates, each wondered how can I handle not knowing my fate, and how does God require me to live my life? As they struggled with these issues, they produced a wide variety of documents that can suggest to us why they made the choice to join the Puritan movement and what that decision meant for the society that they created in New England.

God's Judgment as a Lesson

Increase Mather (1639–1723), an influential Boston minister, wrote a best-selling book that recounted examples of "God's Providence"—that is, God's direct intercession in people's lives. Mather collected stories from all over New England to illustrate that God did take an active role in daily life. In the preface to his book, he related the following incident from an earlier English manuscript that made his point quite well; Mather criticizes then-prevailing religious practices (such as church discipline) even as he approvingly relates the tale of poor Mr. Juxon. From the unpaginated preface to An Essay for the Recording of Illustrious Providences . . . *(Boston, 1684).*

This M. *SS.* [manuscript] doth also mention some most *Remarkable Judgments* of God upon Sinners, as worthy to be Recorded for Posterity to take notice of. It is there said, that when Mr. *Richard Juxon* was a Fellow of *Kings Colledge* in *Cambridge*, he led a most vicious life: and whereas such of the Students as were serious in matters of Religion, did endeavour by solemn Fasting and Prayer to prepare themselves for the Communion which was then (this was about the year 1636) on *Easter-Day.* This *Juxon* spent all the time of preparation in Drunken wild Meetings, and was up late and Drunk on . . . Saturday night. Nevertheless, on the Lords day, he came with others to the Communion, and sat next to the Relator [storyteller], who knowing his Disorder the night before, was much troubled: but had no remedy; Church-Discipline not being then so practiced as ought to have been. The Communion being ended, such of the Scholars as had the fear of God in their hearts, repaired to their Closets [or small rooms]. But this *Juxon* went immediately to a Drunken-meeting, and there to a Cock-fight, where he fell to his accustomed madness, and pouring out a volley of Oaths and Curses; while these were between his Lips, God smote him dead in the twinkle of an eye. And though *Juxon* were but young, and of a comely person, his Carcase was immediately so corrupted as that the stench of it was insufferable,

Preface to "An Essay for the Recording of Illustrious Providences," by Increase Mather, published by Samuel Green for Joseph Browning, Boston, 1684.

insomuch that no house would receive it; and his Friends were forced to hire some base Fellows to watch the Carcase till night; and then with Pitch and such like Gums covered him in a Coffin, and so made a shift to endure his Interment. There stood by a Scholar, whose name was *George Hall*, and who acted his part with *Juxon* in his prophaneness: but he was so astonished with this amazing Providence of God, as that he fell down upon his knees, begging pardoning mercy from Heaven, and vowing a Reformation; which vow the Lord enabled him to keep, so as that afterwards he became an able and famous Minister of the Gospel.

An Artist Contemplates the Struggle to Overcome Sin

The Puritan poet Anne Bradstreet (1612?–1672) approaches the struggle over sin that engaged John Dane and indeed all Puritans from a more philosophical perspective in the poem reprinted below. In "The Flesh and The Spirit" the natural (or sinful) side of the Christian believer debates with the spiritual side. Note that the spirit derides worldly pleasures, contrasting these with spiritual pleasures to come. Reprinted from The Complete Works of Anne Bradstreet, *ed. Joseph R. McElrath, Jr., and Allan P. Robb (Boston, 1981), 175–77.*

The Flesh and the Spirit.

In secret place where once I stood
Close by the Banks of *Lacrim* flood
I heard two sisters reason on
Things that are past, and things to come;
One flesh was call'd, who had her eye
On worldly wealth and vanity;
The other Spirit, who did rear
Her thoughts unto a higher sphere:

"The Flesh and the Spirit," by Anne Bradstreet, reprinted from *The Complete Works of Anne Bradstreet,* Joseph R. McElrath, Jr. and Allan P. Robb, editors. Published by Twayne Publishers, 1981. Copyright © 1981 by G.K. Hall & Co.

Sister, quoth Flesh, what liv'st thou on
Nothing but Meditation?
Doth Contemplation feed thee so
Regardlesly to let earth goe?
Can Speculation satisfy
Notion without Reality?
Dost dream of things beyond the Moon
And dost thou hope to dwell there soon?
Hast treasures there laid up in store
That all in th' world thou count'st but poor?
Art fancy sick, or turn'd a Sot
To catch at shadowes which are not?
Come, come, Ile shew unto thy sence,
Industry hath its recompence.
What canst desire, but thou maist see
True substance in variety?
Dost honour like? acquire the same,
As some to their immortal fame:
And trophyes to thy name erect
Which wearing time shall ne're deject.
For riches dost thou long full sore?
Behold enough of precious store.
Earth hath more silver, pearls and gold,
Then eyes can see, or hands can hold.
Affect's thou pleasure? take thy fill,
Earth hath enough of what you will.
Then let not goe, what thou maist find,
For things unknown, only in mind.
Spir. Be still thou unregenerate part,
Disturb no more my setled heart,
For I have vow'd (and so will doe)
Thee as a foe, still to pursue.
And combate with thee will and must,
Untill I see thee laid in th' dust.
Sisters we are, yea twins we be,
Yet deadly feud 'twixt thee and me;
For from one father are we not,
Thou by old Adam wast begot,
But my arise is from above,
Whence my dear father I do love.
Thou speak'st me fair, but hat'st me sore,

Thy flatt'ring shews Ile trust no more.
How oft thy slave, hast thou me made,
When I believ'd, what thou hast said,
And never had more cause of woe
Then when I did what thou bad'st doe.
Ile stop mine ears at these thy charms,
And count them for my deadly harms.
Thy sinfull pleasures I doe hate,
Thy riches are to me no bait,
Thine honours doe, nor will I love;
For my ambition lyes above.
My greatest honour it shall be
When I am victor over thee,
And triumph shall, with laurel head,
When thou my Captive shalt be led,
How I do live, thou need'st not scoff,
For I have meat thou know'st not off;
The hidden Manna I doe eat,
The word of life it is my meat.
My thoughts do yield me more content
Then can thy hours in pleasure spent.
Nor are they shadows which I catch,
Nor fancies vain at which I snatch,
But reach at things that are so high,
Beyond thy dull Capacity;
Eternal substance I do see,
With which inriched I would be:
Mine Eye doth pierce the heavens, and see
What is Invisible to thee.
My garments are not silk nor gold,
Nor such like trash which Earth doth hold,
But Royal Robes I shall have on,
More glorious then the glistring Sun;
My Crown not Diamonds, Pearls, and gold,
But such as Angels heads infold.
The City where I hope to dwell,
There's none on Earth can parallel;
The stately Walls both high and strong,
Are made of pretious *Jasper* stone;
The Gates of Pearl, both rich and clear,
And Angels are for Porters there;

The Streets thereof transparent gold,
Such as no Eye did e're behold,
A Chrystal River there doth run,
Which doth proceed from the Lambs Throne:
Of Life, there are the waters sure,
Which shall remain for ever pure,
Nor Sun, nor Moon, they have no need,
For glory doth from God proceed:
No Candle there, nor yet Torch light,
For there shall be no darksome night.
From sickness and infirmity,
For evermore they shall be free,
Nor withering age shall e're come there,
But beauty shall be bright and clear;
This City pure is not for thee,
For things unclean there shall not be:
If I of Heaven may have my fill,
Take thou the world, and all that will.

Both Mather and Bradstreet write about overcoming sin. How do their approaches differ? To whom would their respective arguments appeal? Which, to you, is the most persuasive?

"To Walke Together":
The Role of the Puritan Congregation

The preceding selections from Mather and Bradstreet dealt with religion on a personal level, but Puritans believed that their spirituality ought to have a public component as well. One way in which they expressed their commitment publicly was by joining a church. In seventeenth-century Massachusetts and Connecticut, only those who seemed to their peers to be saved—that is, to have undergone a legitimate conversion experience—could become church members. Once accepted into a congregation, new members entered into a church covenant. In many churches, such as the one founded in Salem, Massachusetts in 1629, a written covenant was publicly endorsed by all members. The text of the Salem covenant explains why the Puritans thought it necessary to organize

31

churches. Taken from The Records of the First Church in Salem Massachusetts, *1629–1736, ed. Richard D. Pierce (Salem, Massachusetts, 1974), 3–5.*

Wee whose names are here under written, members of the present Church of Christ in Salem, haveing found by sad experience how dangerous it is to sitt loose to the Covenant wee make with our God: and how apt wee are to wander into by pathes, even to the looseing of our first aimes in entring into Church fellowship: Doe therefore, solemnly in the presence of the Eternall God both for our owne comforts and those which shall or maye be joyned unto us renewe that Church covenant we find this Church bound unto at theire first begining. vizt: That we Covenant with the Lord and one with an other, and doe bynd our selves in the presence of God, to walke together in all his waies, according as he is pleased to reveale him selfe unto us in his Blessed word of truth. And doe more explicitely in the name and feare of God, profess and protest to walke as followeth through the power and grace of our Lord Jesus.

1. first wee avowe the Lord to be our God, and our selves his people in the truth and simplicitie of our Spirits

2. Wee give our selves to the Lord Jesus Christ, and the word of his grace, fore the teaching, ruleing and sanctifyeing of us in matters of worship, and conversation resolveing to cleave to him alone for life and glorie; and oppose all contrarie wayes, cannons and constitutions of men in his worship.

3. Wee promise to walk with our brethren and sisters in the Congregation with all watchfullness, and tendernis avoyding all jelousies, suspitions, backbyteings, conjurings, provoakings, secrete riseings of spirit against them, but in all offences to follow the rule of the Lord Jesus, and to beare and forbeare, give and forgive as he hath taught us.

4. In publick or private, we will willingly doe nothing to the ofence of the Church but will be willing to take advise for ourselves and ours as ocasion shall be presented.

5. Wee will not in the Congregation be forward eyther to show

---

our owne gifts or parts in speaking or scrupuling [2] or there discover the fayling of our brethren or sisters butt attend an orderly cale there unto; knowing how much the Lord may be dishonoured, and his Gospell in the profession of it, sleighted by our distempers, and weaknesses in publyck.

6. Wee bynd ourselves to studdy the advancment of the Gospell in all truth and peace, both in regard of those that are within, or without, noe waye sleighting our sister Churches, but useing theire Counsell as need shalbe; nor laying a stumbling block, before any, noe not the Indians, whose good we desire to promote, and soe to converse, as wee may avoyd the verrye appearance of evill,

7. Wee hereby promise to carrye ourselves in all lawfull obedience, to those that are over us in Church or Common weale, knowing how well pleasing it wilbe to the Lord, that they should have incouragement in theire places, by our not greiveing theyre spirites through our iregulareties.

8. Wee resolve to prove our selves to the Lord in our particular calings, shunning ydlenes as the bane of any state, nor will wee deale hardly, or opressingly with Any, wherein wee are the Lords stewards: alsoe

9. promyseing to our best abilitie to teach our children and servants, the knowledge of God and his will, that they may serve him alsoe and all this, not by any strength of our owne, but by the Lord Christ, whose bloud we desire may sprinckle this our Covenant made in his name.

This covenant between members of a Puritan church demonstrates their very difficult individual and social standards. What was (and is) the appeal of the Puritan way for so many?

The Creation of
New Worlds

INTRODUCTION

In 1675 and early 1676, a series of confrontations occurred along the Potomac River in the Chesapeake region, pitting Doeg and Susquehannock Indians against English planters. Nathaniel Bacon, a well-born Englishman who had recently moved to Virginia, sought official sanction for a general attack against the natives. After Virginia's Governor William Berkeley refused to authorize Bacon's request, he led a group of volunteers to massacre one of the friendly tribes. When Berkeley declared him a rebel and moved to arrest him, Bacon led an attack against the governor, and the entire colony collapsed in civil war. Jamestown, the capital, was burned to the ground by the rebels, and a period of plunder ensued in which partisans on both sides looted the homes and property of their enemies.

For most of 1676 Virginia was engulfed by civil war. The uprising against Berkeley, led by Bacon and named after him, was the largest armed revolt against English authority in the American colonies until the Revolution a century later. It became popular during the revolutionary era to present Bacon as a forerunner of later Virginian revolutionaries like George Washington and Patrick Henry. More recently, scholars have been inclined to see the rebellion as a significant indication of serious divisions within late-seventeenth-century Chesapeake society. Bacon's Rebellion was the only colonial revolt to involve Native Americans, Europeans, and Africans. As such, it offers a glimpse of the social and political development of early Virginia.

36

SCHOLARS DEBATE MOTIVATION

Ironically, Bacon's Rebellion "waited" almost one hundred years after it first erupted in 1676 to become an important historical event. During and after the American Revolution, people like Thomas Jefferson searched for examples of previous resistance to English authority in the American colonies and identified Nathaniel Bacon as a model for a later generation of Virginian rebels. Well into the twentieth century, this view that Bacon's Rebellion was an early example of Americans standing up against English tyranny continued to be widely accepted by historians. Over the last four decades, however, some scholars have questioned its accuracy and reconsidered the evidence to find alternative explanations. The readings below focus on explaining what motivated the colonists to take up arms against their government.

Prelude to the American Revolution

Thomas Jefferson Wertenbaker defends the traditional interpretation of Bacon's Rebellion, explicitly comparing Nathaniel Bacon's revolt against a "tyrannical" Governor Berkeley with the American colonists' later revolution against King George. The excerpt below is abridged from Virginia Under the Stuarts, *which was reprinted as part of* The Shaping of Colonial Virginia *(New York, 1958), 115–16, 123, 127, 130–31, 133, 143–45.*

Never was a people doomed to more bitter disappointment [than the Virginians were after Charles II was restored to the throne of England in 1660]. The years which followed the Restoration were crowded with misfortunes greater than any that had befallen the colony since the ghastly days of the Great Sickness [malaria epidemics]. Charles II, far from showing gratitude to his Old Dominion, overwhelmed it with injustice and oppression. The Virginians were crushed with tremendous duties on their tobacco and with ruinous restrictions upon their trade. The titles to their plantations were threatened by a grant of the entire colony to two unworthy favorites of the King. Governor Berkeley, embittered . . . and growing avaricious and crabbed with advancing years, soon forfeited that respect and love which his former good conduct had gained him. His second administration [1660–1677] was marred by partiality, oppression and inefficiency. The people were deprived of their right of suffrage by continued prorogation [dismissal] of the Assembly. Local government fell into the hands of small aristocratic cliques, while the poor were ground down with unequal and excessive taxes. Two wars with Holland added to the misfortunes of the colonists. Even the Heavens seemed to join with their enemies, for the country was visited by a terrific hurricane which swept over the plantations, destroying crops and wrecking houses. These accumulated misfortunes brought such deep suffering upon the colony that hundreds of families were reduced to poverty and many were forced into debt and ruin. No wonder that the commons, finally driven to desperation, should have risen in insurrection against the Governor and the King.

First among the causes of distress during this unhappy period must be placed the Navigation Acts. . . . [A series of laws intended to force the colonists to trade with England rather than other European countries.] Can there be any doubt that the Navigation Acts and the futility of all attempts to escape their baleful effects, were largely instrumental in bringing on Bacon's Rebellion? As prosperity and contentment are the greatest safeguards of the public peace, so poverty, nakedness and distress are breeders of sedition. Philip Ludwell spoke of Bacon's army as "a Rabble of the basest sort of People; whose Condicion was such as by a chaunge could not admitt of worse". Had England been less selfish in her treatment of Virginia, there would not have been so many indigent men in the colony eager to join in this wild uprising against the government. Berkeley himself admitted, in 1673, that at least one third of the freemen had been rendered so desperate by poverty and debt that in times of foreign war their loyalty to England could not be relied upon.

But Charles II was indifferent to the welfare of these distant subjects and blind to their growing dissatisfaction. Just when the situation was most critical, he aroused their anger and grief to the highest pitch, by making a gift of the entire colony to Lord Culpeper and the Earl of Arlington. . . .

The wars of 1664 and 1672 with Holland added much to the distress in Virginia. The bold Dutch mariners, angered at the injury done them by the Navigation Acts, preyed upon the English merchantmen in every sea. Woe to the tobacco ship that encountered a hostile privateer, in its journey across the Atlantic! The English vessels were not safe even in the Virginia rivers, under the guns of their forts. Twice the daring Dutch came through the capes and into the James River itself, where they wrought great damage to the shipping. . . .

Great as was the distress caused by the depredations of the Dutch, the planters suffered even more during these wars by the stagnation of trade. The great risk incurred in crossing the ocean necessarily brought an increase both in freight rates and in the cost of manufactured goods. In 1667 the Governor and Council declared that the planters were "inforced to pay 12 pounds to £17 per ton freight" on their tobacco "which usually was but at seven pounds". Conditions were even worse during the second war. In 1673 Berkeley complained that the number of vessels that dared come to Virginia was so small, that they had "not brought goods and tools enough for one part of five of the people to go on with their necessary labor". "And those few goods that are brought," he added "have Soe few (and these hard Dealing) Sellers and Soe many Indigent and necessitous buyors that the Poore Planter gets not the fourth part . . . for his tobacco which he usually has had in other times."

In this period, so full of suffering and misfortune, the year 1667 was especially noteworthy for its long series of [natural] disasters. . . .

Perhaps the people of Virginia might have borne patiently all these misfortunes, had their Governor ruled them with wisdom and justice. Certain it is they would never have turned in wild anger to strike down his government, had that government not done much to make their condition intolerable. Sir William Berkeley was accused of destroying the representative character of the Assembly, of initiating a notorious spoils system, of intimidating

Burgesses, of winking at embezzlement of public funds. And, although most of these charges were brought by the Governor's bitter enemies, some of them were undoubtedly true. . . .

It would not be just to give credence to all the accusations made against Berkeley. The King's commissioners who conducted the investigation into his conduct, were his enemies; while many of the charges were brought by those who had taken part in the Rebellion. Thus the testimony against him is in most cases distinctly partisan. Moreover those that were closely associated with Sir William often expressed extravagant admiration for his ability and energy, and love for his character. "He hath," wrote the Council in 1673, "for neare 30 years governed this colony with that prudence and justice which hath gained him both love and reverence from all the Inhabitants here." . . .

But whatever is the verdict of posterity upon the conduct and motives of Sir William Berkeley, the causes of the Rebellion stand out with great clearness:—England's selfish commercial policy, . . . the Dutch wars, storms and pestilence, inefficient if not corrupt government, excessive taxes. The only wonder is that the insurrection did not occur earlier. In fact two mutinies did break out in 1674, when the excessively heavy taxes of that year were announced, but the rebels lacked leaders and were suppressed without great difficulty. As early as 1673 the defection of the planters was so great that it was feared many might attempt to deliver the colony into the hands of the Dutch. Berkeley wrote that a large part of the people were so desperately poor that they might reasonably be expected upon any small advantage of the enemy to "revolt to them in hopes of bettering their Condition by Shareing the Plunder of the Country with them". A certain John Knight reported "that the planters there doe generally desire a trade with the Dutch and all other nations and would not be singly bound to the trade of England, and speake openly there that they are in the nature of slaves, soe that the hearts of the greatest part of them are taken away from his Majesty". Thus the downtrodden planters, alienated from England, angered at the Governor, even distrusting their own Assembly, waited but an occasion and a leader to rise in open rebellion. A new Indian war offered the occasion, and they found their leader in young Nathaniel Bacon.

How does the author compare Bacon's rebellion to the American Revolution?

Conflict on the Frontier

Historian Wilcomb Washburn refutes the consensus Wertenbaker and many others shared on Bacon's Rebellion. He rejects comparisons with the Revolution and argues that the uprising must be understood in the context of Bacon's hatred for Native Americans and his desire for their frontier lands. Excerpted from Wilcomb E. Washburn, The Governor and The Rebel: A History of Bacon's Rebellion in Virginia *(Chapel Hill, 1957), 153, 159–60, 162–63, 166.*

What was the "cause" of Bacon's Rebellion? What motivated the 400 foot and 120 horse who marched with Bacon into Jamestown on June 23, 1676? Romantic historians like to see the rebellion as "a revolt of the lower classes of whites against the aristocratic families who governed Virginia," as "the cause of the poor against the rich, of the humble folk against the grandees.". . .

The more prosaic interests of the rebels have rarely been inquired into. It has been assumed that they were selfless patriots fighting a tyrannical government. We are told that Bacon was "a champion of the weak, a rebel against injustice, the forerunner of Washington, Jefferson and Samuel Adams." Others have compared Bacon to Patrick Henry, to Tiberius Gracchus, to Callimachus, and even to Leonidas at Thermopylae.

It is generally assumed, on the other hand, that the governor and his council were the "grandees" of the colony and that they possessed vast holdings of land while the rest of the colonists eked out a precarious existence on their small plantations. Like so many other assertions about Bacon's Rebellion, this one is not based on a study of the evidence. An investigation of the land holdings of the partisans on both sides reveals a surprising equality between them. The leaders on both sides had large holdings. The followers on both sides had more modest holdings. What is most significant is that the leaders of the rebellion against Governor Berkeley

---

"Causes of the Rebellion," reproduced from *The Governor and the Rebel: A History of Bacon's Rebellion in Virginia,* by Wilcomb E. Washburn. Published for The Institute of Early American History and Culture, Williamsburg, Virginia. Copyright © 1957 by The University of North Carolina Press. Used by permission of the publisher.

almost invariably owned great tracts of land on the frontier, frequently had a record of oppression and aggression against the neighboring Indians, and occasionally had been punished by Berkeley for their crimes against the natives.

Governor Berkeley strove throughout his career to restrain the aggressiveness of the frontier landowners. But his power was limited. For one thing he was not in control of the government from 1652 to 1660 when the most unregulated expansion took place. His ability to control expansion was further restricted when, in 1666, he lost the right to allow or disallow individual grants. The assembly successfully challenged his authority to limit the right to acquire land, and "henceforth it was recognised in practice that the Governor had no more power over land grants than that secured by his individual vote in the Council." . . .

The connection between the colonists' itch for land and the Indian "troubles" is a close one. Since the Indian troubles set off the rebellion, it would seem fair to blame the rebellion in great part on those who caused the Indian troubles. But it seems an inescapable conclusion that the English, and particularly the rebellious frontiersmen themselves, were responsible for the Indian troubles. It was the frontiersmen's continuing violation of Governor Berkeley's efforts to settle the Indian-white relationship with fairness to both sides that precipitated the rebellion.

Colonel Moryson, one of the commissioners [who investigated the rebellion for the King], was well aware from his period in the Virginia government of the propensity of the frontiersmen to push the Indians off their land. He wrote in 1676 that there had not been a war with the Indians for the previous twenty-five years that had not been caused by the English coveting their land. When, therefore, Moryson and his fellow commissioners were presented the "grievance" of Henrico County that no satisfaction had been obtained against the Indians, they commented: "These Complainants never consider that the breach of the Peace and occasion of Bloodshed has still been on the side of the English, which was publickly Justified and affirmed in open Court in the face of a very great Assembly, and denied by none."

The one cause of Bacon's Rebellion that has been consistently overlooked, then, is the aggressiveness of the frontiersmen. The careful [Richard] Hildreth [a nineteenth-century historian] nearly stumbled onto this conception when he wrote, with unconscious humor, that "the Indian war, the immediate cause of all the late disturbances, seems to have subsided so soon as expeditions against the Indians were dropped." What has caused English and American historians to overlook the frontiersmen's aggressiveness? The reason lies partly in the white historian's unconscious immersion in his racial bias. According to the mythology of the white view of the world, the Indian is ever "primitive," "warlike," and "aggressive," while the "civilized" white man is constantly on guard against his attacks. But the aggressiveness of the frontiersmen has been overlooked for another reason, one based on our idea of our political beliefs. Most of the writers and historians who have dealt with Bacon's Rebellion have written from what they regarded as a "liberal" point of view, and it is part of the mythology of this view of history that the American frontiersman symbolizes America's freedom, democracy, and hatred of oppression. Actually the American frontiersman of the seventeenth century paid scant heed to such ideals. . . .

The causes of Bacon's rebellion are complex and profound. They cannot be explained in terms of Berkeley's "greed" and "oppression," Bacon's love of "liberty," the "savagery" of the Indians, or the "patriotism" of the frontiersmen; such explanatory descriptions are meaningless labels pasted on the actors by those who see all history as a morality play. Nor can the rebellion be explained in terms of the concealed identities and mysterious motives of a Gothic romance. Bacon does not change, with the hemispheres, from the spoiled son of a well-to-do English country squire to a dedicated democratic frontier hero. Nor does Governor Berkeley, after being the "Darling of the People" for thirty-five years, suddenly reveal his true identity as their blackest oppressor. Both men remained true to the faults and virtues of their natures.

Nathaniel Bacon would be vastly amused to find himself the sainted hero of the guardians of the liberal traditions of western democratic government. No doubt he would receive the news with an expression of his profane amusement at the idiocy of men. "God damn my blood," he might exclaim; "how easily people are led!"

How does Washburn's view differ from that of Wertenbaker? What might account for the differences?

CONTEMPORARY VIEWS
OF THE REBELLION

Only a few of the participants left records about their roles in the rebellion, and those were mostly the wealthy men who served as leaders of either faction. While we know that several different groups of Native Americans were involved, that women participated actively in both the Bacon and Berkeley camps, and that the last rebels out in the field were mostly European indentured servants and African or African American slaves, we have few, if any, records from these people to explain their actions. The motives of all parties can only be interpreted through the limited existing records. (Throughout these documents, archaic abbreviations have been silently edited for greater clarity.)

Berkeley Declares Bacon a Rebel

When Governor William Berkeley refused to authorize attacks against the Susquehannocks, Nathaniel Bacon, a wealthy planter, took matters into his own hands, leading a group of volunteers in a massacre of friendly Indians. In the selection below, Berkeley defends his own actions and declares Bacon a rebel. Originally printed in the Collections of the Massachusetts Historical Society, *4th Series, (Boston, 1871) 9:178–81.*

Since that time that I returned into the Country [as Governor of Virginia: about 1660], I call the great God, Judge of all things in heaven and earth to wittness, that I doe not know of any thing relateive to this Country, wherein I have acted unjustly, corruptly, or negligently, in distributeing equall Justice to all men, & takeing all possible care to preserue [preserve] their proprietys, & defend them from their barbarous enimies. . . .

And now I will state the Question betwixt me as a Governor and Mr Bacon, and say that if any enimies should invade England, any Councellor Justice of peace, or other interiour officer, might raise what forces they could to protect his Majesty's subiects [subjects], But I say againe, if after the Kings knowledge of this inuasion, any the greatest peere [or nobleman] of England, should raise forces against the kings p'hibition this would be now, & ever was in all ages & Nations accompted [accounted as] treason. Nay I will goe further, that though this peere was truly zealous for the preservation of his King, & subiects, and had better & greater abillitys than all the rest of his fellow subiects, to doe his King and Country seruice, yett if the King (though by false information) should suspect the contrary, itt were treason in this Noble peere to p'ceed after the King's prohibition, and for the truth of this I appeale to all the laws of England, and the Laws and constitutions of all other Nations in the world. . . .

Now my friends I have lived 34 yeares amongst you, as vncorrupt and dilligent as ever [a] Governor was, Bacon is a man of two yeares amongst you, his p'son and qualities vnknowne to most of you, & to all men else, by any vertuous action that ever I heard of, And that very action which he boasts of [the massacre of the Occaneechee Indians], was sickly & fooleishly, & as I am informed treacherously carried to the dishonnor of the English Nation, yett in itt, he lost more men then I did in three yeares Warr [against an Indian uprising several decades earlier], and by the grace of God will putt myselfe to the same daingers & troubles againe when I have brought Bacon to acknowledge the Laws are above him, and I doubt not but by God's assistance to have better success then Bacon hath had, the reason of my hopes are, that I will take Councell of wiser men then my selfe, but Mr Bacon hath none about him, but the lowest of the people.

Yett I must further enlarge, that I cannot without your helpe, doe any thinge in this but dye in defence of my King, his laws, & subiects, which I will cheerefully doe, though alone I doe itt, and considering my poore fortunes, I can not leave my poore Wife and friends a better legacy then by dyeing for my King & you: for his sacred Majesty will easeily distinguish betweene Mr Bacons actions & myne, and Kinges have long Armes, either to reward or punish. . . .

Lastly my most assured friends I would have preserued those Indians that I knew were howerly att our mercy, to have beene our spyes and intelligence, to finde out our bloody enimies, but as soone as I had the least intelligence that they alsoe were trecherous enimies, I gave out Comissions to distroy them all as the Comissions themselues will speake itt.

To conclude, I have don what was possible both to friend and enimy, have granted Mr Bacon three pardons, which he hath scornefully reiected, suppoaseing himselfe stronger to subuert [the laws] than I and you [are] to mainteyne the Laws, by which onely and Gods assisting grace and mercy, all men must hope for peace and safety. I will add noe more though much more is still remaineing to Justifie me & condemne Mr Bacon, but to desier that this declaration may be read in every County Court in the Country.

What arguments does Berkeley offer to defend his actions? Do you find them compelling?

Bacon Justifies Rebellion on Behalf of "the People"

Within months, the colony divided into factions that supported either Berkeley or Bacon, and both sides took up arms. On 30 July 1676, Bacon issued "The Declaration of the People," in which he defended his actions and attacked the policies of Berkeley's government. Reprinted from the Collections of the Massachusetts Historical Society, 4th Series, (Boston, 1871), 9:184–85.

1st. For haveing . . . raised greate unjust taxes vpon the Comonality for the aduancement of private favorites & other sinister ends, but [without having] . . . in any measure aduanced this hopefull Colony either by fortifications Townes or Trade.

2d. For haveing abused & rendred contemptable the Magistrates of Justice, by aduanceing to places of Judicature, scandalous and Ignorant favorites.

3. For haveing wronged his Majestys prerogative & interest, by assumeing Monopolony of the Beaver trade, & for haveing in that unjust gaine betrayed & sold his Majestys Country & the lives of his loyall subiects to the barbarous heathen.

4. For haveing, protected, favoured, & Imboldned the Indians against his Majestys loyall subiects, never contriveing, requireing, or appointing any due or proper meanes of satisfaction for theire many Inuasions, robbories, & murthers comitted vpon vs.

5. For haveing when the Army of English was just vpon the track of those Indians, who now in all places burne, spoyle, murther & when we might with ease have distroyed them who then were in open hostillity, for then haveing expressly counter-manded, & sent back our Army, by passing his word for the peaceable demeanour of the said Indians, who imediately p'secuted theire evill intentions, comitting horred murthers & robberies in all places, being p'tected by the said ingagement & word past of him the said Sir Wm Berkeley, haveing ruined & laid desolate a greate part of his Majestys Country, & have now drawne themselves into such obscure & remote places, & are by theire success soe imboldned & confirmed, by theire confederacy soe strengthned that the cryes of blood are in all places, & the terror, & constirnation of the people soe greate, are now become, not onely a difficult, but a very formidable enimy, who might att first with ease haue beene distroyed.

6th. And lately when vpon the loud outcryes of blood the Assembly had with all care raised & framed an Army for the preventing of further mischiefe & safeguard of this his Majestys Colony.

7th. For haveing with onely the privacy of some few favorites, without acquainting the people, onely by the alteration of a figure, forged a Comission, by we know not what hand, not onely with-out, but even against the consent of the people, for the raiseing & effecting civill warr & destruction, which being happily & without blood shed prevented, for haveing the second time attempted the same, thereby calling downe our forces from the defence of the fronteeres & most weekely expoased places.

8. For the prevention of civill mischeife & ruin amongst ourselues, whilst the barbarous enimy in all places did invade, murther & spoyle vs, his majestys most faithfull subiects.

How does Bacon justify his actions? Who has the better argument, Berkeley or Bacon?

Indentured Servants
and Slaves Resist Surrender

Along with poor freemen, indentured servants and slaves who had deserted their masters formed a large part of Bacon's army. As the rebellion collapsed, they still held the fort at West Point. As the passage below indicates, Berkeley and his supporters were not above lying to trick such people into putting down their arms. Thomas Grantham was a ship captain who helped Berkeley suppress the uprising. From "A Narrative of the Indian and Civil Wars in Virginia . . .," in Tracts and Other Papers . . ., *ed. Peter Force, 1:44–45.*

What number of soulders was, at this time, in Garrisson at West Point, I am not certaine: It is saide about 250, sumed up in freemen, sarvants and slaves; these three ingredience being the compossition of Bacons Army, ever since that the Governour left Towne. These was informed (to prepare the way) two or three days before that Grantham came to them, that there was a treaty on foote betwene there Generall, and the Governour; and that Grantham did manely promote the same, as he was a parson [person] that favoured the cause, that they were contending for.

When that Grantham arived, amongst these fine fellowes, he was receved with more then an ordnary respect; which he haveing repade, with a suteable deportment, he acquaints them with his commission, which was to tell them, that there was a peace concluded betwene the Governour and their Generall; an since himself had (in some measure) used his indeviours, to bring the same to pass, hee begged of the Governour, that he might have the honor to com and acquaint them with the terms; which he saide was such, that they had all cause to rejoyce at, than any ways to thinke hardly of the same; there being a compleate satisfaction to be given (by the Articles of agreement) according to every ones particuler intress; which he sumed up under these heads. And first, those that were now in Arms (and free men) under the Generall, were still to be retained in Arms, if they so pleased, against the Indians. Secondly, and for those who had a desire for to return hom, to their owne abodes, care was taken for to have them satisfide, for the time they had bin out, according to the alowance made the last Assembley. And lastly, those that were sarvants in Arms, and behaved themselves well, in their imployment, should emediately receve discharges from their Indentures, signed by the Governour or Sequetary of State; and their Masters to receve, from the publick, a valluable satisfaction, for every sarvant, so set free (marke the words) proportionably to the time that they have to sarve.

Upon these terms, the soulders forsake West Point, and goe with Grantham to kiss the Governours hands (still at Tindells point) and to receve the benefitt of the Articles, mentioned by Grantham; where when they came (which was by water, themselves in one vessill, and their arms in another; and so contrived by Grantham, as he tould me himselfe, upon good reason) the sarvants and slaves was sent hom to their Masters, there to stay till the Governour had leasure to signe their discharges; or to say better, till they were free according to the custom of the countrey [which meant finishing their indentures, plus serving extra time for being runaways], the rest was made prissoners, or entertained by the Governour, as hee found them inclined.

Convergence and Conflict, 1660s–1763

George Washington's *Rules of Civility in Conversation Amongst Men*

In the late nineteenth century, a school notebook entitled "Forms of Writing" was discovered at Mount Vernon, Virginia, George Washington's plantation home on the Potomac River. The notebook apparently dates from about 1745, when George was fourteen years old and attending school in Fredericksburg, Virginia. Inside, in George's own handwriting, we find the foundation of a solid character education for an eighteenth-century youth: some 110 "Rules of Civility in Conversation Amongst Men." Historical research has shown that young George probably copied them from a 1664 English translation of an even older French work. Most of the rules are still delightfully applicable as a modern code of personal conduct. On the assumption that what was good enough for the first president of the United States is good enough for the rest of us, here are fifty-four of George Washington's "Rules of Civility."

1. Every action in company ought to be with some sign of respect to those present.
2. In the presence of others sing not to yourself with a humming voice, nor drum with your fingers or feet.
3. Speak not when others speak, sit not when others stand, and walk not when others stop.
4. Turn not your back to others, especially in speaking; jog not the table or desk on which another reads or writes; lean not on anyone.
5. Be no flatterer, neither play with anyone that delights not to be played with.
6. Read no letters, books, or papers in company; but when there is a necessity for doing it, you must ask leave. Come not near the books or writings of anyone so as to read them unasked; also look not nigh when another is writing a letter.
7. Let your countenance be pleasant, but in serious matters somewhat grave.

8. Show not yourself glad at the misfortune of another, though he were your enemy.

9. They that are in dignity or office have in all places precedency, but whilst they are young, they ought to respect those that are their equals in birth or other qualities, though they have no public charge.

10. It is good manners to prefer them to whom we speak before ourselves, especially if they be above us, with whom in no sort we ought to begin.

11. Let your discourse with men of business be short and comprehensive.

12. In visiting the sick do not presently play the physician if you be not knowing therein.

13. In writing or speaking give to every person his due title according to his degree and the custom of the place.

14. Strive not with your superiors in argument, but always submit your judgment to others with modesty.

15. Undertake not to teach your equal in the art he himself professes; it savors of arrogancy.

16. When a man does all he can, though it succeeds not well, blame not him that did it.

17. Being to advise or reprehend anyone, consider whether it ought to be in public or in private, presently or at some other time, also in what terms to do it; and in reproving show no signs of choler, but do it with sweetness and mildness.

18. Mock not nor jest at anything of importance; break no jests that are sharp or biting; and if you deliver anything witty or pleasant, abstain from laughing thereat yourself.

19. Wherein you reprove another be unblamable yourself, for example is more prevalent than precept.

20. Use no reproachful language against anyone, neither curses nor revilings.

21. Be not hasty to believe flying reports to the disparagement of anyone.

22. In your apparel be modest, and endeavor to accommodate nature rather than procure admiration. Keep to the fashion of your equals, such as are civil and orderly with respect to time and place.

23. Play not the peacock, looking everywhere about you to see if you be well decked, if your shoes fit well, if your stockings set neatly and clothes handsomely.

24. Associate yourself with men of good quality if you esteem your own reputation, for it is better to be alone than in bad company.

25. Let your conversation be without malice or envy, for it is a sign of tractable and commendable nature; and in all causes of passion admit reason to govern.

26. Be not immodest in urging your friend to discover a secret.

27. Utter not base and frivolous things amongst grown and learned men, nor very difficult questions or subjects amongst the ignorant, nor things hard to be believed.

28. Speak not of doleful things in time of mirth nor at the table; speak not of melancholy things, as death and wounds; and if others mention them, change, if you can, the discourse. Tell not your dreams but to your intimate friends.

29. Break not a jest when none take pleasure in mirth. Laugh not aloud, nor at all without occasion. Deride no man's misfortunes, though there seem to be some cause.

30. Speak not injurious words, neither in jest or earnest. Scoff at none, although they give occasion.

31. Be not forward, but friendly and courteous, the first to salute, hear and answer, and be not pensive when it is time to converse.

32. Detract not from others, but neither be excessive in commending.

33. Go not thither where you know not whether you shall be welcome or not. Give not advice without being asked; and when desired, do it briefly.

34. If two contend together, take not the part of either unconstrained, and be not obstinate in your opinion; in things indifferent be of the major side.

35. Reprehend not the imperfection of others, for that belongs to parents, masters, and superiors.

36. Gaze not on the marks or blemishes of others, and ask not how they came. What you may speak in secret to your friend deliver not before others.

37. Speak not in an unknown tongue in company, but in your own language; and that as those of quality do, and not as the vulgar. Sublime matters treat seriously.

38. Think before you speak; pronounce not imperfectly, nor bring out your words too hastily, but orderly and distinctly.

39. When another speaks, be attentive yourself, and disturb not the audience. If any hesitate in his words, help him not, nor prompt him without being desired; interrupt him not, nor answer him till his speech be ended.

40. Treat with men at fit times about business, and whisper not in the company of others.

41. Make no comparisons; and if any of the company be commended for any brave act of virtue, commend not another for the same.

42. Be not apt to relate news if you know not the truth thereof. In discoursing of things you have heard, name not your author always. A secret discover not.

43. Be not curious to know the affairs of others, neither approach to those that speak in private.

44. Undertake not what you cannot perform; but be careful to keep your promise.

45. When you deliver a matter, do it without passion and indiscretion, however mean the person may be you do it to.

46. When your superiors talk to anybody, hear them; neither speak or laugh.

47. In disputes be not so desirous to overcome as not to give liberty to each one to deliver his opinion, and submit to the judgment of the major part, especially if they are judges of the dispute.

48. Be not tedious in discourse, make not many digressions, nor repeat often the same matter of discourse.

49. Speak no evil of the absent, for it is unjust.

50. Be not angry at table, whatever happens; and if you have reason to be so show it not; put on a cheerful countenance, especially if there be strangers, for good humor makes one dish a feast.

51. Set not yourself at the upper end of the table; but if it be your due, or the master of the house will have it so, contend not, lest you should trouble the company.

52. When you speak of God or his attributes, let it be seriously, reverence and honor, and obey your natural parents.

53. Let your recreations be manful, not sinful.

54. Labor to keep alive in your breast that little spark of celestial called conscience.

What role did the idea of personal virtue play in the development of the revolutionary generation as personified by Washington?

John Locke, from *An Essay Concerning Understanding in the Age of Enlightenment*

Chapter I. *Introduction*

1. *An Inquiry into the Understanding, pleasant and useful.*— Since it is the understanding that sets man above the rest of sensible beings, and gives him all the advantage and dominion which he has over them, it is certainly a subject, even for its nobleness, worth our labour to inquire into. The understanding, like the eye, whilst it makes us see and perceive all other things, takes no notice of itself; and it requires art and pains to set it at a distance, and make it its own object. But whatever be the difficulties that lie in the way of this inquiry, whatever it be that keeps us so much in the dark to ourselves, sure I am that all the light we can let in upon our own minds, all the acquaintance we can make with our own understandings, will not only be very pleasant, but bring us great advantage in directing our thoughts in the search of other things.

2. *Design.*—This, therefore, being my purpose, to inquire into the original, certainty, and extent of human knowledge, together with the grounds and degrees of belief, opinion, and assent, I shall not at present meddle with the physical consideration of the mind, or trouble myself to examine wherein its essence consists, or by what motions of our spirits or alterations of our bodies we come to have any sensations by our organs, or any ideas in our understandings; and whether those ideas do, in their formation, any or all of them, depend on matter or not. These are speculations which, however curious and entertaining, I shall decline, as lying out of my way in the design I am now upon. . . .

3. *Method.*—It is therefore worth while to search out the bounds between opinion and knowledge, and examine by what measures, in things whereof we have no certain knowledge, we ought to regulate our assent and moderate our persuasions. In order whereunto I shall pursue this following method.

First, I shall inquire into the original of those ideas, notions, or whatever else you please to call them, which a man observes and is conscious to himself he has in his mind; and the ways whereby the understanding comes to be furnished with them.

Secondly, I shall endeavour to show what knowledge the understanding hath by those ideas, and the certainty, evidence, and extent of it.

Thirdly, I shall make some inquiry into the nature and grounds of faith, or opinion; whereby I mean that assent which we give to any proposition as true, of whose truth yet we have no certain knowledges and here we shall have occasion to examine the reasons and degrees of assent.

7. *Occasion of this Essay.*—This was that which gave the first rise to this essay concerning the understanding. For I thought that the first step towards satisfying several inquiries the mind of man was very apt to run into, was to take a survey of our own understandings, examine our own powers, and see to what things they were adapted. All that was done, I suspected we began at the wrong end, and in vain sought for satisfaction in a quiet and sure possession of truths that most concerned us, whilst we let loose our thoughts into the vast ocean of being; as if all that boundless extent were the natural and undoubted possession of our understandings, wherein there was nothing exempt from its decisions, or that escaped its comprehension.

What is the difference between opinions and knowledge or the understanding? How does Locke intend to go about his task?

Jonathan Edwards, *Sinners in the Hands of an Angry God*[1]

Deuteronomy 32:35—*Their foot shall slide in due time.*[2]

In this verse is threatened the vengeance of God on the wicked unbelieving Israelites, that were God's visible people, and lived under means of grace;[3] and that notwithstanding all God's wonderful works that He had wrought towards that people, yet remained, as is expressed verse 28,[4] void of counsel, having no understanding in them; and that, under all the cultivations of heaven, brought forth bitter and poisonous fruit; as in the two verses next preceding the text.

The expression that I have chosen for my text, *their foot shall slide in due time,* seems to imply the following things relating to the punishment and destruction that these wicked Israelites were exposed to.

1. That they are always exposed to *destruction,* as one that stands or walks in slippery places is always exposed to fall. This is implied in the manner of their destruction's coming upon them, being represented by their foot's sliding. The same is expressed, Psalm 73:18: "Surely thou didst set them in slippery places: thou castedst them down into destruction."

2. It implies that they were always exposed to sudden, unexpected destruction. As he that walks in slippery places is every moment liable to fall, he cannot foresee one moment whether he shall stand or fall the next; and when he does fall, he falls at once, without warning, which is also expressed in that Psalm 73:18–19: "Surely thou didst set them in slippery places: thou castedst them down into destruction. How are they brought into desolation as in a moment."

3. Another thing implied is that they are liable to fall of *themselves,* without being thrown down by the hand of another, as he that stands or walks on slippery ground needs nothing but his own weight to throw him down.

4. That the reason why they are not fallen already, and do not fall now, is only that God's appointed time is not come. For it is said that when that due time or appointed time comes, *their foot shall slide.* Then they shall be left to fall, as they are inclined by their own weight. God will not hold them up in these slippery places any longer but will let them go; and then, at that very instant, they shall fall into destruction; as he that stands on such slippery declining ground on the edge of a pit that he cannot stand alone, when he is let go he immediately falls and is lost.

The observation from the words that I would now insist upon is this.

There is nothing that keeps wicked men at any one moment out of hell, but the mere pleasure of God.

By the *mere* pleasure of God, I mean His *sovereign* pleasure, His arbitrary will, restrained by no obligation, hindered by no manner of difficulty, any more than if nothing else but God's mere will had in the least degree, or in any respect whatsoever, any hand in the preservation of wicked men one moment.

The truth of this observation may appear by the following considerations.

1. There is no want of *power* in God to cast wicked men into hell at any moment. Men's hands cannot be strong when God rises up: the strongest have no power to resist Him, nor can any deliver[5] out of His hands.

He is not only able to cast wicked men into hell, but He can most easily do it. Sometimes an earthly prince meets with a great deal of difficulty to subdue a rebel that has found means to fortify himself and has made himself strong by the number his followers. But it is not so with God. There is no fortress that is any defence against the power of God. Though hand join in hand, and vast multitudes of God's enemies combine and associate themselves, they are easily broken in pieces; they are as great heaps of light chaff before the whirlwind, or large quantities of dry stubble before devouring flames. We find it easy to tread on and crush a worm that we see crawling on the earth; so it is easy for us to cut or singe a slender thread that any thing hangs by; thus easy is it for God, when He pleases, to cast his enemies down to hell. What are we, that we should think to stand before Him, at whose rebuke the earth trembles and before Whom the rocks are thrown down!

2. They *deserve* to be cast into hell; so that divine justice never stands in the way, it makes no objection against God's using His power at any moment to destroy them. Yea, on the contrary, justice calls aloud for an infinite punishment of their sins. Divine justice says of the tree that brings forth such grapes of Sodom, "Cut it down, why cumbereth it the ground?" Luke 13:7. The sword of divine justice is every moment brandished over their heads, and it is nothing but the hand of arbitrary mercy, and God's mere will, that holds it back.

3. They are already under a sentence of *condemnation* to hell. They do not only justly deserve to be cast down thither, but the sentence of the law of God, that eternal and immutable rule of righteousness that God has fixed between Him and mankind, is gone out against them and stands against them, so that they are bound over already to hell: John 3:18, "He that believeth not is condemned already." So that every unconverted man properly belongs to hell; that is his place; from thence he is: John 8:23, "Ye are from beneath," and thither he is bound; it is the place that justice, and God's word, and the sentence of his unchangeable law, assign to him.

4. They are now the objects of that very same *anger* and wrath of God, that is expressed in the torments of hell; and the reason why they do not go down to hell at each moment, is not because God, in whose power they are, is not then very angry with them, as angry as He is with many of those miserable creatures that He is now tormenting in hell, and do there feel and bear the fierceness of His wrath. Yea, God is a great deal more angry with great numbers that are now on earth, yea, doubtless, with many that are now in this congregation, that, it may be, are at ease and quiet, than He is with many of those that are now in the flames of hell.

So that it is not because God is unmindful of their wickedness, and does not resent it, that He does not let loose his hand and cut them off. God is not altogether such a one as themselves, though they may imagine Him to be so. The wrath of God burns against them; their damnation does not slumber; the pit is prepared; the fire is made ready; the furnace is now hot, ready to receive them; the flames do now rage and glow. The glittering sword is whet,[6] and held over them, and the pit hath opened its mouth under them.

5. The *devil* stands ready to fall upon them, and seize them as his own, at what moment God shall permit him. They belong to him; he has their souls in his possession, and under his dominion. The Scripture represents them as his goods, Luke 11:21.[7] The devils watch them; they are ever by them, at their right hand; they stand waiting for them, like greedy hungry lions that see their prey, and expect to have it, but are for the present kept back; if God should withdraw His hand, by which they are restrained, they would in one moment fly upon their poor souls. The old serpent is gaping for them, hell opens its mouth wide to receive them; and if God should permit it, they would be hastily swallowed up and lost.

6. There are in the souls of wicked men those hellish *principles* reigning, that would presently kindle and flame out into hell-fire, if it were not for God's restraints. There is laid in the very nature of carnal men, a foundation for the torments of hell; there are those corrupt principles, in reigning power in them, and in full possession of them, that are the beginnings of hell-fire. These principles are active and powerful, exceeding violent in their nature, and if it were not for the restraining hand of God upon them, they would soon break out; they would flame out after the same manner as the same corruptions, the same enmity does in the hearts of damned

souls, and would beget the same torments in them as they do in them. The souls of the wicked are in Scripture compared to the troubled sea, Isaiah 57:20.[8] For the present, God restrains their wickedness by His mighty power, as He does the raging waves of the troubled sea, saying, "Hitherto shalt thou come, but no further;"[9] but if God should withdraw that restraining power, it would soon carry all before it. Sin is the ruin and misery of the soul; it is destructive in its nature; and if God should leave it without restraint, there would need nothing else to make the soul perfectly miserable. The corruption of the heart of man is a thing that is immoderate and boundless in its fury; and while wicked men live here, it is like fire pent up by God's restraints; whereas if it were let loose, it would set on fire the course of nature; and as the heart is now a sink of sin, so, if sin was not restrained, it would immediately turn the soul into a fiery oven or a furnace of fire and brimstone.

7. It is no security to wicked men for one moment, that there are no visible means of death at hand. It is no security to a natural man, that he is now in health, and that he does not see which way he should now immediately go out of the world by any accident, and that there is no visible danger in any respect in his circumstances. The manifold and continual experience of the world in all ages shows that this is no evidence that a man is not on the very brink of eternity and that the next step will not be into another world. The unseen, unthought of ways and means of persons going suddenly out of the world are innumerable and inconceivable. Unconverted men walk over the pit of hell on a rotten covering, and there are innumerable places in this covering so weak that they will not bear their weight, and these places are not seen. The arrows of death fly unseen at noonday;[10] the sharpest sight cannot discern them. God has so many different, unsearchable ways of taking wicked men out of the world and sending them to hell, that there is nothing to make it appear that God had need to be at the expense of a miracle, or go out of the ordinary course of His providence, to destroy any wicked man, at any moment. All the means that there are of sinners going out of the world, are so in God's hands and so absolutely subject to His power and determination, that it does not depend at all less on the mere will of God, whether sinners shall at any moment go to hell, than if means were never made use of or at all concerned in the case.

8. Natural men's *prudence* and *care* to preserve their own lives, or the care of others to preserve them, do not secure them a moment. This, divine providence and universal experience do also bear testimony to. There is this clear evidence that men's own wisdom is no security to them from death, that if it were otherwise we should see some difference between the wise and politic men of the world and others, with regard to their liableness to early and unexpected death; but how is it in fact? Ecclesiastes 2:16, "How dieth the wise man? As the fool."

9. All wicked men's *pains* and *contrivance* they use to escape hell, while they continue to reject Christ and so remain wicked men, do not secure them from hell one moment. Almost every natural man that hears of hell, flatters himself that he shall escape it; he depends upon himself for his own security; he flatters himself in what he has done, in what he is now doing, or what he intends to do; everyone lays out matters in his own mind how he shall avoid damnation and flatters himself that he contrives well for himself, and that his schemes will not fail. They hear indeed that there are but few saved and that the bigger part of men that have died heretofore are gone to hell; but each one imagines that he lays out matters better for his own escape than others have done; he does not intend to come to that place of torment; he says within himself that he intends to take care that shall be effectual and to order matters so for himself as not to fail.

But the foolish children of men do miserably delude themselves in their own schemes and in their confidence in their own strength and wisdom; they trust to nothing but a shadow. The greater part of those that heretofore have lived under the same means of grace, and are now dead, are undoubtedly gone to hell; and it was not because they were not as wise as those that are now alive; it was not because they did not lay out matters as well for themselves to secure their own escape. If it were so that we could come to speak with them, and could inquire of them, one by one, whether they expected, when alive, and when they used to hear about hell, ever to be subjects of that misery, we, doubtless, should hear one and another reply, "No, I never intended to come here; I had laid out matters otherwise in my mind; I thought I should contrive well for myself; I thought my scheme good; I intended to take effectual care; but it came upon me unexpectedly; I did not look for it at that time, and in that manner; it came as a thief; death outwitted me; God's wrath was too quick for me; O my cursed foolishness! I was flattering myself and pleasing myself with vain dreams of what I would do hereafter; and when I was saying, peace and safety, then sudden destruction came upon me."

10. God has laid Himself under *no obligation*, by any promise, to keep any natural man out of hell one moment; God certainly has made no promises either of eternal life, or of any deliverance or preservation from eternal death, but what are contained in the covenant of grace,[11] the promises that are given in Christ, in whom all the promises are yea and amen. But surely they have no interest in the promises of the covenant of grace that are not the children of the covenant, and that do not believe in any of the promises of the covenant, and have no interest in the Mediator of the covenant.

So that, whatever some have imagined and pretended about promises made to natural men's earnest seeking and knocking, it is plain and manifest that whatever pains a natural man takes in religion, whatever prayers he makes, till he believes in Christ, God is under no manner of obligation to keep him a moment from eternal destruction.

So that thus it is, that natural men are held in the hand of God, over the pit of hell; they have deserved the fiery pit and are already sentenced to it; and God is dreadfully provoked; His anger is as great towards them as to those that are actually suffering the executions of the fierceness of His wrath in hell, and they have done nothing in the least to appease or abate that anger; neither is God in the least bound by any promise to hold them up one moment; the devil is waiting for them; hell is gaping for them; the flames gather and flash about them, and would fain lay hold on them and swallow them up; the fire pent up in their own hearts is struggling to break out; and they have no interest in any Mediator; there are no means within reach that can be any security to them. In short, they have refuge, nothing to take hold of; all that preserves them every moment is the mere arbitrary will and uncovenanted, unobliged forbearance of an incensed God.

Application

The use of this awful subject may be of awakening unconverted persons in this congregation. This that you have heard is the case of every one of you that are out of Christ. That world of mercy, that lake of burning brimstone, is extended abroad under you.

There is the dreadful pit of the glowing flames of the wrath of God; there is hell's wide gaping mouth open; and you have nothing to stand upon, nor any thing to take hold of. There is nothing between you and hell but the air; it is only the power and mere pleasure of God that holds you up.

You probably are not sensible of this; you find you are kept out of hell but do not see the hand of God in it; but look at other things, as the good state of your bodily constitution, your care of your own life, and the means you use for your own preservation. But indeed these things are nothing; if God should withdraw His hand, they would avail no more to keep you from falling than the thin air to hold up a person that is suspended in it.

Your wickedness makes you, as it were, heavy as lead and to tend downwards with great weight and pressure towards hell; and if God should let you go, you would immediately sink and swiftly descend and plunge into the bottomless gulf, and your healthy constitution, and your own care and prudence, and best contrivance, and all your righteousness, would have no more influence to uphold you and keep you out of hell, than a spider's web would have to stop a falling rock. Were it not that so is the sovereign pleasure of God, the earth would not bear you one moment; for you are a burden to it; the creation groans with you; the creature is made subject to the bondage of your corruption, not willingly; the sun does not willingly shine upon you to give you light to serve sin and Satan; the earth does not willingly yield her increase to satisfy your lusts; nor is it willingly a stage for your wickedness to be acted upon; the air does not willingly serve you for breath to maintain the flame of life in your vitals while you spend your life in the service of God's enemies. God's creatures are good, and were made for men to serve God with, and do not willingly subserve to any other purpose, and groan when they are abused to purposes so directly contrary to their nature and end. And the world would spew you out, were it not for the sovereign hand of Him who hath subjected it in hope. There are the black clouds of God's wrath now hanging directly over your heads, full of the dreadful storm and big with thunder; and were it not for the restraining hand of God, it would immediately burst forth upon you. The sovereign pleasure of God, for the present, stays His rough wind; otherwise it would come with fury, and your destruction would come like a whirlwind, and you would be like the chaff of the summer threshing floor.

chapter 4

The wrath of God is like great waters that are dammed for the present; they increase more and more, and rise higher and higher, till an outlet is given; and the longer the stream is stopped, the more rapid and mighty is its course when once it is let loose. It is true that judgment against your evil works has not been executed hitherto; the floods of God's vengeance have been withheld; but your guilt in the meantime is constantly increasing, and you are every day treasuring up more wrath, the waters are continually rising and waxing more and more mighty; and there is nothing but the mere pleasure of God that holds the waters back that are unwilling to be stopped and press hard to go forward. If God should only withdraw His hand from the floodgate, it would immediately fly open, and the fiery floods of the fierceness and wrath of God would rush forth with inconceivable fury and would come upon you with omnipotent power; and if your strength were ten thousand times greater than it is, yea, ten thousand times greater than the strength of the stoutest, sturdiest devil in hell, it would be nothing to withstand or endure it.

The bow of God's wrath is bent, and the arrow made ready on the string, and justice bends the arrow at your heart and strains the bow, and it is nothing but the mere pleasure of God, and that of an angry God, without any promise or obligation at all, that keeps the arrow one moment from being made drunk with your blood.

Thus are all you that never passed under a great change of heart, by the mighty power of the Spirit of God upon your souls; all that were never born again, and made new creatures, and raised from being dead in sin, to a state of new, and before altogether unexperienced light and life (however you may have reformed your life in many things, and may have had religious affections, and may keep up a form of religion in your families, and closets, and in the houses of God, and may be strict in it), you are thus in the hands of an angry God; it is nothing but His mere pleasure that keeps you from being this moment swallowed up in everlasting destruction.

However unconvinced you may now be of the truth of what you hear, by and by you will be fully convinced of it. Those that are gone from being in the like circumstances with you, see that it was so with them; for destruction came suddenly upon most of them, when they expected nothing of it and while they were saying, "Peace and safety;" now they see that those things that

66

they depended on for peace and safety were nothing but thin air and empty shadows.

The God that holds you over the pit of hell, much as one holds a spider, or some loathsome insect, over the fire, abhors you and is dreadfully provoked; His wrath towards you burns like fire; He looks upon you as worthy of nothing else but to be cast into the fire; He is of purer eyes than to bear to have you in His sight; you are ten thousand times more abominable in His eyes than the most hateful and venomous serpent is in ours. You have offended Him infinitely more than ever a stubborn rebel did his prince; and yet it is nothing but His hand that holds you from falling into the fire every moment; it is to be ascribed to nothing else, that you did not go to hell the last night, that you were suffered to awake again in this world, after you closed your eyes to sleep; and there is no other reason to be given, why you have not dropped into hell since you arose in the morning, but that God's hand has held you up; there is no other reason to be given why you have not gone to hell, since you have sat here in the house of God, provoking His pure eyes by your sinful, wicked manner of attending His solemn worship; yea, there is nothing else that is to be given as a reason why you do not this very moment drop down into hell.

O sinner! consider the fearful danger you are in; it is a great furnace of wrath, a wide and bottomless pit, full of the fire of wrath, that you are held over in the hand of that God, whose wrath is provoked and incensed as much against you, as against many of the damned in hell; you hang by a slender thread, with the flames of divine wrath flashing about it and ready every moment to singe it and burn it asunder; and you have no interest in any Mediator and nothing to lay hold of to save yourself, nothing to keep off the flames of wrath, nothing of your own, nothing that you ever have done, nothing that you can do to induce God to spare you one moment.

And consider here more particularly several things concerning that wrath that you are in such danger of.

1. *Whose* wrath it is. It is the wrath of the infinite God. If it were only the wrath of man, though it were of the most potent prince, it would be comparatively little to be regarded. The wrath of kings is very much dreaded, especially of absolute monarchs that have the possessions and lives of their subjects wholly in their power, to be disposed of at their mere will. Proverbs 20:2, "The fear of a

king is as the roaring of a lion; whoso provoketh him to anger sinneth against his own soul." The subject that very much enrages an arbitrary prince is liable to suffer the most extreme torments that human art can invent or human power can inflict. But the greatest earthly potentates, in their greatest majesty and strength, and when clothed in their greatest terrors, are but feeble, despicable worms of the dust, in comparison of the great and almighty Creator and King of heaven and earth; it is but little that they can do, when most enraged and when they have exerted the utmost of their fury. All the kings of the earth, before God, are as grasshoppers; they are nothing and less than nothing; both their love and their hatred is to be despised. The wrath of the great King of kings is as much more terrible than theirs, as His majesty is greater. Luke 12:4–5, "And I say unto you, my friends, Be not afraid of them that kill the body, and after that, have no more that they can do. But I will forewarn you whom ye shall fear: Fear him, which after he hath killed, hath power to cast into hell; yea, I say unto you, Fear him."

2. It is the *fierceness* of His wrath that you are exposed to. We often read of the fury of God; as in Isaiah 59:18. "According to their deeds, accordingly he will repay fury to his adversaries." So Isaiah 66:15, "For behold, the Lord will come with fire, and with his chariots like a whirlwind, to render his anger with fury, and his rebuke with flames of fire." And so in many other places. So Revelation 19:15.[12] There we read of "the winepress of the fierceness and wrath of Almighty God." The words are exceedingly terrible; if it had only been said, "the wrath of God," the words would have implied that which is infinitely dreadful; but it is not only said so, but "the fierceness and wrath of God," the fury of God! the fierceness of Jehovah! Oh how dreadful must that be! Who can utter or conceive what such expressions carry in them! But it is also "the fierceness and wrath of Almighty God." As though there would be a very great manifestation of His almighty power in what the fierceness of His wrath should inflict, as though omnipotence should be, as it were, enraged and exerted, as men are wont to exert their strength in the fierceness of their wrath. Oh! then, what will be the consequence! What will become of the poor worm that shall suffer it! Whose hands can be strong! And whose heart endure! To what a dreadful, inexpressible, inconceivable depth of misery must the poor creature be sunk who shall be the subject of this!

Consider this, you that are here present, that yet remain in an unregenerate state. That God will execute the fierceness of His anger, implies that He will inflict wrath without any pity; when God beholds the ineffable extremity of your case, and sees your torment so vastly disproportioned to your strength, and sees how your poor soul is crushed and sinks down, as it were, into an infinite gloom, He will have no compassion upon you; He will not forbear the executions of his wrath or in the least lighten His hand; there shall be no moderation or mercy, nor will God then at all stay His rough wind; He will have no regard to your welfare, nor be at all careful lest you should suffer too much in any other sense, than only that you should not suffer beyond what strict justice requires; nothing shall be withheld because it is so hard for you to bear. Ezekiel 8:18, "Therefore will I also deal in fury: mine eye shall not spare, neither will I have pity: and though they cry in mine ears with a loud voice, yet will I not hear them." Now God stands ready to pity you; this is a day of mercy; you may cry now with some encouragement of obtaining mercy; but when once the day of mercy is past, your most lamentable and dolorous cries and shrieks will be in vain; you will be wholly lost and thrown away of God, as to any regard to your welfare; God will have no other use to put you to but to suffer misery; you shall be continued in being to no other end; for you will be a vessel of wrath fitted to destruction; and there will be no other use of this vessel but to be filled full of wrath; God will be so far from pitying you when you cry to him, that it is said he will only "laugh and mock," Proverbs 1:25–26,[13] & c.

How awful are those words, Isaiah 63:3, which are the words of the great God: "I will tread them in mine anger, and trample them in my fury; and their blood shall be sprinkled upon my garments, and I will stain all my raiment." It is perhaps impossible to conceive of words that carry in them greater manifestations of these three things, viz., contempt, and hatred, and fierceness of indignation. If you cry to God to pity you, He will be so far from pitying you in your doleful case, or showing you the least regard or favor, that instead of that He will only tread you under foot; and though He will know that you cannot bear the weight of omnipotence treading upon you, He will not regard that, but He will crush you under His feet without mercy; He will crush out your blood and make it fly, and it shall be sprinkled on His garments, so as to stain all His raiment. He will not only hate you, but He will have you in the utmost contempt; no place shall be thought fit for you but under His feet, to be trodden down as the mire in the streets.

3. The *misery* you are exposed to is that which God will inflict to that end, that He might show what that wrath of Jehovah is. God hath had it on His heart to show to angels and men both how excellent His love is and also how terrible His wrath is. Sometimes earthly kings have a mind to show how terrible their wrath is, by the extreme punishments they would execute on those that provoke them. Nebuchadnezzar, that mighty and haughty monarch of the Chaldean empire, was willing to show his wrath when enraged with Shadrach, Meshech, and Abednego[14] and accordingly gave order that the burning fiery furnace should be heated seven times hotter than it was before; doubtless, it was raised to the utmost degree of fierceness that human art could raise it; but the great God is also willing to show His wrath and magnify His awful Majesty and mighty power in the extreme sufferings of His enemies. Romans 9:22, "What if God, willing to show his wrath, and to make his power known, endured with much long-suffering, the vessels of wrath fitted to destruction?" And seeing this is His design, and what He has determined, to show how terrible the unmixed, unrestrained wrath, the fury, and fierceness of Jehovah is, He will do it to effect. There will be something accomplished and brought to pass that will be dreadful with a witness. When the great and angry God hath risen up and executed His awful vengeance on the poor sinner and the wretch is actually suffering the infinite weight and power of his indignation, then will God call upon the whole universe to behold that awful majesty and mighty power that is to be seen in it. Isaiah 33:12-14, "And the people shall be as the burnings of lime: as thorns cut up shall they be burnt in the fire. Hear, ye that are afar off, what I have done; and ye that are near, acknowledge my might. The sinners in Zion are afraid; fearfulness hath surprised the hypocrites," &c.

Thus it will be with you that are in an unconverted state, if you continue in it; the infinite might, and majesty, and terribleness of the Omnipotent God shall be magnified upon you in the ineffable strength of your torments; you shall be tormented in the presence of holy angels, and in the presence of the Lamb; and when you shall be in this state of suffering, the glorious inhabitants of heaven shall go forth and look on the awful spectacle, that they may see what the wrath and fierceness of the Almighty is;

and when they have seen it, they will fall down and adore that great power and majesty. Isaiah 66:23-24, "And it shall come to pass, that from one new moon to another, and from one Sabbath to another, shall all flesh come to worship before me, saith the Lord. And they shall go forth and look upon the carcasses of the men that have transgressed against me; for their worm shall not die, neither shall their fire be quenched; and they shall be an abhorring unto all flesh."

4. It is *everlasting* wrath. It would be dreadful to suffer this fierceness and wrath of Almighty God one moment; but you must suffer it to all eternity; there will be no end to this exquisite, horrible misery; when you look forward, you shall see a long forever, a boundless duration before you which will swallow up your thoughts and amaze your soul; and you will absolutely despair of ever having any deliverance, any end, any mitigation, any rest at all; you will know certainly that you must wear out long ages, millions of millions of ages, in wrestling and conflicting with this Almighty merciless vengeance; and then when you have so done, when so many ages have actually been spent by you in this manner, you will know that all is but a point to what remains. So that your punishment will indeed be infinite. Oh, who can express what the state of a soul in such circumstances is! All that we can possibly say about it, gives but a very feeble, faint representation of it; it is inexpressible and inconceivable; for "who knows the power of God's anger?"[15]

How dreadful is the state of those that are daily and hourly in danger of this great wrath and infinite misery! But this is the dismal case of every soul in this congregation that has not been born again, however moral and strict, sober and religious, they may otherwise be. Oh that you would consider it, whether you be young or old! There is reason to think that there are many in this congregation now hearing this discourse, that will actually be the subjects of this very misery to all eternity. We know not who they are, or in what seats they sit, or what thoughts they now have. It may be they are now at ease, and hear all these things without much disturbance, and are now flattering themselves that they are not the persons, promising themselves that they shall escape. If we knew that there was one person, and but one, in the whole congregation that was to be the subject of this misery, what an awful thing it would be to think of! If we knew who it was, what an awful sight would it be to see such a person! How might all the rest of the congregation lift up a lamentable and bitter cry over him! But alas! Instead of one, how many is it likely will remember this discourse in hell! And it would be a wonder if some that are now present should not be in hell in a very short time, even before this year is out. And it would be no wonder if some persons, that now sit here in some seats of this meeting-house, in health, and quiet and secure, should be there before tomorrow morning. Those of you that finally continue in a natural condition, that shall keep out of hell longest will be there in a little time! Your damnation does not slumber; it will come swiftly, and, in all probability, very suddenly upon many of you. You have reason to wonder that you are not already in hell. It is doubtless the case of some whom you have seen and known, that never deserved hell more than you, and that heretofore appeared as likely to have been now alive as you. Their case is past all hope; they are crying in extreme misery and perfect despair; but here you are in the land of the living and in the house of God, and have an opportunity to obtain salvation. What would not those poor damned hopeless souls give for one day's opportunity such as you now enjoy!

And now you have an extraordinary opportunity, a day wherein Christ has thrown the door of mercy wide open and stands in, calling and crying with a loud voice to poor sinners, a day wherein many are flocking to Him and pressing into the kingdom of God. Many are daily coming from the east, west, north and south; many that were very lately in the same miserable condition that you are in, are now in a happy state, with their hearts filled with love to Him who has loved them and washed them from their sins in His own blood, and rejoicing in hope of the glory of God. How awful it is to be left behind at such a day! To see so many others feasting, while you are pining and perishing! To see so many rejoicing and singing for joy of heart, while you have cause to mourn for sorrow of heart and howl for vexation of spirit! How can you rest one moment in such a condition? Are not your souls as precious as the souls of the people at Suffield,[16] where they are flocking from day to day to Christ?

Are there not many here who have lived long in the world, and are not to this day born again? and so are aliens from the commonwealth of Israel, and have done nothing ever since they have lived, but treasure up wrath against the day of wrath? Oh, sirs, your case, in an especial manner, is extremely dangerous. Your guilt and hardness of heart is extremely great. Do you not see how generally persons of your years are passed over and left, in the present remarkable and wonderful dispensation of God's mercy? You had need to consider yourselves and awake thoroughly out of sleep. You cannot bear the fierceness and wrath of the infinite God. And you, young men and young women, will you neglect this precious season which you now enjoy, when so many others of your age are renouncing all youthful vanities and flocking to Christ? You especially have now an extraordinary opportunity; but if you neglect it, it will soon be with you as with those persons who spent all the precious days of youth in sin and are now come to such a dreadful pass in blindness and hardness. And you, children, who are unconverted, do not you know that you are going down to hell, to bear the dreadful wrath of that God who is now angry with you every day and every night? Will you be content to be the children of the devil, when so many other children in the land are converted and are become the holy and happy children of the King of kings?

And let every one that is yet of Christ, and hanging over the pit of hell, whether they be old men and women, or middle aged, or young people, or little children, now hearken to the loud calls of God's word and providence. This acceptable year of the Lord, a day of such great favors to some, will doubtless be a day of as remarkable vengeance to others. Men's hearts harden, and their guilt increases apace at such a day as this, if they neglect their souls; and never was there so great danger of such persons being given up to hardness of heart and blindness of mind. God seems now to be hastily gathering in His elect in all parts of the land; and probably the greater part of adult persons that ever shall be saved will be brought in now in a little time and that it will be as it was on the great out-pouring of the Spirit upon the Jews in the apostles' days; the election will obtain, and the rest will be blinded. If this should be the case with you, you will eternally curse this day, and will curse the day that ever you were born to see such a season of the pouring out of God's Spirit, and will wish that you had died and gone to hell before you had seen it. Now undoubtedly it is, as it was in the days of John the Baptist, the axe is in an extraordinary manner laid at the root of the trees, that every tree which brings not forth good fruit may be hewn down and cast into the fire.[17]

Therefore, let every one that is out of Christ, now awake and fly from the wrath to come. The wrath of Almighty God is now undoubtedly hanging over a great part of this congregation: Let every one fly out of Sodom: "Haste and escape for your lives, look not behind you, escape to the mountain, lest you be consumed."[18]

How does Edwards differ from Locke in his beliefs concerning the ability of people to gain knowledge or use reason?

Endnotes

1. In 1741, in the midst of the Great Awakening, Edwards delivered this, his most famous sermon. His description of the impending and awesome wrath of an inscrutable and arbitrary God and the exquisite tortures to be suffered by men was meant to destroy the religious complacency of his audience, the "loose and indolent" congregation at Enfield, Connecticut. Witnesses recorded that his words, spoken with dramatic calmness and restraint, brought comfort to some of his listeners but roused others to shrieks, groans, and writhing and left them "bowed down with awful conviction of their sin and danger."

2. "To me belongeth vengeance, and recompence; their foot shall slide in due time: for the day of their calamity is at hand, and the things that shall come upon them make haste." Edwards' references to Deuteronomy are drawn from Chapter 32 in which Moses speaks God's words of warning to the Israelites and exhorts them to obey God's commands lest He forsake and destroy them.

3. The Decalogue, or Ten Commandments, under which the Israelites were to live and thereby remain God's chosen people.

4. "They are a nation void of counsel, neither is there any understanding in them."

5. I.e., rescue others.

6. Sharpenend.

7. "When a strong man armed keepeth his palace, his goods are in peace."

8. "But the wicked are like the troubled sea, when it cannot rest, whose waters cast up mire and dirt."

9. Job 38:11.

10. Cf. "Thou shalt not be afraid for the terror by night; nor for the arrow that flieth by day." Psalms 91:5.

11. The covenant, or agreement, by which God, because of Jesus' atonement, restored the possibility of grace, or salvation, that had previously been lost to mankind by the fall of Adam.

12. "He treadeth the winepress of the fierceness and wrath of Almighty God."

13. "But ye have set at nought all my counsel, and would none of my reproof: I also will laugh at your calamity; I will mock you when your fear cometh."

14. Described in Daniel 3:1-30.

15. "Who knoweth the power of thine anger? even according to thy fear, so is thy wrath." Psalms 90:11.

16. "A town in the neighborhood."—Edwards' note.

17. An adaptation of Luke 3:9.

18. Genesis 19:17.

John Woolman, from
The Journal of John Woolman

"In the Service of the Gospel"

Henceforth I might not consider myself as a distinct or separate person.
—John Woolman

"I Was Taught to Watch the Pure Opening"

[FROM *Journal*]

JOHN WOOLMAN

[John Woolman (1720–1772) was a moral and religious genius. His life, in the realm of action, is to the lives of other individuals what a poet's use of words is to the nonpoetic. He was equipped with moral antennae which caused him to feel about slavery, and indeed about the conditions under which all people worked, what others would not feel for another century. He had insights about the use of time and of money and the waging of war which it may take most of us another thousand years to attain. One

feels ashamed to understand Woolman's words without imitating his life.

He was no born idol-breaker like Fox, not natively courageous and built for bufferings. He was a frail man, often in poor health and with no stomach for facing warring peoples, traversing the wilderness, and telling others anything-let alone that, by his lights, they were wrong. So before he could do any of these things he had to combat and conquer the naturally diffident, retiring, fearful Woolman. He did conquer him. Fox's belief—and bones—were so strong that, when beaten on the arm with a stave until the onlookers cried that he would never again have the use of his hand, he was able to control, within the hour, the injury and swelling. One feels that Woolman's arm would have been broken, that, as the crowd prophesied, he would never again have use of it—but that, nevertheless, he would have gone on, exactly as before.

Fox, a man cast in the mold of the physical hero, and burning with a belief not yet completely voiced, preached the inner light. Woolman harkened to Fox, lived in that light, and disseminated it.

Woolman went to the native American tribes with a characteristically modest and honest statement. He intended to live with them, he said, not as a missionary but so that, "haply, I might receive some instruction from them, or they might in any degree be helped forward by my following the leadings of truth among them." If every missionary had approached the mission field with this concept, how different would have been the history of foreign missions. Woolman possessed no truth, extraneous to these people. He intended only, among this particular people, to follow "the leadings of truth." He would speak to their condition.

One Woolman in a hundred, one Woolman in a thousand, might be enough to change the face of the earth. Shall we see his like again? It was a part of Woolman's, as of Fox's belief that perfection is possible to all. If they were right, we may.]

I have often felt a Motion of Love to leave some Hints in Writing of my Experience of the Goodness of God; and now, in the thirty-sixth Year of my Age, I begin this Work.

I was born in Northampton, in Burlington County, West Jersey, in the Year 1720; and before I was seven years old, I began to be acquainted with the Operations of divine Love. Through the Care of my Parents, I was taught to read nearly as soon as I was capable of it; and, as I went from School one seventh Day, I remember, while my Companions went to play by the Way, I went forward out of Sight, and, sitting down, I read the 22d

Chapter of the Revelations: "He shewed me a pure River of Water of Life, clear as Crystal, proceeding out of the Throne of God and of the Lamb, etc." and, in reading it, my Mind was drawn to seek after that pure Habitation, which, I then believed, God had prepared for his Servants. The Place where I sat, and the Sweetness that attended my Mind, remain fresh in my Memory.

This, and the like gracious Visitations, had that Effect upon me, that when Boys used ill Language it troubled me; and, through the continued Mercies of God, I was preserved from it.

The pious Instructions of my Parents were often fresh in my Mind when I happened to be among wicked Children, and were of Use to me. My Parents, having a large Family of Children, used frequently, on first Days after Meeting, to put us to read in the holy Scriptures, or some religious Books, one after another, the rest sitting by without much Conversation; which, I have since often thought, was a good Practice. From what I had read and heard, I believed there had been, in past Ages, People who walked in Uprightness before God, in a Degree exceeding any that I knew, or heard of, now living: And the Apprehension of there being less Steadiness and Firmness, amongst People in this Age than in past Ages, often troubled me while I was a Child.

A Thing remarkable in my Childhood was, that once, going to a Neighbour's House, I saw, on the Way, a Robin sitting on her Nest, and as I came near she went off, but, having young ones, flew about, and with many Cries expressed her Concern for them; I stood and threw Stones at her, till, one striking her, she fell down dead: At first I was pleased with the Exploit, but after a few Minutes was seized with Horror, as having, in a sportive Way, killed an innocent Creature while she was careful for her Young: I beheld her lying dead, and thought these young ones, for which she was so careful, must now perish for want of their Dam to nourish them; and, after some painful Considerations on the Subject, I climbed up the Tree, took all the young Birds, and killed them; supposing that better than to leave them to pine away and die miserably: And believed, in this Case, that Scripture-proverb was fulfilled, "The tender Mercies of the Wicked are cruel." I then went on my Errand, but, for some Hours, could think of little else but the Cruelties I had committed, and was much troubled. Thus he, whose tender Mercies are over all his Works, hath placed a Principle in the human Mind, which incited to exercise Goodness towards every living Creature; and this being singly attended to,

People become tender hearted and sympathizing; but being frequently and totally rejected, the Mind becomes shut up in a contrary Disposition. . . .

Having attained the Age of sixteen Years, I began to love wanton Company; and though I was preserved from prophane Language, or scandalous Conduct, still I perceived a Plant in me which produced much wild Grapes; yet my merciful Father forsook me not utterly, but, at Times, through his Grace, I was brought seriously to consider my Ways; and the Sight of my Backslidings affected me with Sorrow; but, for want of rightly attending to the Reproofs of Instruction, Vanity was added to Vanity, and Repentance to Repentance: Upon the whole, my Mind was more and more alienated from the Truth, and I hastened toward Destruction. While I meditate on the Gulph towards which I travelled, and reflect on my youthful Disobedience, for these Things I weep, mine Eyes run down with Water.

Advancing in Age, the Number of my Acquaintances increased, and thereby my Way grew more difficult; though I had found Comfort in reading the holy Scriptures, and thinking on heavenly Things, I was now estranged therefrom: I knew I was going from the Flock of Christ, and had no Resolution to return; hence serious Reflections were uneasy to me, and youthful Vanities and Diversions my greatest Pleasure. Running in this Road I found many like myself; and we associated in that which is the reverse of true Friendship. . . .

Thus Time passed on: My Heart was replenished with Mirth and Wantonness, and pleasing Scenes of Vanity were presented to my Imagination, till I attained the Age of eighteen Years; near which Time I felt the Judgments of God, in my Soul, like a consuming Fire; and, looking over my past Life, the Prospect was moving. I was often sad, and longed to be delivered from those Vanities; then again, my Heart was strongly inclined to them, and there was in me a sore Conflict: At Times I turned to Folly, and then again, Sorrow and Confusion took hold of me. In a while, I resolved totally to leave off some of my Vanities; but there was a secret Reserve, in my Heart, of the more refined Part of them, and I was not low enough to find true Peace. Thus, for some Months, I had great Troubles; there remaining in me an unsubjected Will, which rendered my Labours fruitless, till at length, through the merciful Continuance of heavenly Visitations, I was made to bow down in Spirit before the Lord. I remember one Evening I had spent some Time in reading a pious Author; and walking out alone, I humbly prayed to the Lord for his Help, that I might be delivered from all those Vanities which so ensnared me. Thus, being brought low, he helped me; and, as I learned to bear the Cross, I felt Refreshment to come from his Presence; but, not keeping in that Strength which gave Victory, I lost Ground again; the Sense of which greatly affected me; and I sought Desarts and lonely Places, and there, with Tears, did confess my Sins to God, and humbly craved Help of him. And I may say with Reverance, he was near to me in my Troubles, and in those Times of Humiliation opened my Ear to Discipline. I was now led to look seriously at the Means by which I was drawn from the pure Truth, and learned this, that, if I would live in the life which the faithful Servants of God lived in, I must not go into Company as heretofore in my own Will; but all the Cravings of Sense must be governed by a divine Principle. In Times of Sorrow and Abasement these Instructions were sealed upon me, and I felt the Power of Christ prevail over selfish Desires, so that I was preserved in a good degree of Steadiness; and, being young, and believing at that Time that a single Life was best for me, I was strengthened to keep from such Company as had often been a Snare to me.

I kept steadily to Meetings; spent First-day Afternoons chiefly in reading the Scriptures and other good Books; and was early convinced in Mind, that true Religion consisted in an inward Life, wherein the Heart doth love and reverence God the Creator, and learns to exercise true Justice and Goodness, not only toward all Men, but also toward the brute Creatures. That as the Mind was moved, by an inward Principle, to love God as an invisible incomprehensible Being, by the same Principle, it was moved to love him in all his Manifestations in the visible World. That, as by his Breath the Flame of Life was kindled in all animal sensible Creatures, to say we love God, and, at the same Time exercise Cruelty toward the least Creature, is a Contradiction in itself.

I found no Narrowness respecting Sects and Opinions; but believed, that sincere upright-hearted People, in every Society, who truly love God, were accepted of him. . . .

All this Time I lived with my Parents, and wrought on the Plantation; and, having had Schooling pretty well for a Planter, I used to improve it in Winter Evenings, and other leisure Times; and, being now in the twenty-first Year of my Age, a Man, in much Business at shop-keeping and baking, asked me, if I would hire with him to tend Shop and keep Books. I acquainted my Father with the Proposal; and, after some Deliberation, it was agreed for me to go.

At Home I had lived retired; and now, having a Prospect of being much in the Way of Company, I felt frequent and fervent Cries in my Heart to God, the Father of Mercies, that he would preserve me from all Corruption; that in this more publick Employment, I might serve him, my gracious Redeemer, in that Humility and Self-denial, with which I had been, in a small Degree, exercised in a more private Life. The Man, who employed me, furnished a Shop in Mount-Holly, about five Miles from my Father's House, and six from his own; and there I lived alone, and tended his Shop. Shortly after my Settlement here I was visited by several young People, my former Acquaintance, who knew not but Vanities would be as agreeable to me now as ever, and, at these Times, I cried to the Lord in secret, for Wisdom and Strength; for I felt myself encompassed with Difficulties, and had fresh Occasion to bewail the Follies of Time past, in contracting a Familiarity with libertine People; and, as I now had left my Father's House outwardly, I found my heavenly Father to be merciful to me beyond what I can express. . . .

I went to Meetings in an awful Frame of Mind, and endeavoured to be inwardly acquainted with the Language of the true Shepherd; and, one Day, being under a strong Exercise of Spirit, I stood up, and said some Words in a Meeting; but, not keeping close to the divine Opening, I said more than was required of me; and being soon sensible of my Error, I was afflicted in Mind some Weeks, without any Light or Comfort, even to that Degree that I could not take Satisfaction in any Thing: I remembered God, and was troubled, and, in the Depth of my Distress, he had Pity upon me, and sent the Comforter: I then felt Forgiveness for my Offence, and my Mind became calm and quiet, being truly thankful to my gracious Redeemer for his Mercies; and, after this, feeling the Spring of divine Love opened, and a Concern to speak, I said a few Words in a Meeting, in which I found Peace; this, I believe, was about six Weeks from the first Time: And, as I was thus humbled and disciplined under the Cross, my Understanding became more strengthened to distinguish the pure Spirit which inwardly moves upon the Heart, and taught me to wait in Silence sometimes many Weeks together, untill I felt that rise which prepares the Creature.

From an inward purifying, and stedfast abiding under it, springs a lively operative Desire for the Good of others: All the Faithful are not called to the public Ministry; but whoever are, are called to minister of that which they have tasted and handled spiritually. The outward Modes of Worship are various; but, wherever any are true Ministers of Jesus Christ, it is from the Operation of his Spirit upon their Hearts, first purifying them, and thus giving them a just Sense of the Conditions of others.

This Truth was clearly fixed in my Mind; and I was taught to watch the pure Opening, and to take Heed, lest, while I was standing to speak, my own Will should get uppermost, and cause me to utter Words from worldly Wisdom, and depart from the Channel of the true Gospel-Ministry. . . .

About the Time called Christmas, I observed many People from the Country, and Dwellers in Town, who, resorting to Public-Houses, spent their Time in drinking and vain Sports, tending to corrupt one another; on which Account I was much troubled. At one House, in particular, there was much Disorder; and I believed it was a Duty incumbent on me to go and speak to the Master of that House. I considered I was young, and that several elderly Friends in town had Opportunity to see these Things; but though I would gladly have been excused, yet I could not feel my Mind clear.

The Exercise was heavy; and as I was reading what the Almighty said to Ezekiel, respecting his Duty as a Watchman, the Matter was set home more clearly; and then, with Prayers and Tears, I besought the Lord for his Assistance, who, in Lovingkindness, gave me a resigned Heart: Then, at a suitable Opportunity, I went to the Public-house, and, seeing the Man amongst much Company, I went to him, and told him, I wanted to speak with him; so we went aside, and there, in the Fear of the Almighty, I expressed to him what rested on my Mind; which he took kindly, and afterward shewed more Regard to me than before. In a few Years afterwards he died, middle-aged; and I often thought that, had I neglected my Duty in that Case, it would have given me great Trouble ; and I was humbly thankful to my gracious Father, who had supported me herein.

My Employer having a Negro Woman, sold her, and desired me to write a Bill of Sale, the Man being waiting who bought her: The Thing was sudden; and, though the Thoughts of writing an Instrument of Slavery for one of my Fellow-creatures felt uneasy, yet I remembered I was hired by the Year, that it was my Master who directed me to do it, and that it was an elderly Man, a Member of our Society, who bought her; so, through Weakness, I gave way, and wrote; but, at the executing it, I was so afflicted in my Mind, that I said, before my Master and the Friend, that I believed Slave-keeping to be a Practice inconsistent with the Christian Religion: This in some Degree abated my Uneasiness; yet, as often as I reflected seriously upon it, I thought I should have been clearer, if I had desired to have been excused from it, as a Thing against my Conscience; for such it was. And, some Time after this, a young Man, of our Society, spoke to me to write a Conveyance of a Slave to him, he having lately taken a Negro into his House: I told him I was not easy to write it; for, though many of our Meeting and in other Places kept Slaves, I still believed the Practice was not right, and desired to be excused from the writing. I spoke to him in Good-will; and he told me that keeping Slaves was not altogether agreeable to his Mind; but that the Slave being a Gift to his Wife, he had accepted of her.

Having now been several Years with my Employer, and he doing less at Merchandize than heretofore, I was thoughtful of some other Way of Business; perceiving Merchandize to be attended with much Cumber, in the Way of trading in these Parts.

My Mind, through the Power of Truth, was in a good degree weaned from the Desire of outward Greatness, and I was learning to be content with real Conveniences, that were not costly; so that a Way of Life, free from much Entanglement, appeared best for me, though the Income might be small. I had several Offers of Business that appeared profitable, but did not see my Way clear to accept of them; as believing the Business proposed would be attended with more outward Care than was required of me to engage in.

I saw that a humble Man, with the blessing of the Lord, might live on a little; and that where the Heart was set on Greatness, Success in Business did not satisfy the craving; but that commonly, with an Increase of Wealth, the Desire of Wealth increased. There was a Care on my Mind so to pass my Time, that nothing might hinder me from the most steady Attention to the Voice of the true Shepherd.

My Employer, though now a Retailer of Goods, was by Trade a Taylor, and kept a Servant-man at that Business; and I began to think about learning the Trade, expecting that, if I should settle, I

CONVERGENCE AND CONFLICT, 1660s–1763

might, by this Trade, and a little retailing of Goods, get a Living in a plain Way, without the Load of great Business: I mentioned it to my Employer, and we soon agreed on Terms; and then, when I had Leisure from the Affairs of Merchandize, I worked with his Man. . . .

Woolman also gains knowledge or understanding through religious belief. How is his view different from that of Edwards?

Imperial Breakdown, 1763–1774

INTRODUCTION

A number of tensions shaped colonial political culture in the century before the Revolution. On the one hand, economic, cultural, and political ties with England grew stronger in the 1700s. Many Americans gloried in the privileges and "rights of Englishmen" that they enjoyed as members of the British empire. They also praised the British Constitution as the best form of government. Rather than a single document or frame of government, the British Constitution referred to the three estates of English society—the king, the aristocracy, and the people. English men and women regarded a proper tension and balance between these groups as essential to the stability of their nation. They believed that the king and the English Parliament—which included the House of Lords and the House of Commons—gave each group proper representation in government and prevented any one group from dominating the rest. Americans believed that they replicated this perfect system in their colonial assemblies, where the royal governor took the place of the king, an upper house or council took the place of the Lords, and the lower house or assembly represented all the people. Yet despite their approving rhetoric, the colonists' actions challenged English notions of balance and power. During the eighteenth century, the lower houses of the colonial assemblies regularly challenged the royal governors' authority; most colonies also lacked a hereditary aristocracy capable of turning colonial councils into another House of Lords. This meant that the elective colonial assemblies exerted far more influence than was proper under the British Constitution, which worried many imperial authorities.

The distribution of political power within the colonies themselves generated another set of tensions. Both religious teachings and social custom instructed people to obey political authorities. England, including its colonies, was a monarchy, and the king occupied the top position in a hierarchical social structure. Few Americans questioned the justice of this inequality in the colonial period; indeed, most believed that inequality and the deference of inferiors to superiors were crucial to the maintenance of political and social order. Members of the colonial elite—merchants in northern port cities, slaveholding planters in the South—dominated political office in the colonies. Women, blacks, and those white men without property were prevented from voting. Yet because of the availability of land and economic opportunity, many colonists (as many as 50 to 90 percent of white males over twenty-one in some areas) were able to meet the property requirements for voting. Far more Americans could participate in political life and influence elections than in contemporary England, where, by the mid-eighteenth century, a man needed the equivalent of $80,000 to vote. But did the right to participate translate into democracy? Or did customs of deference and hierarchy continue to influence voters? Did the growing power of the assemblies translate into a fairer, more democratic government for all?

STATE AND SOCIETY: THEORY AND PRACTICE

The following documents either offer insight into the political theories of the seventeenth and eighteenth centuries or explore the relationship between economic and political equality in colonial America. In sermons, diaries, public speeches, and pamphlets, civil and religious leaders discussed the duty of citizens to obey and of rulers to guard the people's well-being; they defined patriotism and public service in exalted terms as an unselfish desire to advance the common good. These selections represent an ideal, not necessarily a reality; nonetheless, they reveal important concepts that shaped the colonists' political understanding.

The Rulers and the Ruled: John Winthrop's Definition of Liberty

One of the original planners of the Massachusetts Bay Colony, John Winthrop (1588–1649) served as governor or deputy governor almost every year from 1630 until his death. He delivered the following speech after his acquittal in a trial in which he was accused of exceeding his authority. Excerpted from The History of New England from 1630 to 1649, *ed. James Savage (Boston, 1826), 2:228–30.*

The great questions that have troubled the country, are about the authority of the magistrates [officeholders] and the liberty of the people. It is yourselves who have called us to this office, and being called by you, we have our authority from God, in way of an ordinance, such as hath the image of God eminently stamped upon it, the contempt and violation whereof hath been vindicated with examples of divine vengeance. I entreat you to consider, that when you choose magistrates, you take them from among yourselves, men subject to like passions as you are. Therefore when you see infirmities in us, you should reflect upon your own, and that would make you bear the more with us, and not be severe censurers of the failings of your magistrates. . . .

For the other point concerning liberty, I observe a great mistake in the country about that. There is a twofold liberty, natural (I mean as our nature is now corrupt) and civil or federal. The first is common to man with beasts and other creatures. By this, man, as he stands in relation to man simply, hath liberty to do what he lists [likes]; it is a liberty to evil as well as to good. This liberty is incompatible and inconsistent with authority, and cannot endure the least restraint of the most just authority. The exercise and maintaining of this liberty makes men grow more evil, and in time to be worse than brute beasts. . . . This is that great enemy of truth and peace, that wild beast, which all the ordinances of God are bent against, to restrain and subdue it. The other kind of liberty I call civil or federal, it may also be termed moral, in reference to the covenant between God and man, in the moral law, and the politic covenants and constitutions, amongst men themselves. This liberty is the proper end and object of authority, and cannot subsist without it; and it is a liberty to that only which is good, just and honest. This liberty you are to stand for, with the hazard (not only of your goods, but) of your lives, if need be. Whatsoever crosseth this, is not authority, but a distemper thereof. This liberty is maintained and exercised in a way of subjection to authority; it is of the same kind of liberty wherewith Christ hath made us free. The woman's own choice makes such a man her husband; yet being so chosen, he is her lord, and she is to be subject to him, yet in a way of liberty, not of bondage; and a true wife accounts her subjection her honour and freedom, and would not think her condition safe and free, but in her subjection to her husband's authority. Such is the liberty of the church under the authority of Christ, her king and husband; his yoke is so easy and sweet to her as a bride's ornaments; and if through frowardness or wantonness &c. she shake it off, at any time, she is at no rest in her spirit, until she take it up again; and whether her lord smiles upon her, and embraceth her in his arms, or whether he frowns, or rebukes, or smites her, she apprehends the sweetness of his love in all, and is refreshed, supported and instructed by every such dispensation of his authority over her. On the other side, ye know who they are that complain of this yoke and say, let us break their bands &c. we will not have this man to rule over us. Even so, brethren, it will be between you and your magistrates. If you stand for your natural corrupt liberties, and will do what is good in your own eyes, you will not endure the least weight of authority, but will murmur, and oppose, and be always striving to shake off that yoke; but if you will be satisfied to enjoy such civil and lawful liberties, such as Christ allows you, then will you quietly and cheerfully submit unto that authority which is set over you, in all the administrations of it, for your good. Wherein, if we fail at any time, we hope we shall be willing (by God's assistance) to hearken to good advice from any of you, or in any other way of God; so shall your liberties be preserved, in upholding the honour and power of authority amongst you.

The great concerns of politics are the desire for liberty and the need for order and authority. For Winthrop, what is the source of his authority? What are the two kinds of liberty?

William Livingston on Patriotism and the Duty of Public Service

---

New York lawyer and politician William Livingston (1723–1790) published a series of essays on politics in a periodical called The Independent Reflector. *In this essay, Livingston defined patriotism as a willingness to suppress selfish interest in favor of the common good. Because of his stress on unity, Livingston viewed political parties as illegitimate, since they represented special interest groups and created political conflict. Taken from William Livingston, "Of Patriotism,"* The Independent Reflector, *3 May 1753, 93–94.*

He is a Patriot who prefers the Happiness of the Whole, to his own private Advantage, who, when properly called upon, is ready to rise up in its Defence, and with a manly Fortitude, shield it from Danger. He is a Patriot, the ruling Object of whose Ambition, is the public Welfare: Whose Zeal, chastised by Reflection, is calm, steady and undaunted: He whom lucrative Views cannot warp from his Duty: Whom no partial Ties can prevail on to act traitorously to the Community, and sacrifice the Interest of the *Whole* to that of a *Part*: He whom Flattery cannot seduce, nor Frowns dismay, from supporting the public Interest when it is in his Power: Who mourns for their Vices, and exerts his Abilities to work a Reformation: Who compassionates their Ignorance, and endeavours to improve their Understandings: He who aims to cultivate Urbanity and social Harmony. To conclude, he is a true Patriot whose Love for the Public is not extinguished, either by their Insensibility or Ingratitude; but goes on with unwearied Benevolence in every public-spirited Attempt. . . .

The noisy intemperate Froth of a political Enthusiast, is as far removed from a steady Principle of Patriotism, as the Dignity of solid Understanding from the Fumes of poetical Madness.—

Party-Faction and personal Resentment, have often imposed themselves upon Mankind for the divine Operations of public Spirit. We shall find Hypocrites of this sort, more frequently inveighing against Men, than reasoning upon Facts: Ridicule is their favourite Engine—to mislead the Judgment by warming the Imagination, is their peculiar Art.

The superstitious Zealot, and the religious Bigot, have not so much as an Idea of a Public: When they presume to act the Part of Patriots, there is something so unnatural and absurd in their Manner, that they can scarcely deceive any but their own Herd.

When these Characters lay Claim to Patriotism, we may be sure they are Imposters, and we should treat them as Hypocrites.

According to Livingston, what is a patriot? Would you define patriotism in the same way?

The Practice of Politics: How to Get Elected— An Eighteenth-Century Guide

In 1770, Robert Munford, a colonel in the Virginia militia and office-holder at many levels of local government, wrote a play about electioneer-

ing in his home colony. Although satirical and comic, The Candidates contains some realistic accounts of political practices in pre-revolutionary Virginia. The main character, Mr. Wou'dbe (i.e. "would be"), wishes to run for the House of Burgesses. As a gentleman, Wou'dbe scorns campaigning and expresses mixed feelings about serving in public office. He believes that voters should recognize the quality of gentlemen candidates and automatically elect them to office. But in order to defeat his opponents—Sir John Toddy, Mr. Strutabout, and Mr. Smallhopes—Wou'dbe adopts a number of not-so-idealistic strategies. Munford describes the practice of "treating" voters with rum, barbecues, and breakfasts before elections and recounts conversations in which candidates make various promises to the freeholder constituents. Taken from "Robert Munford's The Candidates," ed. Jay B. Hubbell and Douglass Adair The William and Mary Quarterly 5 (April 1948): 231, 237–44.

Act I. Scene I. *Mr. Wou'dbe's house. Enter Wou'dbe with a newspaper in his hand.*

. . . Well, our little world will soon be up, and very busy towards our next election. Must I again be subject to the humours of a fickle croud? Must I again resign my reason, and be nought but what each voter pleases? Must I cajole, fawn, and wheedle, for a place that brings so little profit? . . .

[*In the next scene, Wou'dbe discusses the proper qualifications for serving in the House of Burgesses with a freeholder (voter), Guzzle.*]

Wou'dbe. I'm sorry Mr. Guzzle, you are so ignorant of the necessary qualifications of a member of the house of burgesses. . . . I'll make it a point of duty to dispatch the business, and my study to promote the good of my county.

Guzzle. Yes, damn it, you all promise mighty fair, but the devil a bit do you perform; there's Strutabout, now, he'll promise to move mountains. He'll make the rivers navigable, and bring the tide over the tops of the hills, for a vote.

Strutabout. You may depend, Mr. Guzzle, I'll perform whatever I promise.

Guzzle. I don't believe it, damn me if I like you. . . .

Wou'dbe. Don't be angry, John, let our actions hereafter be the test of our inclinations to serve you. . . . who are you for?

Guzzle. For the first man that fills my bottle. so Mr. Wou'dbe, your servant.

Wou'dbe. Ralpho, go after him, and fill his bottle. . . .

Wou'dbe. (pulling out his watch.) 'Tis now the time a friend of mine has appointed for me to meet the freeholders at a barbecue; well, I find, in order to secure a seat in our august senate, 'tis necessary a man should either be a slave or a fool; a slave to the people, for the privilege of serving them, and a fool himself, for thus begging a troublesome and expensive employment.

To sigh, while toddy-toping sots rejoice,
To see you paying for their empty voice,
From morn to night your humble head decline,
To gain an honour that is justly thine,
Intreat a fool, who's your's at this day's treat,
And next another's, if another's meat,
Is all the bliss a candidate acquires,
In all his wishes, or his vain desires. . . .

[The next scene takes place at a barbecue Wou'dbe has sponsored in order to woo the voters. Freeholders Twist, Stern, Prize, and their wives discuss the candidates. Sir John Toddy arrives with his aide, Guzzle, and proceeds to "glad-hand" the voters. Note that Guzzle has to whisper their names to Sir John, who pretends that he knows his constituents. Finally, Twist presses Mr. Wou'dbe about what he specifically would do for the voters once in office.]

Stern. Pray, gentlemen, what plausible objection have you against Mr. Wou'dbe? he's a clever civil gentleman as any, and as far as my poor weak capacity can go, he's a man of as good learning, and knows the punctilios of behaving himself, with the best of them. . . .

Lucy. If the wives were to vote, I believe they would make a better choice than their husbands.

Twist. You'd be for the funnyest—wou'dn't you?

Lucy. Yes, faith; and the wittiest, and prettiest, and the wisest, and the best too; you are all for ugly except when you choose me.

Catharine. Well done, Lucy, you are right, girl. If we were all to speak to our old men as freely as you do, there would be better doings.

Stern. Perhaps not, Kate. . . .

Catharine. Husband, you know Mr. Wou'dbe is a clever gentleman; he has been a good friend to us.

Stern. I agree to it, and can vote for him without your clash.

Guzzle. I'll be bound when it comes to the pinch, they'll all vote for him. . . .

Enter Sir John Toddy.

Sir John. Gentlemen and ladies, your servant, hah! my old friend Prize, how goes it? how does your wife and children do?

Sarah. At your service, sir. *(making a low courtsey.)*

Prize. How the devil come he to know me so well, and never spoke to me before in his life? *(aside.)*

Guzzle. *(whispering [to] Sir John)* Dick Stern.

Sir John. Hah! Mr. Stern, I'm proud to see you; I hope your family are well; how many children? does the good woman keep to the old stroke?

Catharine. Yes, an't please your honour, I hope my lady's well, with your honour.

Sir John. At your service, madam.

Guzzle. *(whispering [to] Sir John)* Roger Twist.

Sir John. Hah! Mr. Roger Twist! your servant, sir. I hope your wife and children are well.

Twist. There's my wife. I have no children, at your service. . . .

Twist. [to Mr. Wou'dbe] . . . I've heard a 'sponsible man say, he could prove you were the cause of these new taxes.

Wou'dbe. Do you believe that too? or can you believe that it's in the power of any individual member to make a law himself? If a law is enacted that is displeasing to the people, it has the concurrence of the whole legislative body, and my vote for, or against it, is of little consequence.

Guzzle. And what the devil good do you do then?

Wou'dbe. As much as I have abilities to do.

Guzzle. Suppose, Mr. Wou'dbe, we were to want you to get the price of rum lower'd—wou'd you do it?

Wou'dbe. I cou'd not.

Guzzle. Huzza for Sir John! he has promised to do it, huzza for Sir John!

Twist. Suppose, Mr. Wou'dbe, we should want this tax taken off—cou'd you do it?

Wou'dbe. I could not.

Twist. Huzza for Mr. Strutabout! he's damn'd, if he don't. Huzza for Mr. Strutabout!

Stern. Suppose, Mr. Wou'dbe, we that live over the river, should want to come to church on this side, is it not very hard we should pay ferryage; when we pay as much to the church as you do?

Wou'dbe. Very hard.

Stern. Suppose we were to petition the assembly could you get us clear of that expence?

Wou'dbe. I believe it to be just; and make no doubt but it would pass into a law.

Stern. Will you do it?

Wou'dbe. I will endeavour to do it.

Stern. Huzza for Mr. Wou'dbe! Wou'dbe forever!

Prize. Why don't you burgesses, do something with the damn'd pickers [*tobacco inspectors*]? If we have a hogshead of tobacco refused, away it goes to them; and after they have twisted up the best of it for their own use, and taken as much as will pay them for their trouble, the poor planter has little for his share.

Wou'dbe. There are great complaints against them; and I believe the assembly will take them under consideration.

Prize. Will you vote against them?

Wou'dbe. I will, if they deserve it.

Prize. Huzza for Mr. Wou'dbe! you shall go, old fellow; don't be afraid; I'll warrant it.

How do democratic leaders get elected according to Mumford? Does his critique still hold up today?

AMERICAN COLONISTS SPEAK FOR THEMSELVES

In the eleven years between the Stamp Act and the Declaration of Independence, American colonists tried to understand the events that were alienating them from England. Most were relieved when the Stamp Act was repealed and allowed themselves to believe that there would be no more difficulty. With subsequent acts (the Townshend Duties, the Tea Act, the "Intolerable Acts," and others) many came slowly to the conclusion that separation from England was necessary. Most were very slow to blame the king: well into the 1770s, they believed instead that officials such as Lord Bute, Lord Grenville, Lord Mansfield, Lord North, and others were deceiving the king and plotting against America. They drew upon all of the ideas at their disposal—religious ideas and Whig ideology as well—to interpret the developments of their day.

A Clergyman's Understanding of Liberty

Jonathan Mayhew (1720–1766), a Harvard-educated Congregational minister in Boston, was one of the first to preach against the Stamp Act. In his mind, the Stamp Act and the proposal for a colonial bishop were two parts of a plot—the Stamp Act would give the government control over newspapers while a colonial bishop would give it control over churches. The following excerpt reveals how his religious training and his exposure to Whig ideology combined to shape his reaction to the Stamp Act in November 1765 and to its repeal in June 1766. Taken from Jonathan Mayhew, The Snare Broken: A Thanksgiving-Discourse. . . . Occasioned by the Repeal of the Stamp-Act *(Boston, 1766), 35–37.*

Having been initiated, in youth, in the doctrines of civil liberty, as they were taught by such men as Plato, Demosthenes, Cicero and other renowned persons among the ancients; and such as Sidney and Milton, Locke and Hoadley, among the moderns; I liked them; they seemed rational. Having, earlier still learnt from the holy scriptures, that wise, brave and vertuous men were always friends to liberty; that God gave the Israelites a King [or absolute Monarch] in his anger, because they had not sense and virtue enough to like a free common-wealth, and to have himself for their King; that the Son of God came down from heaven, to make us "free indeed"; and that "where the Spirit of the Lord is, there is liberty"; this made me conclude, that freedom was a great blessing. Having, also, from my childhood up, by the kind providence of my God, and the tender care of a good parent now at rest with Him, been educated to the love of liberty, tho' not of licentiousness; which chaste and virtuous passion was still increased in me, as I advanced towards, and into, manhood; I would not, I cannot now, tho' past middle age, relinquish the fair object of my youthful affections, LIBERTY; whose charms, instead of decaying with time in my eyes, have daily captivated me more and more. I was, accordingly, penetrated with the most sensible grief, when,

Reprinted from *The Life and Letters of Charles Inglis: His Ministry in America and Consecration as First Colonial Bishop, from 1759–1787* by John Wolfe Lydekker, M.A. Copyright © 1936 by Macmillan.

about the *first of November last,* that day of darkness, a day hardly to be numbered with the other days of the year, SHE seemed about to take her final departure from America, and to leave that ugly Hag *Slavery,* the deformed child of Satan, in her room. I am now filled with a proportionable degree of joy in God, on occasion of HER speedy return, with new smiles on her face, with augmented beauty and splendor.—Once more then, Hail! celestial Maid, the daughter of God, and, excepting his Son, the first-born of heaven! Welcome to these shores again; welcome to every expanding heart! Long mayest thou reside among us, the delight of the wise, good and brave; the protectress of innocence from wrongs and oppression, the patroness of learning, arts, eloquence, virtue, rational loyalty, religion! And if any miserable people on the continent or isles of Europe, after being weakened by luxury, debauchery, venality, intestine quarrels, or other vices, should, in the rude collisions, or now-uncertain revolutions of kingdoms, be driven, in their extremity, to seek a safe retreat from slavery in some far-distant climate; let them find, O let them find one in America under thy brooding, sacred wings; where *our* oppressed fathers once found it, and we now enjoy it, by the favor of Him, whose service is the most glorious freedom! Never, O never may He permit thee to forsake us, for our unworthiness to enjoy thy enlivening presence! By His high permission, attend us thro' life AND DEATH to the regions of the blessed, thy original abode, there to enjoy forever the "glorious liberty of the sons of God!"

How do Mayhew's religion and his philosophical readings combine? What are the political results of this combination?

A Loyalist Perspective

Charles Inglis was an Anglican employed by the Society for the Propagation of the Gospel and a Tory. His letter to the secretary of the society on 31 October 1776 reveals the loyalism of many Anglicans and the persecution that they suffered from their neighbors. The following excerpt is from John Wolfe Lydekker, The Life and Letters of Charles Inglis: His Ministry in America and Consecration as First Colonial Bishop, from 1759 to 1787 (London, 1936), 156–60.

REVEREND SIR,

I have the Pleasure to assure you that *all* the Society's Missionaries, without excepting one, in New Jersey, New York, Connecticut, &, so far as I can learn, in the other New England Colonies, have proved themselves faithful, loyal Subjects in these trying Times; & have to the utmost of their Power opposed the Spirit of Disaffection & Rebellion which has involved this Continent in the greatest Calamities. . . .

You have, doubtless, been long since informed . . . to what an Height our violences were risen, so early as May 1775. . . . Those violences have been gradually increasing ever since; & this, with the Delay of sending over Succours, & the King's Troops totally abandoning this Province, reduced the Friends of Government here to a most disagreeable & dangerous Situation; particularly the Clergy, who were viewed with peculiar envy and Malignity by the Disaffected. For altho Civil Liberty was the ostensible Object, the Bait that was flung out to catch the Populace at large, & engage them in the Rebellion; yet it is now past all Doubt, that an Abolition of the Church of England was one of the principal Springs of the Dissenting Leaders' Conduct. . . . I have it from good Authority that the Presbyterian Ministers, at a Synod where most of them in the Middle Colonies were collected, passed a Resolve to support the Continental Congress in all their Measures. This, & this *only* can account for the Uniformity of their Conduct. . . .

The Clergy, amidst this Scene of Tumult & Disorder, went on steadily with their Duty; in their Sermons, confirming themselves to the Doctrines of the Gospel, without touching on politics; using their Influence to allay our Heats, & cherish a Spirit of Loyalty among their People. This Conduct, however harmless, gave great offence to our flaming Patriots, who laid it down as a Maxim— "that those who were not for them, were against them." The Clergy were everywhere threatened; often reviled with the most approbrious Language; sometimes treated with brutal Violence. . . . Some have been flung into Jails by Committees, for frivolous Suspicions of Plots, of which even their Persecutors afterwards acquitted them. Some who were obliged to fly their Own Province to save their Lives, have been taken Prisoners, sent back, & are threatened to be tried for their Lives because they fled from Danger. Some have been pulled out of the Reading Desk, because they prayed for the King, & that before Independency was declared. . . .

The present Rebellion is certainly one of the most causeless, unprovoked and unnatural that ever disgraced any Country—a Rebellion marked with peculiarly aggravated Circumstances of Guilt & Ingratitude. Yet amidst this general Defection, there are very many who have exhibited Instances of Fortitude & Adherence to their Duty. . . . It is but Justice to say . . . there is not one of the Clergy in the Provinces I have specified, of whom this may not be affirmed; & very few of the Laity who were respectable, or Men of Property, have joined in the Rebellion.

Thus matters continued, the Clergy proceeding regularly in the Discharge of their Duty, where the Hand of Violence did not interfere, untill the Beginning of last July, when the Congress thought proper to make an explicit Declaration of Independency. . . . This Declaration increased the Embarrassment of the Clergy. To officiate publickly, & not pray for the King & Royal Family according to the Liturgy, was against their Duty & Oath, as well as Dictates of their Consciences; & yet to use the Prayers for the King & Royal Family, would have drawn inevitable Destruction on them. The only Course which they could pursue to avoid both evils, was to suspend the public Exercise of their Function, & shut up their Churches. This accordingly was done.

How does Inglis feel about the colonial rebellion? What does he think is the role of the clergy?

The War for
Independence,
1774–1783

INTRODUCTION

Americans have debated the meaning of the Revolution for more than two hundred years. Was the Revolution "a war for home rule, or a war for who should rule at home?" For those scholars who believe that the break with Britain was merely a colonial war for independence, the Revolution has been portrayed as hardly revolutionary. In the case of those scholars who believe that the challenge to British authority was part of a broader social and political transformation, the Revolution appears as a distinctly revolutionary event.

Historians have explored many different aspects of the Revolution. The political and constitutional ideas of the Revolution have been analyzed in great detail. The Revolution has also produced a large body of scholarship devoted to exploring "history from the bottom up." In contrast to traditional political and constitutional history, history from the bottom up focuses on the experience of non-elite groups, including artisans, farmers, women, and slaves. The Revolution did not mean the same thing to all Americans. Nor did the Revolution have the same impact on all groups in American society. Given the complexity of the revolutionary experience, it is easy to understand why scholars would be divided when asked to assess the radicalism of the Revolution.

RADICALISM OF THE AMERICAN REVOLUTION

Historical debate over the meaning of the Revolution has been dominated by the question first posed by the Progressive historian Carl Becker—Was the Revolution "a war for home rule, or a war for who should rule at home?" For historians interested in the political and constitutional ideas of the Revolution, the achievements of the American Revolution are impressive. The right of revolution, the idea of limited government, and the beginnings of a new, more democratic conception of politics are among the most important examples of the profound changes wrought by the Revolution. Social historians, by contrast, have been more interested in documenting how the Revolution changed the lives of Americans. When viewed from the perspective of social history, the legacy of the Revolution is more complicated. The selections in this section explore the meaning of the Revolution from a variety of different viewpoints. The ideas of the revolutionaries, the governments they created, and the fortunes of Americans from all walks of life have been examined by scholars. How we assess the radicalism of the Revolution ultimately depends as much on the criteria we use as on the events of 1776.

Forming New Governments

Political scientist Donald Lutz focuses on the constitutional documents drafted by Americans. The period between the Revolution and the ratification of the federal Constitution was a period of lively political experimentation. For Lutz, the meaning of the Revolution can best be understood by analyzing the kinds of governments Americans created after

*independence. Abridged from Donald S. Lutz, "State Constitution-mak-
ing, Through 1781," in* The Blackwell Encyclopedia of the American Revolution, *ed. Jack P. Greene and J. R. Pole (Cambridge, Massachusetts, 1991), 278-81, 287-88.*

MASSACHUSETTS, NEW HAMPSHIRE, AND SOUTH CAROLINA

The first state constitution put into effect was that of Massachusetts. On 16 May 1775 the Provincial Congress of Massachusetts suggested that the Continental Congress write a model constitution for it and the other colonies. Afraid of alarming those
who still hoped for reconciliation with Britain, the Continental
Congress did not oblige. But on 2 June 1775 it did suggest that
Massachusetts consider its charter of 1691 as still in force and the
offices of governor and lieutenant-governor as temporarily va-
cated. It also recommended that new elections be held and a new
governor's council be elected by the Provincial Congress. On 19
June 1775 the Massachusetts Congress elected a 28-member council that replaced the governor as executive. With this one alteration, the replacement of the governor with an executive council,
the Massachusetts Charter of 1691 became the first state constitution. It was replaced in 1780 but in the meantime constituted,
along with the Connecticut and Rhode Island charters, the most
obvious link between colonial and statehood political institutions.

On 18 October 1775 New Hampshire put to the Continental
Congress the same question that Massachusetts had asked the
previous May. The intent of the request was to press the issue of
independence, since a recommendation to frame a state constitution would be regarded by many as a declaration of independence. There was no functioning colonial charter which the Continental Congress could use to dodge the issue, so it advised the
New Hampshire provincial congress to "establish such a government, as in their judgment will best produce the happiness of the
people." The letter to the New Hampshire Provincial Congress
added, however, that such reorganization should endure only
until the conflict with Britain was over. In the face of this ambigu-

---

ous recommendation, on 21 December 1775 the New Hampshire Provincial Congress met to draft a document. Prominent during these proceedings were Matthew Thornton, Meshech Weare, John Langdon, and John Sullivan. On 5 January 1776 New Hampshire became the first state to write a new constitution. As in Massachusetts, the major change from colonial practice was the election of a council by the House of Representatives. The council, the upper house in what was now a bicameral legislature, in turn elected a president who replaced the Crown-appointed governor.

South Carolina received the same recommendation from the Continental Congress on 4 November 1775. Prominent figures during the proceedings included John Rutledge, Christopher Gadsden, Henry Laurens, Charles Pinckney, and Rawlins Lowndes. As elsewhere, there was great hesitation to break openly with Britain, and the document approved on 26 March 1776 by the provincial congress of South Carolina amounted only minimally to a constitution. Designed to be in effect only until hostilities with Britain were over and passed as a normal piece of legislation by a legislature that underwent no special election to frame such a document, the "constitution" did not carry enormous authority and would be replaced in 1778. The indeterminate nature of the constitution reflected the position of the South Carolina Congress that wrote and adopted it. When it wrote the document, this body was simultaneously the old revolutionary legislature, the constitutional convention, and the new legislature created by the old legislature. During the morning of 25 March 1776, the men in this group acted in the first two capacities; in the afternoon of the same day they acted as an Assembly under the new government and elected the Council, which became the new upper house in the new bicameral legislature.

These first three state constitutions had a half-hearted quality to them. Rather short and incomplete as foundation documents, written and adopted by a sitting legislature in a manner indistinguishable from normal legislation, and bearing the marks of compromise between proponents for independence and supporters of reconciliation, they could in truth be viewed either as temporary expedients implying no significant alteration in colonial status or as manifestations of the intent to break with Britain. If the American Revolution had not been successful, perhaps history would have recorded them as the former. However, since the Revolution did conclude successfully and no other constitutional action was necessary for Massachusetts, New Hampshire, and South Carolina to assert their independence, we can view these three documents as being the constitutions of states establishing their independence. Still, their transitional status is clearly reflected in the fact that, by the time the United States Constitution was written in 1787, only these three states of the original 13 felt the need to write and adopt a second state constitution—South Carolina in 1778, Massachusetts in 1780, and New Hampshire in 1784.

VIRGINIA AND NEW JERSEY

There was no half-heartedness about the next constitution. The Virginia Provincial Congress had its share of reluctance about writing a state constitution, since such an action was viewed as equivalent to a declaration of independence. However, by 15 May 1776 the Virginia Congress had instructed its delegates at the Continental Congress to vote for independence. Thus, when Virginia turned to writing a declaration of rights and a state constitution, there was no doubt in the minds of the delegates about what they were doing. Although a committee of the provincial congress was charged with the task, George Mason was largely responsible for both the Declaration of Rights adopted on 27 May 1776 and the new constitution adopted unanimously on 29 June 1776. The similarity in wording between Virginia's Declaration of Rights and that found in the first two paragraphs of the Declaration of Independence can probably be accounted for by the close juxtaposition in time between the two documents, and Mason's close connections with his fellow Virginian Thomas Jefferson. Many of Virginia's most visible leaders were not available. George Washington was leading the army, and Jefferson was away serving in the Continental Congress, as were Richard Henry Lee and George Wythe. However, Virginia was blessed with a host of good minds, and among these Edmund Pendleton, Richard Bland, James Madison, Patrick Henry, Edmund Randolph, and Mason were in attendance and prominent in debates.

The New Jersey Provincial Congress barely missed beating Virginia. Although it did not start drafting a document until 21 June 1776, it was able to adopt a new constitution on 2 July 1776, only nine days after starting. The Virginia Congress had put in very long hours to write its document in 45 days, so one might conclude that the New Jersey Congress either worked around the clock, or, as is likely, was not scrupulously concerned about its new document. It is doubtful that such speed would have been possible in either Virginia's or New Jersey's case if there had not been a long colonial experience upon which to draw and an existing form of government successful enough to warrant close approximation. That New Jersey's hastily framed and adopted constitution lasted 44 years before being replaced is testimony to the utility of having an existing political system upon which to model a new constitution. Prominent in New Jersey's deliberations were the Reverend Jacob Greene, John Cleves Symmes, Lewis Ogden, Jonathan D. Sergeant, and Theophilus Elmer. Greene was the most influential and is reputed to have received considerable help from another cleric, the famous John Witherspoon.

PENNSYLVANIA AND DELAWARE

Thus, by the time the Declaration of Independence was adopted, seven fully constituted states were already in existence, counting Connecticut and Rhode Island. Almost three months elapsed before another group of state constitutions appeared, during late 1776. The brief hiatus allowed enough time for experience and evolving constitutional theory to support a number of innovations. The first of these was to use a specially elected rather than an already sitting legislature to write a constitution. Pennsylvania initiated the innovation, but Delaware, copying its neighbor, was the first to finish a constitution using the method.

Among proponents for independence there were two viewpoints concerning the method for writing new state constitutions. On the one hand were those who wished to emphasize the continuity between colonial and statehood institutions in service of the basic premise that Americans were breaking with Britain in order to preserve their constitutional tradition. The provincial congresses were the bearers of that continuity and thus were the bodies that should write constitutions. Also, during the colonial era constitution-like documents had occasionally been adopted by the legislature.

On the other hand, there were those who felt that the American commitment to popular sovereignty and the need to engage as many people as possible in support of the legitimacy of the new governments required both a distinction between constitutions and normal legislation and a more direct linkage with popular sentiment. Since masses of people could not directly write a constitution, the best alternative seemed to be a body elected specifically for the purpose. The second group gradually won its point as constitution-writing progressed. Americans would eventually move a step further and require that constitutions written by a special convention also be approved by the people at large in a referendum. As logical as this next step was, it was not taken until 1780, in the fifteenth state constitution adopted.

Delaware was slow in moving from a colonial assembly to a provincial congress, and did so only on 15 June 1776, when all public officials were requested to continue their power from that date forward in the name of the people of specific counties rather than in the name of the King. On 27 July 1776 elections were called for a legislature that was first to sit as a constitutional convention. This specially elected legislature convened on 2 September 1776 and adopted a declaration of rights nine days later. The process was speeded along by copying much of Pennsylvania's declaration. The convention adopted a constitution on 20 September 1776, with both George Read and Thomas McKean being mentioned as the document's primary authors. Despite the haste, the document would not be replaced for 39 years.

Pennsylvania's new state constitution was interesting for far more than its being written by a specially elected legislature sitting as a constitutional convention. More than any other state until that of Massachusetts in 1778-80, Pennsylvania worked at developing a constitution that would reflect the latest in constitutional theory. The result was the most radical document of the era, certainly the most innovative, and until the adoption of the 1780 Massachusetts document the primary contender as a model for future state constitutions. It was at least partially adopted by several states.

Like Delaware, Pennsylvania was slow to move to provincial status, and for the same reason—there were many who did not wish to replace the old government. The legal assembly proved unwilling to act, and the election of 1 May 1776 failed to alter significantly the make-up of the legislative assembly. The proponents for independence absented themselves from the legislature, thereby denying the assembly its quorum and rendering it impotent. Then a convention of county committees of inspection was called by the Philadelphia Committee of Inspection in an attempt to bypass the legal assembly. This convention met for a week in Philadelphia, and its 108 delegates in June scheduled an election for 8 July 1776. Ninety-six men were elected by an electorate that was potentially broader than usual, since the normal property requirements were waived, but was in fact narrower than usual, since it excluded from voting anyone who did not attest to their support for independence. These men became a legislature parallel to the legal one, but they first assembled as a constitutional convention and met across the street from the Continental Congress in Philadelphia.

The Pennsylvania Constitutional Convention was dominated by pro-independence men, and several of its more radically democratic members were prominent in writing the new constitution. Benjamin Franklin had a considerable impact on the document, but James Cannon, Timothy Matlack, and Cannon's good friend George Bryan (who was not a delegate but worked closely with Cannon nonetheless) were the primary authors.

Pennsylvania's Declaration of Rights owed much to Virginia's, although Pennsylvania's was both longer and more far reaching. The resulting constitution, adopted along with the Declaration of Rights on 28 September 1776, was distinguished by creating a unicameral legislature, an extremely broad electorate, and a set of institutions designed to make the government as responsive to popular consent as possible. For example, in order to become a law a bill had to be passed in two consecutive sessions of the legislature. Since Pennsylvania had what became the standard American practice of annual elections, and bills approved the first time had to be published for public perusal, legislators were subject to explain their past and future votes between elections. Also, the constitution established a state-wide grand jury, called a Council of Censors, which was to be elected every seven years to review and evaluate all aspects of governmental action. Vermont would later copy most of this constitution, including its council of censors, and Georgia would emulate its unicameral legislature. Indeed, during the 1820s, 1830s, and 1840s the next generation of state constitutions would bring to widespread fruition many of the potentially highly democratic aspects of Pennsylvania's 1776 constitution. . . .

THE COMMON POLITICAL CULTURE OF THE COLONIES

What is striking about the early state constitutions as a group is that, despite some institutional diversity, there were strong similarities among them that reflected a common political culture. That is, the political institutions developed in relative isolation by each colony converged over time, and during the revolutionary era the similarities became even stronger. To a certain extent this can be explained by the common practice of borrowing from other state constitutions, but it is doubtful that such borrowing would have been likely, or so successful, unless fundamental similarities had not already existed.

A general look at the 15 state constitutions adopted between 1775 and 1781 reveals the following patterns. All but two states used a bicameral legislature. Georgia went bicameral when it replaced its 1777 document in 1789, and Pennsylvania did so when it replaced its 1776 document in 1790. In all 15 constitutions the lower house was elected directly by the people. Although the percentage of white adult males enfranchised varied from state to state, on average the percentage was at least four times larger than it was in Britain.

Of the 13 constitutions creating bicameral legislatures, all but one had the upper house (senate) elected directly by the people, usually using the same electorate for both houses. Maryland, the one exception, used an electoral college to elect its senate. With only one exception, 1776 South Carolina, all constitutions provided for annual elections for the lower house. Of the 13 bicameral states, eight had annual elections for the senate, two had biennial elections, and three had staggered, multi-year elections.

In nine of the constitutions the executive was elected by the legislature, three used a popular election, and three used a popular election to identify the major candidates from among whom the legislature picked the governor. Eleven constitutions provided for annual elections for the governor, two for biennial elections, and two for triennial elections. Twelve of the constitutions required voters to own property, usually about 50 acres or the equivalent, and three required voters to have paid taxes. Of the 13 bicameral legislatures, ten had the same property requirement to vote for the upper house as for the lower house. Of the nine states that involved the people in selecting the governor, eight used the same property requirement to vote for the governor as was required to vote for the lower house. All but one of the constitutions had property requirements to run for office, and nine [of the constitutions] for the 13 bicameral legislatures required more property to run for the upper house than for the lower house.

Ten of the early state constitutions included bills of rights. These bills of rights varied in length and detail, but generally had similar content. Virtually all rights later found in the United States Bill of Rights could be found in an earlier state constitution, usually in several.

Fourteen of the 15 constitutions were written and adopted by the respective state legislature, usually after an election where it was made clear that the new legislature would also write a new constitution.

Far from exhausting the similarities, the ones listed here indicate that, despite differences resulting from colonial experiences, regionalism, size, diversity, or degree of radicalism, there was a coherent shared political culture underlying the early state constitutions. Perhaps most obvious is the manner in which they produced political systems dominated by a bicameral legislature. The executive was invariably quite weak and a creature of the legislature. This was in keeping with both the colonial tendency to focus upon the legislature as the embodiment of the people, and the colonial distrust of executives and executive privilege.

Typical provisions in state constitutions towards this end, in addition to having the legislature elect the executive, included the requirement that the legislature approve executive appointments, the creation of a small body drawn from the legislature to assist the governor in giving executive approval to legislation, granting pardons, or just generally telling him what to do. The extent to which separation of powers was actually found in state constitutions, aside from the 1780 Massachusetts document, it was limited to a prohibition on anyone holding simultaneously a position in the legislative and executive branches.

In this regard, the United States Constitution built upon and evolved out of state constitutionalism. The national executive was stronger than state executives, although only somewhat more so than the Massachusetts governor. The movement away from the radical model of direct, popular consent was also only a matter of degree with respect to the Massachusetts constitution. When taken together, some believe, the state constitutions and the politi-

cal process that produced them shows [show] the extent to which
the national constitution was in most respects a logical development out of, or deflection from, what had come before rather than
a radical departure or a conservative reaction. Regardless, the
early state constitutions were the American laboratory for liberty,
the base upon which the Continental Congress rested as it successfully prosecuted the war of independence and the first true
written constitutions in world history. Even those who prefer to
minimize the impact of these documents upon the United States
Constitution admit the importance of the early state constitutions
in these other respects.

*What are the major similarities in the state constitutions described
by Lutz? What do these similarities tell us about the causes of the
Revolution?*

Popular Radicalism

*For historians interested in writing "history from the bottom up," it is
important to distinguish the views of commonfolk from those of the elite.
The most important spokesman for this radical tradition was Thomas
Paine. His pamphlet,* Common Sense, *expressed the more egalitarian
and democratic ideals of commonfolk. In the view of historian Edward
Countryman, the popular voice of the Revolution was distinctly radical.
Popular radicalism contrasted sharply with the conservative views of the
men who led the revolutionary movement. Taken from Edward Country-
man, "Social Protest and the Revolutionary Movement, 1765-1776," in*
The Blackwell Encyclopedia of the American Revolution, *ed. Jack
P. Greene and J. R. Pole (Cambridge, Massachusetts, 1991), 193-96.*

REVOLUTION AND RADICALISM IN PHILADELPHIA

As the independence movement gained strength, social protest and political experience began combining to create new public identities. The case of Philadelphia shows the process particularly well. Pennsylvania's capital took little part in the great upris-
ings of the Stamp Act period; its stamp distributor resigned with

little ado and there was virtually no rioting. But by the end of the 1760s relations within the city were growing tense. The issue was the non-importation movement with which the colonies had responded to Parliament's Townshend Duties of 1767. These were an attempt to meet the supposed colonial objection to "internal" taxes, such as the Stamp Tax, by imposing "external" duties on colonial imports. The colonials had long accepted Parliament's right to impose duties in order to control their behavior, such as the Molasses Act of 1733. By and large they were even paying the duties imposed by the Sugar Act of 1764. It seemed to the British that they had made the external-internal distinction themselves. On all counts, it looked as if Parliament had found a way of taxing the colonials that the colonials would accept.

They did not accept it. Instead, they agreed to boycott British commerce until the taxes were repealed. To the merchants of the great ports it was a disagreeable necessity: they would not accept Parliament's right to tax them, but transatlantic commerce was their life. But to Philadelphia's artisans it was another matter. Like New Yorkers and Bostonians, Philadelphians were enduring the depression that had settled on the colonies at the end of the Seven Years' War. It seemed to the artisans that nonimportation offered a chance to bring prosperity back. Without British imports there would be more of a market for their own goods. But when Parliament repealed four of the five Townshend Duties in 1770, leaving only the duty on tea in place, nonimportation began to collapse.

To the merchants the issue was simple: they were the traders and they had the right to decide whether to import or not. But to one Philadelphia "tradesman" the "consent of the majority of the tradesmen, farmers and other freemen . . . should have been obtained." A "lover of liberty and a mechanic's friend" wrote that a "good mechanic" was "one of the most serviceable, one of the most valuable members of society" but that merchants were only "weak and babbling boys—clerks of yesterday." "Brother Chip" asked Philadelphia artisans whether they did not have "an equal right of electing or being elected. . . . Are there no . . . men well acquainted with the constitution and laws of their country among the tradesmen and mechanics?"

"Social Protest and the Revolutionary Movement, 1765–1776" by Edward Countryman from *The Blackwell Encyclopedia of the American Revolution*, Jack P. Greene and J.R. Pole, eds. Copyright © 1991 by Blackwell Publishers.

The issue was one of social and political consciousness more than it was one of overt social conflict. The Philadelphia artisans wanted an equal voice in the making of their community's major decisions. But in their self-assertion they were also redefining the terms of their membership in the community. In the colonial period they may have accepted that their political position and their social rank were inferior. Now they were casting such beliefs aside and developing instead the ideology of equal rights which would become dominant in American political culture.

From its slow start in 1765, Philadelphia went on to become the most radical urban center in revolutionary America. Politically the culmination came in June 1776, when the old provincial government was forcibly overthrown. One element in the coalition that overthrew it was the militant members of the Continental Congress, who were determined to have independence and who recognized that the Pennsylvania Assembly formed the last major obstacle to it. But they were joined by Pennsylvanians whose vision of America demanded transformation as well as independence. Many of them were master artisans, the people who had asserted their right to an equal political voice in 1770. But now they were joined by lesser men, most notably the journeymen and laborers who formed the bulk of the city's revolutionary militia. The artisans had found the means to express themselves in the city's committee of safety. Like similar committees elsewhere this had begun to take shape in the aftermath of the Boston Tea Party, and by 1776 its voice was dominant in the city's popular politics. The emergence and triumph of such committees was the surest possible sign that a full political revolution was underway. The spread of their membership to include men who would never have had such a voice in running the old order was as sure a sign that the Revolution had a profound social dimension.

But Philadelphians took it further. They met the final crisis as a bitterly divided people. For reasons of both religion and self-interest the city's old elite of Quaker and Anglican merchants were rejecting the revolution. The non-Quaker patriot elite, typified by the lawyer and pamphleteer John Dickinson, proved unwilling to accept the consequences of what they had helped to begin. In 1768 Dickinson's own *Letters From a Farmer in Pennsylvania* had been enormously influential in rousing opposition to the Townshend Duties and his "Liberty Song" had been sung from New Hampshire to Georgia. In it he had urged, "Come join hand in hand, brave Americans all, and rouse your bold hearts at fair liberty's call," but now his own heart was timid and he held back from joining his own hand to the cause of independence. It was Dickinson and his like, not open loyalists, who were using the old provincial assembly to put the moment of independence off, and it was their power that dissolved when the popular committee and the Continental Congress joined their own hands to bring the assembly down.

Meanwhile another group had also taken on shape and consciousness: the privates of the city's militia. Philadelphia's Quaker pacifist heritage meant that it had no military tradition, which meant that there were no established lines of military authority. When a militia became necessary its officers were drawn from the better and middling sorts, and the privates came from the city's journeymen, apprentices, laborers, and servants. But the terms of the militia law were lenient, and a man who had conscientious objections could easily avoid service. To the city's Quakers it was a matter of religious belief. But to the militiamen liability to military service became a matter of political principle.

The consequence was that the militiamen established their own committee and formulated their own program for the Revolution. Equal liability to service was only one of the points they put forward. They scorned the paternalistic willingness of some of their officers to equip the troops they commanded; instead they wanted officers and men alike to be uniformed in simple hunting shirts. They wanted to elect their officers themselves, rather than serve under men appointed by higher authority. Their demands found echoes elsewhere. Hunting shirts became the costume of revolutionary commitment in Virginia. A committee of artisans took shape in New York City, and in May 1776 it issued a strident set of demands to the "elected delegates" in the province's provincial congress. One of those demands was that under the new order the system of popular committees that had taken power during the final crisis be able to reconstitute itself whenever the people might choose.

The need for governmental simplicity and responsiveness became one of the dominant themes in popular political discourse. No one put the point more clearly than the pamphleteer Thomas Paine. His first great piece in a long career of radical political writing was *Common Sense*, published in Philadelphia in January 1776. Paine was a former corset-maker and British customs official, and he had migrated from England only in 1774. He had known Benjamin Franklin there, and through the famous former printer he found an entrée to the artisan community just at the point when it was awakening to political consciousness.

Paine set himself three distinct projects in *Common Sense*. One, after nine inconclusive months of war, was to convince Americans that reconciliation was impossible. Full independence was the only course worth following: "the weeping voice of nature cries 'tis time to part." The second was to argue the case for simple republicanism: "let the assemblies be annual, with a president only." The third was to put his case in a political language that would be sophisticated but also simple. Paine's predecessors in the Revolution's pamphlet literature had been gentlemen and they had written for other gentlemen. Paine's own roots were plebeian, and he wrote for people like himself.

His impact was enormous. *Common Sense* sold some 150,000 copies and was read and discussed from one end of the 13 provinces to the other. People had been waiting for an unequivocal call for independence. Artisans and farmers were ready for a major piece of political writing that was neither beyond them nor condescending to them. Paine had made himself the voice of these people. The power with which he spoke for them was a measure of their own importance to the revolutionary movement. It was also a measure of how much their consciousness and situation had changed over the decade since the crisis first began. His call for republican institutions of the simplest sort, directly responsive, open to anyone's participation, devoid of the complications and balances of the old order, expressed the conclusions that the people who devoured *Common Sense* were drawing from their experience in the revolutionary movement.

LATER DEVELOPMENTS

The fullest measure of social protest in revolutionary America came after 1776, and it is beyond the main scope of this article. Independence brought the collapse of existing political institutions, and the collapse provided opportunity for many sorts of Americans to try to change their situations. Paine's people—white working men pressed for institutional settlements of the sort he sketched in *Common Sense*. Their fullest opportunity came in Pennsylvania itself, where the patriot wing of the old elite gave way to panic and lost control. The result was the state's radical constitution of1776, and its provisions found echoes elsewhere. It was copied directly in the Green Mountains, where the New England settlers seized the moment and cut themselves free of New York. Their choice of the Pennsylvania model suggests the political mentality of revolutionary rural America. So does the equally simple New England proposal called *The People the Best Governors*. Following Paine, the Pennsylvanians repudiated the whole idea of a governorship, appointing a "president only" to see to public business. The title bore none of the quasi-regal meaning it would later take on in American political culture, and others proposed it as well: South Carolina, Delaware, and New Hampshire in their first constitutions and New York in a constitutional proposal of 1776.

All of these changes took place among white men. [Historians] Mary Beth Norton, Linda Kerber, and Ira Berlin have pointed the way for understanding the terms on which women and African-Americans confronted the Revolution, entered it, and tried to take advantage of the possibilities it presented.... Enough here to make four points. The first is that they started from situations far less privileged than those of any white males. The second, springing from the first, is that neither women nor Blacks found themselves in a position to claim full political equality or direct political power. The third is that members of each group were to at least some extent actors in the main events between 1765 and 1776. The most notable case is that of Crispus Attucks, who was black and who was one of the five Bostonians slain in the King Street Riot in 1770. The fourth is that some members of both groups did make the most they could of the political and the ideological opportunities that the Revolution presented.

The American Revolution does not, perhaps, fit a mechanistic model of a social revolution. But that is not to say that the Revolution did not have a profound social dimension, both in its origins, to which this article has referred, and in its short-term and long-term consequences. One starting point for the people who made the Revolution was their common membership in a dependent, colonial yet British society. The other was their many different situations within that society and their relations with one another. During the political crisis with Britain they found themselves confronting their own social situations and relationships as well as the large imperial issues. The process and the great transformations of the Revolution grew from its domestic and social aspects as well as from its imperial and political ones.

How did the views of the average citizen differ from those of the colonial elite? Is this difference still in evidence today?

Women and the Revolution

Abigail Adams implored her husband John to "remember the ladies" and reminded him that "all Men would be tyrants if they could." The experience of war and the ideological struggle waged against Britain had important consequences for women's lives. Historian Betty Wood explores the mixed legacy that the Revolution bequeathed to women. Taken from Betty Wood, "The Impact of the Revolution on the Role, Status, and Experience of Women," in The Blackwell Encyclopedia of the American Revolution, *ed. Jack P. Greene and J. R. Pole (Cambridge, Massachusetts, 1991), 404-7.*

Examples of the female commitment to the patriot cause, and the support given by women to that cause both before and during the War for Independence, are manifold. Among the best known is the Edenton resolution. In October 1774, 51 women from Edenton, North Carolina, signed a statement in which they declared their unwavering commitment to the patriot cause and their intent to do all that they could to further the same. Equally well known are the 36 women in Philadelphia who in 1780 launched what was to prove an immensely successful campaign to raise money to help equip American troops. Within a matter of weeks they managed to collect around $300,000.

In Edenton and Philadelphia, and elsewhere on the mainland also, some women were taking the initiative. But there was a very real sense in which women were participating in a political campaign devised and orchestrated by men. And those men had fairly

---

explicit ideas about the most appropriate ways in which women could help them. During the 1760s and early 1770s male patriots freely acknowledged that the success of the most important weapon in their political armoury, the boycotting of British goods, depended upon the cooperation of women, upon their willingness to change their patterns of consumption. It is abundantly clear that many women in all social classes were willing to do precisely that. However, male patriots went on to suggest that women could express their support for the American cause not only by wearing homespun clothes but also by making them. It was in their homes, in an essentially domestic context, sitting at their wheels and looms, that women could most appropriately assist their menfolk. And, it must be said, that is precisely what many women from all walks of life did, often with great gusto and enthusiasm. Patriot men were concerned to ensure that the horizons of women did not extend very far beyond their wheels and looms.

In a purely practical sense, the War for Independence, when it came, was to have essentially similar consequences for women as had all previous colonial wars. Out of necessity, women were required to fill various economic roles often closed to them in peacetime. As their fathers, husbands, sons, and brothers went off to fight, for whichever side, so many women found themselves left to run the family farm or business. For those who had worked alongside the men in their family and in the process acquired invaluable knowledge and expertise, this might have been an unwelcome prospect, but was certainly not daunting. It was a rather different proposition for women whose husbands and fathers had effectively denied them any detailed knowledge of their business affairs. But in either case, the assumption was that when men returned from the war they would resume their usual role and responsibilities in the family. And more often than not that is exactly what did happen. But of course many men did not return from the war. For their wives this meant not only the trauma of bereavement but also the psychological and sometimes material problems of adjusting to widowhood.

It would seem reasonable to suggest that, in the longer term at any rate, the War for Independence *per se* did not result in any significant or permanent changes in the status, roles and daily lives of most white women. However, the dislocations of war, especially in the southern theater, did offer possibilities of escape and flight to black women. An unknown number of slave women did run away, but their freedom was often to prove both precarious and temporary.

In some respects it was patriot ideology rather than the War for Independence *per se* which seemed to hold out the best prospect of freedom, if not complete equality, for black men and women, both in the North and in the South. To some degree, that prospect began to be realized during the 1770s and 1780s, albeit often gradually and grudgingly in the North and, through the device of private manumission, on a limited scale in parts of the South. In the South, however, most black men and women ended the revolutionary era as they had begun it: as chattel slaves. The accommodations and compromises made in Philadelphia in 1787 ruled out the possibility that this situation would change in the foreseeable future.

Many people, on both sides of the Atlantic, had pointed to the apparent inconsistency, if not hypocrisy, of a patriot ideology which demanded freedom, liberty, and equality for white Americans but which denied those self-same things to black Americans. But, with the notable exception of Thomas Paine, no patriot pamphleteer or politician suggested or even hinted that women too might legitimately claim full and equal participation in the political society which men were so busy defining and bringing into existence. Neither did American women make the same claim on their own behalf or, during the 1790s, enthusiastically applaud Mary Wollstonecraft when she did.

The New Republican Woman

Yet the social and political discourse of the revolutionary era did not, and arguably could not, totally avoid the question of women. In many respects, it was the greater visibility of women in the America of the 1760s and 1770s, the part which they were playing and ought to be playing in the revolutionary movement, that prompted an intense examination of various attitudes and assumptions which previously had been largely taken for granted by both sexes. During the 1780s, with the achievement of American independence, the debate focused on the attributes which made for the "ideal" republican woman, the role of women in the new republic, and how they might best be prepared for that role. The outcome of that debate, in which women participated and with which they by and large concurred, was to return women to the private, domestic sphere from which it seemed by their actions if not by their words they might be trying to escape.

The fact of the matter was, however, that the political upheavals and disruptions of the revolutionary era did not dramatically change the self-perception of American women, or at least of those middle- and upper-class women who committed their thoughts and opinions to paper. Both before, during, and after the War for Independence, these women were arguing vociferously not for a complete redefinition of their role and status which, amongst other things, would have accorded them complete political equality with men, but for the acknowledgment by men of the equal importance and value of the private sphere in which they operated and were content to continue operating. As Abigail Adams put it—and she was by no means atypical of women in her social class—"if man is Lord, women is *Lordess*—that is what I contend for." When she urged the delegates meeting in Philadelphia to "Remember the Ladies," she was not and probably would not have dreamed of suggesting that Jefferson amend the Declaration of Independence to read "All men and women are created equal." Rather, she was emphasizing the importance of and claiming an equality of status for the private sphere in which women operated. Abigail Adams, and women like her, subscribed to many of the same social attitudes, assumptions, and values as American men.

Abigail Adams would not have dissented from the almost universally held view of the social and moral role, function, and importance of marriage and the family. Virtually every woman of her social class was truly appalled by Paine and Wollstonecraft's critiques of marriage and horrified by the way in which the latter practiced what she preached. The path suggested by Paine and Wollstonecraft pointed, or seemed to be pointing, to a complete breakdown of society—to social chaos, disorder, and anarchy. For women to step from the private to the public sphere, assuming that they had the time to combine the roles of wife, mother, and homemaker with the demands of a public career, would be one step along that infinitely dangerous path. In fact, the vehement denunciation by women such as Abigail Adams of state constitutions and election laws which, with the notable exception of those of New Jersey, explicitly denied women even the possibility of formal participation in political life, would have been more surprising and difficult to explain than their apparently placid acceptance of this state of affairs. Because of a dearth of first-hand written evidence, the perceptions of women further down the social scale are much more difficult to unravel.

If one of the principal concerns and preoccupations of some upper- and middle-class women during the 1780s was with establishing the importance and equality of the private sphere, then another, and one which they shared with some men—most notably perhaps with Benjamin Rush—was defining the attributes of the "ideal" republican woman and determining how girls and women might best be prepared to fulfill their assigned role in the new Republic.

In some ways, the "ideal" republican woman shared many of the same attributes and was required to display many of the same virtues as the "ideal" Roman matron. Her civic duty lay in the benign, almost civilizing, influence which she exerted over her husband and sons in ensuring that they became wise, virtuous, just, and, compassionate members of the body politic and, if called upon, good rulers.

The "ideal" republican woman was not a frivolous, empty headed ornament. On the contrary, she was expected and required to be a competent partner who could engage in serious discourse on a wide range of matters with her husband and sons. The problem was, as Benjamin Rush, Judith Sargent Murray, and others realized, that the traditional modes and methods of educating girls, when they were educated at all, scarcely fitted them for such an awesome responsibility. Girls had to be educated, and suitably educated, if they were ever to live up to the high expectations, of the republican woman. The "ideal" republican woman had to know how to cook and manage an efficient household, but she also had to know something about those subjects which would be of interest and concern to her husband. In what was to be one of the more tangible benefits accruing to women as a direct result of the American Revolution, much greater attention than ever before came to be paid to the formal education of girls and, not least, to the devising of curricula more in keeping with those available to boys.

Comparatively few female lives, black or white, in North or South, town or countryside, remained completely untouched or unaffected by the ideas and events of the American Revolution But although, because of their commitment and contribution to the revolutionary cause, white women came to be regarded in a rather more positive light during the 1780s and 1790s, these years did not witness a "revolutionary" change in the status, role, and daily lives of American women.

How did the ideology behind the Revolution hold the best promise for women even if the leaders of the Revolution did not recognize it at the time?

REVOLUTIONARY RHETORIC
AND REALITY

One way of measuring the revolutionary character of the events of 1776 is to consider the nature of the social change brought about by Americans. Studies of the American Revolution have used other social upheavals like the English Revolution, the French Revolution, or the Russian Revolution as a yardstick against which the events of 1776 should be judged. In all of these European revolutions there was an ideological challenge to the ideals of aristocracy and monarchy. In each of these historical episodes a revolutionary ideology emerged that championed some form of political and social equality. In all of these revolutions the effort to implement these ideals also resulted in profound and rapid social change.

Another way of exploring the meaning of the Revolution is to consider the relationship between the ideals of the Revolution and the political and economic changes that accompanied the break with Britain. In the Declaration of Independence, Jefferson asserted that:

> *[A]ll men are created equal, that they are endowed by their Creator with certain unalienable Rights, that among these are Life, Liberty, and the pursuit of Happiness—That, to secure these rights, Governments are instituted among Men, deriving their just powers from the consent of the governed,—That whenever any Form of Government becomes destructive of these ends, it is the Right of the People to alter or to abolish it, and to institute new Government. . . .*

To evaluate the degree to which revolutionary rhetoric translated into reality one might begin by asking how radical were Jefferson's claims in the Declaration. The next question that needs to be considered is to what extent did the Revolution fulfill the promise of Jefferson's words. The selections that follow provide different perspectives on these important questions.

Property and the Right to Vote

Patriot leader John Adams was among the most influential political theorists of the revolutionary generation. His pamphlet, Thoughts on Government, *helped define the principles of republican government for Americans. Adams was an avid and prolific correspondent. Like so many of his generation, he used his personal correspondence to explore important political issues of the day. In his letter to John Sullivan, Adams makes clear the republican idea that ownership of property ought to be a prerequisite for the exercise of the right to vote. Abridged from* Papers of John Adams, *ed. Robert J. Taylor (Cambridge, Massachusetts, 1979), 4:208, 210–12.*

Philadelphia May. 26. 1776

Dear Sir

. . . It is certain in Theory, that the only moral Foundation of Government is the Consent of the People. But to what an Extent Shall We carry this Principle? Shall We Say, that every Individual of the Community, old and young, male and female, as well as rich and poor, must consent, expressly to every Act of Legislation? No, you will Say. This is impossible. How then does the Right arise in the Majority to govern the Minority, against their Will? Whence arises the Right of the Men to govern Women, without their Consent? Whence the Right of the old to bind the Young, without theirs.

But let us first Suppose, that the whole Community of every Age, Rank, Sex, and Condition, has a Right to vote. This Community, is assembled—a Motion is made and carried by a Majority of one Voice. The Minority will not agree to this. Whence arises the Right of the Majority to govern, and the Obligation of the Minority to obey? from Necessity, you will Say, because there can be no other Rule. But why exclude Women? You will Say, because their Delicacy renders them unfit for Practice and Experience, in the great Business of Life, and the hardy Enterprizes of War, as well as the arduous Cares of State. Besides, their attention is So much engaged with the necessary Nurture of their Children, that Nature has made them fittest for domestic Cares. And Children have not Judgment or Will of their own. True. But will not these Reasons apply to others? Is it not equally true, that Men in general in every Society, who are wholly destitute of Property, are also too little acquainted with public Affairs to form a Right Judgment, and too dependent upon other Men to have a Will of their own? If this is a Fact, if you give to every Man, who has no Property, a Vote, will you not make a fine encouraging Provision for Corruption by your fundamental Law? Such is the Frailty of the human Heart, that very few Men, who have no Property, have any Judgment of their own. They talk and vote as they are directed by Some Man of Property, who has attached their Minds to his Interest. . . .

Harrington has Shewn that Power always follows Property. This I believe to be as infallible a Maxim, in Politicks, as, that Action and Re-action are equal, is in Mechanicks. Nay I believe We may advance one Step farther and affirm that the Ballance of Power in a Society, accompanies the Ballance of Property in Land. The only possible Way then of preserving the Ballance of Power on the side of equal Liberty and public Virtue, is to make the Acquisition of Land easy to every Member of Society: to make a Division of the Land into Small Quantities, So that the Multitude may be possessed of landed Estates. If the Multitude is possessed of the Ballance of real Estate, the Multitude will have the Ballance of Power, and in that Case the Multitude will take Care of the Liberty, Virtue, and Interest of the Multitude in all Acts of Government. . . .

The Same Reasoning, which will induce you to admit all Men, who have no Property, to vote, . . . will prove that you ought to admit Women and Children: for generally Speaking, Women and Children, have as good Judgment, and as independent Minds as those Men who are wholly destitute of Property: these last being to all Intents and Purposes as much dependent upon others, who will please to feed, cloath, and employ them, as Women are upon their Husbands, or Children on their Parents. . . .

Depend upon it, sir, it is dangerous to open So fruitfull a Source of Controversy and Altercation, as would be opened by attempting to alter the Qualifications of Voters. There will be no End of it. New Claims will arise. Women will demand a Vote. Lads from 12 to 21 will think their Rights not enough attended to, and every Man, who has not a Farthing, will demand an equal Voice with any other in all Acts of State. It tends to confound and destroy all Distinctions, and prostrate all Ranks, to one common Levell.

According to Adams, why should the ownership of property be necessary in order to vote? How does this concept manifest itself in today's electoral politics?

The Problem of Women's Suffrage

The logic of Adams's argument excluded women who were not property owners from the vote. But what of widows, the group of women who did own property? In this letter, patriot Richard Henry Lee discusses the possibility of allowing suffrage for widows. In the case of widows the connection between the right to vote and the ownership of property need not have presented a barrier to their participation. This contradiction did not go unnoticed by women at the time, as this letter to Mrs. Hannah Corbin suggests. While female suffrage was hardly common in this period, the state constitution New Jersey adopted enfranchised "all free inhabitants." Women voted in New Jersey until an explicit prohibition on female voting was enacted in 1807. Excerpted from The Letters of Richard Henry Lee, *ed. James Curtis Ballagh (New York, 1911), 1:392–93.*

[March 17, 1778]

You complain that widows are not represented. . . . The doctrine of representation is a large subject, and it is certain that it ought to be extended as far as wisdom and policy can allow; nor do I see that either of these forbid widows having property from voting, notwithstanding it has never been the practice either here or in England. Perhaps 'twas thought rather out of character for women to press into those tumultuous assemblages of men where the business of choosing representatives is conducted. And it might also have been considered as not so necessary, seeing that the representatives themselves, as their immediate constituents, must suffer the tax imposed in exact proportion as does all other property taxed, and that, therefore, it could not be supposed that taxes would be laid where the public good did not demand it. This, then, is the widow's security as well as that of the never married women, who have lands in their own right, for both of whom I have the highest respect, and would at any time give my consent to establish their right of voting. . . . When we complained of British taxation we did so with much reason, and there is great difference between our case and that of the unrepresented in this country. The English Parliament nor their representatives would pay a farthing of the tax they imposed on us but quite otherwise. . . . Oppressions, therefore, without end and taxes without reason or public necessity would have been our fate had we submitted to British usurpation.

How does Lee handle the issue of women who own property? What are the implications of his position?

The First Republic,
1776–1789

Benjamin Franklin's Speech at the Conclusion of the Constitutional Convention

---

Philadelphia, September 17, 1787

I confess that I do not entirely approve of this Constitution at present, but Sir, I am not sure I shall never approve it: For having lived long, I have experienced many Instances of being oblig'd, by better Information or fuller Consideration, to change Opinions even on important Subjects, which I once thought right, but found to be otherwise. It is therefore that the older I grow the more apt I am to doubt my own Judgment and to pay more Respect to the Judgment of others. Most Men indeed as well as most Sects in Religion, think themselves in Possession of all Truth, and that wherever others differ from them it is so far Error. Steele, a Protestant, in a Dedication tells the Pope, that the only Difference between our two Churches in their Opinions of the Certainty of their Doctrine, is, the Romish Church is infallible, and the Church of England is never in the Wrong. But tho' many private Persons think almost as highly of their own Infallibility, as that of their Sect, few express it so naturally as a certain French lady, who in a little Dispute with her Sister, said, I don't know how it happens, Sister, but I meet with no body but myself that's *always* in the right. *Il n'y a que moi qui a toujours raison.*

In these Sentiments, Sir, I agree to this Constitution, with all its Faults, if they are such: because I think a General Government necessary for us, and there is no *Form* of Government but what may be a Blessing to the People if well administered; and I believe farther that this is likely to be well administered for a Course of Years, and can only end in Despotism as other Forms have done before it, when the People shall become so corrupted as to need Despotic Government, being incapable of any other. I doubt too whether any other Convention we can obtain, may be able to make a better Constitution: For when you assemble a Number of Men to have the Advantage of their joint Wisdom, you inevitably assemble with those Men all their Prejudices, their Passions, their Errors of Opinion, their local Interests, and their selfish Views. From such an Assembly can a perfect Production be expected? It therefore astonishes me, Sir, to find this System approaching so near to Perfection as it does; and I think it will astonish our Enemies, who are waiting with Confidence to hear that our Councils are confounded, like those of the Builders of Babel, and that our States are on the Point of Separation, only to meet hereafter for the Purpose of cutting one another's Throats. Thus I consent, Sir, to this Constitution because I expect no better, and because I am not sure that it is not the best. The Opinions I have had of its Errors, I sacrifice to the Public Good. I have never whisper'd a Syllable of them abroad. Within these Walls they were born, & here they shall die. If every one of us in returning to our Constituents were to report the Objections he has had to it, and endeavour to gain Partizans in support of them, we might prevent its being generally received, and thereby lose all the salutary Effects & great Advantages resulting naturally in our favour among foreign Nations, as well as among ourselves, from our real or apparent Unanimity. Much of the Strength and Efficiency of any Government, in procuring & securing Happiness to the People depends on Opinion, on the general Opinion of the Goodness of that Government as well as of the Wisdom & Integrity of its Governors. I hope therefore that for our own Sakes, as a Part of the People, and for the Sake of our Posterity, we shall act heartily & unanimously in recommending this Constitution, wherever our Influence may extend, and turn our future Thoughts and Endeavours to the Means of having it well administred.—

On the whole, Sir, I cannot help expressing a Wish, that every Member of the Convention, who may still have Objections to it, would with me on this Occasion doubt a little of his own Infallibility, and to make *manifest* our *Unanimity*, put his Name to this Instrument.—

Then the Motion was made for adding the last Formula, viz Done in Convention by the unanimous Consent &c—which was agreed to and added—accordingly.

On what grounds does Franklin urge compromise and the acceptance of the Constitution?

"VIGOUR OF GOVERNMENT IS ESSENTIAL TO THE SECURITY OF LIBERTY"

"Publius," The Federalist I
[Alexander Hamilton]

Independent Journal (New York), October 27, 1787

To the People of the State of New York

After an unequivocal experience of the inefficacy of the sub-sisting Federal Government, you are called upon to deliberate on a new Constitution for the United States of America. The subject speaks its own importance; comprehending in its consequences, nothing less than the existence of the UNION, the safety and welfare of the parts of which it is composed, the fate of an empire, in many respects, the most interesting in the world. It has been frequently remarked, that it seems to have been reserved to the people of this country, by their conduct and example, to decide the important question, whether societies of men are really capable or not, of establishing good government from reflection and choice, or whether they are forever destined to depend, for their political constitutions, on accident and force. If there be any truth in the remark, the crisis, at which we are arrived, may with propriety be regarded as the æra in which that decision is to be made; and a wrong election of the part we shall act, may, in this view, deserve to be considered as the general misfortune of mankind.

This idea will add the inducements of philanthropy to those of patriotism to heighten the sollicitude, which all considerate and good men must feel for the event. Happy will it be if our choice should be decided by a judicious estimate of our true interests, unperplexed and unbiassed by considerations not connected with the public good. But this is a thing more ardently to be wished, than seriously to be expected. The plan offered to our deliberations, affects too many particular interests, innovates upon too many local institutions, not to involve in its discussion a variety of objects foreign to its merits, and of views, passions and prejudices little favourable to the discovery of truth.

Among the most formidable of the obstacles which the new Constitution will have to encounter, may readily be distinguished the obvious interests of a certain class of men in every State to resist all changes which may hazard a diminution of the power, emolument and consequence of the offices they hold under the State-establishments—and the perverted ambition of another class of men, who will either hope to aggrandise themselves by the confusions of their country, or will flatter themselves with fairer prospects of elevation from the subdivision of the empire into several partial confederacies, than from its union under one government.

It is not, however, my design to dwell upon observations of this nature. I am well aware that it would be disingenuous to resolve indiscriminately the opposition of any set of men (merely because their situations might subject them to suspicion) into interested or ambitious views: Candour will oblige us to admit, that even such men may be actuated by upright intentions; and it cannot be doubted, that much of the opposition which has made its appearance, or may hereafter make its appearance, will spring from sources, blameless at least, if not respectable, the honest errors of minds led astray by preconceived jealousies and fears. So numerous indeed and so powerful are the causes, which serve to give a false bias to the judgment, that we upon many occasions, see wise and good men on the wrong as well as on the right side of questions, of the first magnitude to society. This circumstance, if duly attended to, would furnish a lesson of moderation to those, who are ever so much persuaded of their being in the right, in any controversy. And a further reason for caution, in this respect, might be drawn from the reflection, that we are not always sure, that those who advocate the truth are influenced by purer principles than their antagonists. Ambition, avarice, personal animosity, party opposition, and many other motives, not more laudable than these, are apt to operate as well upon those who support as upon those who oppose the right side of a question. Were there not even these inducements to moderation, nothing could be more illjudged than that intolerant spirit, which has, at all times, characterised political parties. For, in politics as in religion, it is equally absurd to aim at making proselytes by fire and sword. Heresies in either can rarely be cured by persecution.

And yet however just these sentiments will be allowed to be, we have already sufficient indications, that it will happen in this as in all former cases of great national discussion. A torrent of angry and malignant passions will be let loose. To judge from the conduct of the opposite parties, we shall be led to conclude, that they will mutually hope to evince the justness of their opinions, and to increase the number of their converts by the loudness of their declamations, and by the bitterness of their invectives. An enlightened zeal for the energy and efficiency of government will be stigmatised, as the off-spring of a temper fond of despotic power and hostile to the principles of liberty. An overscrupulous jealousy of danger to the rights of the people, which is more commonly the fault of the head than of the heart, will be represented as mere pretence and artifice; the bait for popularity at the expence of public good. It will be forgotten, on the one hand, that jealousy is the usual concomitant of violent love, and that the noble enthusiasm of liberty is too apt to be infected with a spirit of narrow and illiberal distrust. On the other hand, it will be equally forgotten, that the vigour of government is essential to the security of liberty; that, in the contemplation of a sound and well informed judgment, their interest can never be separated; and that a dangerous ambition more often lurks behind the specious mask of zeal for the rights of the people, than under the forbidding appearance of zeal for the firmness and efficiency of government. History will teach us, that the former has been found a much more certain road to the introduction of despotism, than the latter, and that of those men who have overturned the liberties of republics the greatest number have begun their career, by paying an obsequious court to the people, commencing Demagogues and ending Tyrants.

In the course of the preceeding observations I have had an eye, my Fellow Citizens, to putting you upon your guard against all attempts, from whatever quarter, to influence your decision in a matter of the utmost moment to your welfare by any impressions other than those which may result from the evidence of truth. You will, no doubt, at the same time, have collected from the general scope of them that they proceed from a source not unfriendly to the new Constitution. Yes, my Countrymen, I own to you, that, after having given it an attentive consideration, I am clearly of opinion, it is your interest to adopt it. I am convinced, that this is the safest course for your liberty, your dignity, and your happiness. I affect not reserves, which I do not feel. I will not amuse you with an appearance of deliberation, when I have decided. I frankly acknowledge to you my convictions, and I will freely lay before you the reasons on which they are founded. The consciousness of good intentions disdains ambiguity. I shall not however multiply professions on this head. My motives must remain in the depositary of my own breast: My arguments will be open to all, and may be judged of by all. They shall at least be offered in a spirit, which will not disgrace the cause of truth.

I propose in a series of papers to discuss the following interesting particulars—*The utility of the* UNION *to your political prosperity*—*The insufficiency of the present Confederation to preserve that Union*—*The necessity of a government at least equally energetic with the one proposed to the attainment of this object*—*The conformity of the proposed Constitution to the true principles of republican government*—*Its analogy to your own state constitution*—and lastly, *the additional security, which its adoption will afford to the preservation of that species of government, to liberty and to property.*

In the progress of this discussion I shall endeavour to give a satisfactory answer to all the objections which shall have made their appearance that may seem to have any claim to your attention.

It may perhaps be thought superfluous to offer arguments to prove the utility of the UNION, a point, no doubt, deeply engraved on the hearts of the great body of the people in every state, and one, which it may be imagined has no adversaries. But the fact is, that we already hear it whispered in the private circles of those who oppose the new constitution, that the Thirteen States are of too great extent for any general system, and that we must of necessity resort to separate confederacies of distinct portions of the whole.* This doctrine will, in all probability, be gradually propagated, till it has votaries enough to countenance an open avowal of it. For nothing can be more evident, to those who are able to take an enlarged view of the subject, than the alternative of an adoption of the new Constitution, or a dismemberment of the Union. It will therefore be of use to begin by examining the advantages of that Union, the certain evils and the probable dangers, to which every State will be exposed from its dissolution. This shall accordingly constitute the subject of my next address.

*The same idea, tracing the arguments to their consequences, is held out in several of the late publications against the New Constitution.

What is Hamilton's strategy in the First Federalist for gaining popular support for the new Constitution?

"TO BREAK AND CONTROL THE VIOLENCE OF FACTION"

"Publius," The Federalist X [James Madison]

Daily Advertiser (New York), November 22, 1787

To the People of the State of New York

Among the numerous advantages promised by a well constructed Union, none deserves to be more accurately developed than its tendency to break and control the violence of faction. The friend of popular governments, never finds himself so much alarmed for their character and fate, as when he contemplates their propensity to this dangerous vice. He will not fail therefore to set a due value on any plan which, without violating the principles to which he is attached, provides a proper cure for it. The instability, injustice and confusion introduced into the public councils, have in truth been the mortal diseases under which popular governments have every where perished; as they continue to be the favorite and fruitful topics from which the adversaries to liberty derive their most specious declamations. The valuable improvements made by the American Constitutions on the popular models, both ancient and modern, cannot certainly be too much admired; but it would be an unwarrantable partiality, to contend that they have as effectually obviated the danger on this side as was wished and expected. Complaints are every where heard from our most considerate and virtuous citizens, equally the friends of public and private faith, and of public and personal liberty; that our governments are too unstable; that the public good is disregarded in the conflicts of rival parties; and that measures are too often decided, not according to the rules of justice, and the rights of the minor party; but by the superior force of an interested and over-bearing majority. However anxiously we may wish that these complaints had no foundation, the evidence of known facts will not permit us to deny that they are in some degree true. It will be found indeed, on a candid review of our situation, that some of the distresses under which we labor, have been erroneously charged on the operation of our governments; but it will be found, at the same time, that other causes will not alone account for many of our heaviest misfortunes; and particularly, for that prevailing and increasing distrust of public engagements, and alarm for private rights, which are echoed from one end of the continent to the other. These must be chiefly, if not wholly, effects of the unsteadiness and injustice, with which a factious spirit has tainted our public administration.

By a faction I understand a number of citizens, whether amounting to a majority or minority of the whole, who are united and actuated by some common impulse of passion, or of interest, adverse to the rights of other citizens, or to the permanent and aggregate interests of the community.

There are two methods of curing the mischiefs of faction: the one, by removing its causes; the other, by controling its effects.

There are again two methods of removing the causes of faction: the one by destroying the liberty which is essential to its existence; the other, by giving to every citizen the same opinions, the same passions, and the same interests.

It could never be more truly said than of the first remedy, that it is worse than the disease. Liberty is to faction, what air is to fire, an aliment without which it instantly expires. But it could not be a less folly to abolish liberty, which is essential to political life, because it nourishes faction, than it would be to wish the annihilation of air, which is essential to animal life, because it imparts to fire its destructive agency

The second expedient is as impracticable, as the first would be unwise. As long as the reason of man continues fallible, and he is at liberty to exercise it, different opinions will be formed. As long as the connection subsists between his reason and his self-love, his opinions and his passions will have a reciprocal influence on each other; and the former will be objects to which the latter will attach themselves. The diversity in the faculties of men from which the rights of property originate, is not less an insuperable obstacle to a uniformity of interests. The protection of these faculties is the first object of Government. From the protection of different and unequal faculties of acquiring property, the possession of different degrees and kinds of property immediately results: and from the influence of these on the sentiments and views of the respective proprietors, ensues a division of the society into different interests and parties.

The latent causes of faction are thus sown in the nature of man; and we see them every where brought into different degrees of activity, according to the different circumstances of civil society. A zeal for different opinions concerning religion, concerning Government, and many other points, as well of speculation as of practice; an attachment to different leaders ambitiously contending for pre-eminence and power; or to persons of other descriptions whose fortunes have been interesting to the human passions, have in turn divided mankind into parties, inflamed them with mutual animosity, and rendered them much more disposed to vex and oppress each other, than to co-operate for their common good. So strong is this propensity of mankind to fall into mutual animosities, that where no substantial occasion presents itself, the most frivolous and fanciful distinctions have been sufficient to kindle their unfriendly passions, and excite their most violent conflicts. But the most common and durable source of factions, has been the various and unequal distribution of property. Those who hold, and those who are without property, have ever formed distinct interests in society. Those who are creditors, and those who are debtors, fall under a like discrimination. A landed interest, a manufacturing interest, a mercantile interest, a monied interest, with many lesser interests, grow up of necessity in civilized nations, and divide them into different classes, actuated by different sentiments and views. The regulation of these various and interfering interests forms the principal task of modern Legislation, and involves the spirit of party and faction in the necessary and ordinary operations of Government.

No man is allowed to be a judge in his own cause; because his interest would certainly bias his judgment, and, not improbably, corrupt his integrity. With equal, nay with greater reason, a body of men, are unfit to be both judges and parties, at the same time; yet, what are many of the most important acts of legislation, but so many judicial determinations, not indeed concerning the rights of single persons, but concerning the rights of large bodies of citizens; and what are the different classes of legislators, but advocates and parties to the causes which they determine? Is a law proposed concerning private debts? It is a question to which the creditors are parties on one side, and the debtors on the other. Justice ought to hold the balance between them. Yet the parties are and must be themselves the judges; and the most numerous party, or, in other words, the most powerful faction must be expected to prevail. Shall domestic manufactures be encouraged, and in what degree, by restrictions on foreign manufactures? are questions which would be differently decided by the landed and the manufacturing classes; and probably by neither, with a sole regard to justice and the public good. The apportionment of taxes on the various descriptions of property, is an act which seems to require the most exact impartiality; yet there is perhaps no legislative act in which greater opportunity and temptation are given to a predominant party, to trample on the rules of justice. Every shilling with which they over-burden the inferior number, is a shilling saved to their own pockets.

It is in vain to say, that enlightened statesmen will be able to adjust these clashing interests, and render them all subservient to the public good. Enlightened statesmen will not always be at the helm: Nor, in many cases, can such an adjustment be made at all, without taking into view indirect and remote considerations, which will rarely prevail over the immediate interest which one party may find in disregarding the rights of another, or the good of the whole.

The inference to which we are brought, is, that the *causes* of faction cannot be removed; and that relief is only to be sought in the means of controling its *effects*.

If a faction consists of less than a majority, relief is supplied by the republican principle, which enables the majority to defeat its sinister views by regular vote: It may clog the administration, it may convulse the society; but it will be unable to execute and mask its violence under the forms of the Constitution. When a majority is included in a faction, the form of popular government on the other hand enables it to sacrifice to its ruling passion or interest, both the public good and the rights of other citizens. To secure the public good, and private rights, against the danger of such a faction, and at the same time to preserve the spirit and the form of popular government, is then the great object to which our enquiries are directed: Let me add that it is the great desideratum, by which alone this form of government can be rescued from the opprobrium under which it has so long labored, and be recommended to the esteem and adoption of mankind.

By what means is this object attainable? Evidently by one of two only. Either the existence of the same passion or interest in a majority at the same time, must be prevented; or the majority, having such co-existent passion or interest, must be rendered, by their number and local situation, unable to concert and carry into effect schemes of oppression. If the impulse and the opportunity be suffered to coincide, we well know that neither moral nor religious motives can be relied on as an adequate control. They are not found to be such on the injustice and violence of individuals, and lose their efficacy in proportion to the number combined together; that is, in proportion as their efficacy becomes needful.

From this view of the subject, it may be concluded, that a pure Democracy, by which I mean, a Society, consisting of a small number of citizens, who assemble and administer the Government in person, can admit of no cure for the mischiefs of faction. A common passion or interest will, in almost every case, be felt by a majority of the whole; a communication and concert results from the form of Government itself; and there is nothing to check the inducements to sacrifice the weaker party, or an obnoxious individual. Hence it is, that such Democracies have ever been spectacles of turbulence and contention; have ever been found incompatible with personal security, or the rights of property; and have in general been as short in their lives, as they have been violent in their deaths. Theoretic politicians, who have patronized this species of Government, have erroneously supposed, that by reducing mankind to a perfect equality in their political rights, they would, at the same time, be perfectly equalized and assimilated in their possessions, their opinions, and their passions.

A Republic, by which I mean a Government in which the scheme of representation takes place, opens a different prospect, and promises the cure for which we are seeking. Let us examine the points in which it varies from pure Democracy, and we shall comprehend both the nature of the cure, and the efficacy which it must derive from the Union.

The two great points of difference between a Democracy and a Republic are, first, the delegation of the Government, in the latter, to a small number of citizens elected by the rest: secondly, the greater number of citizens, and greater sphere of country, over which the latter may be extended.

The effect of the first difference is, on the one hand to refine and enlarge the public views, by passing them through the medium of a chosen body of citizens, whose wisdom may best discern the true interest of their country, and whose patriotism and love of justice, will be least likely to sacrifice it to temporary or partial considerations. Under such a regulation, it may well happen that the public voice pronounced by the representatives of the people, will be more consonant to the public good, than if pronounced by the people themselves convened for the purpose. On the other hand, the effect may be inverted. Men of factious tempers, of local prejudices, or of sinister designs, may by intrigue, by corruption or by other means, first obtain the suffrages, and then betray the interests of the people. The question resulting is, whether small or extensive Republics are most favorable to the election of proper guardians of the public weal; and it is clearly decided in favor of the latter by two obvious considerations.

In the first place it is to be remarked that however small the Republic may be, the Representatives must be raised to a certain number, in order to guard against the cabals of a few; and that however large it may be, they must be limited to a certain number, in order to guard against the confusion of a multitude. Hence the number of Representatives in the two cases, not being in proportion to that of the Constituents, and being proportionally greatest in the small Republic, it follows, that if the proportion of fit characters, be not less, in the large than in the small Republic, the former will present a greater option, and consequently a greater probability of a fit choice.

In the next place, as each Representative will be chosen by a greater number of citizens in the large than in the small Republic, it will be more difficult for unworthy candidates to practise with success the vicious arts, by which elections are too often carried; and the suffrages of the people being more free, will be more likely to centre on men who possess the most attractive merit, and the most diffusive and established characters.

It must be confessed, that in this, as in most other cases, there is a mean, on both sides of which inconveniencies will be found to lie. By enlarging too much the number of electors, you render the representative too little acquainted with all their local circumstances and lesser interests; as by reducing it too much, you render him unduly attached to these, and too little fit to comprehend and pursue great and national objects. The Federal Constitution forms a happy combination in this respect; the great and aggregate interests being referred to the national, the local and particular, to the state legislatures.

The other point of difference is, the greatest number of citizens and extent of territory which may be brought within the compass of Republican, than of Democratic Government; and it is this circumstance principally which renders factious combinations less to be dreaded in the former, than in the latter. The smaller the society, the fewer probably will be the distinct parties and interests composing it; the fewer the distinct parties and interests, the more frequently will a majority be found of the same party; and the smaller the number if individuals composing a majority, and the smaller the compass within which they are placed, the more easily will they concert and execute their plans of oppression. Extend the sphere, and you take in a greater variety of parties and interests; you make it less probable that a majority of the whole will have a common motive to invade the rights of other citizens; or if such a common motive exists, it will be more difficult for all who feel it to discover their own strength, and to act in unison with each other. Besides other impediments, it may be remarked, that where there is a consciousness of unjust or dishonorable purposes, communication is always checked by distrust, in proportion to the number whose concurrence is necessary.

Hence it clearly appears, that the same advantage, which a Republic has over a Democracy, in controling the effects of faction, is enjoyed by a large over a small Republic—is enjoyed by the Union over the States composing it. Does this advantage consist in the substitution of Representatives, whose enlightened views and virtuous sentiments render them superior to local prejudices, and to schemes of injustice? It will not be denied, that the Representation of the Union will be most likely to possess these requisite endowments. Does it consist in the greater security afforded by a greater variety of parties, against the event of any one party being able to outnumber and oppress the rest? In an equal degree does the encreased variety of parties, comprised within the Union, encrease this security. Does it, in fine, consist in the greater obstacles opposed to the concert and accomplishment of the secret wishes of an unjust and interested majority? Here, again, the extent of the Union gives it the most palpable advantage.

The influence of factious leaders may kindle a flame within their particular States, but will be unable to spread a general conflagration through the other States: a religious sect, may degenerate into a political faction in a part of the Confederacy; but the variety of sects dispersed over the entire face of it, must secure the national Councils against any danger from that source: a rage for paper money, for an abolition of debts, for an equal division of property, or for any other improper or wicked project, will be less apt to pervade the whole body of the Union, than a particular member of it; in the same proportion as such a malady is more likely to taint a particular county or district, than an entire State.

In the extent and proper structure of the Union, therefore, we behold a Republican remedy for the diseases most incident to Republican Government. And according to the degree of pleasure and pride, we feel in being Republicans, ought to be our zeal in cherishing the spirit, and supporting the character of Federalists.

How, according to Madison, does the new Constitution propose to handle the issue of factions? Looking at American politics today, would you say that he was correct?

THE DESPOTISM AND MISERY OF A UNIFORM NATIONAL STATE

"Agrippa" IV [James Winthrop]

Massachusetts Gazette (Boston), December 4, 1787

To the People.

Having considered some of the principal advantages of the happy form of government under which it is our peculiar good fortune to live, we find by experience, that it is the best calculated of any form hitherto invented, to secure to us the rights of our persons and of our property, and that the general circumstances of the people shew an advanced state of improvement never before known. We have found the shock given by the war in a great measure obliterated, and the publick debt contracted at that time to be considerably reduced in the nominal sum. The Congress lands are fully adequate to the redemption of the principal of their debt, and are selling and populating very fast. The lands of this state, at the west, are, at the moderate price of eighteen pence an acre, worth near half a million pounds in our money. They ought, therefore, to be sold as quick as possible. An application was made lately for a large tract at that price, and continual applications are made for other lands in the eastern part of the state. Our resources are daily augmenting.

We find, then, that after the experience of near two centuries our separate governments are in full vigour. They discover, for all the purposes of internal regulation, every symptom of strength, and none of decay. The new system is, therefore, for such purposes, useless and burdensome.

Let us now consider how far it is practicable consistent with the happiness of the people and their freedom. It is the opinion of the ablest writers on the subject, that no extensive empire can be governed upon republican principles, and that such a government will degenerate to a despotism, unless it be made up of a confederacy of smaller states, each having the full powers of internal regulation. This is precisely the principle which has hitherto preserved our freedom. No instance can be found of any free government of considerable extent which has been supported upon any other plan. Large and consolidated empires may indeed dazzle the eyes of a distant spectator with their splendour, but if examined more nearly are always found to be full of misery. The reason is obvious. In large states the same principles of legislation will not apply to all the parts. The inhabitants of warmer climates are more dissolute in their manners, and less industrious, than in colder countries. A degree of severity is, therefore, necessary with one which would cramp the spirit of the other. We accordingly find that the very great empires have always been despotick. They have indeed tried to remedy the inconveniences to which the people were exposed by local regulations; but these contrivances have never answered the end. The laws not being made by the people, who felt the inconveniences, did not suit their circumstances. It is under such tyranny that the Spanish provinces languish, and such would be our misfortune and degradation, if we should submit to have the concerns of the whole empire managed by one legislature. To promote the happiness of the people it is necessary that there should be local laws; and it is necessary that those laws should be made by the representatives of those who are immediately subject to the want of them. By endeavouring to suit both extremes, both are injured.

It is impossible for one code of laws to suit Georgia and Massachusetts. They must, therefore, legislate for themselves. Yet there is, I believe, not one point of legislation that is not surrendered in the proposed plan. Questions of every kind respecting property are determinable in a continental court, and so are all kinds of criminal causes. The continental legislature has, therefore, a right to make rules *in all cases* by which their judicial courts shall proceed and decide causes. No rights are reserved to the citizens. The laws of Congress are in all cases to be the supreme law of the land, and paramount to the constitutions of the individual states. The Congress may institute what modes of trial they please, and no plea drawn from the constitution of any state can avail. This new system is, therefore, a consolidation of all the states into one large mass, however diverse the parts may be of which it is to be composed. The idea of an uncompounded republick, on an average, one thousand miles in length, and eight hundred in breadth, and containing six millions of white inhabitants all reduced to the same standard of morals, or habits, and of laws, is in itself an absurdity, and contrary to the whole experience of mankind. The attempt made by Great-Britain to introduce such a system, struck us with horrour, and when it was proposed by some theorists that we should be represented in parliament, we uniformly declared that one legislature could not represent so many different interests for the purposes of legislation and taxation. This was the leading principle of the revolution, and makes an essential article in our creed. All that part, therefore, of the new system, which relates to the internal government of the states, ought at once to be rejected.

How does the argument of James Winthrop differ from Hamilton and Madison? Who do you think gets the better of the argument?

"To Lick the Feet of Our Well Born Masters"

"John Humble"

Independent Gazetteer (Philadelphia), October 29, 1787

The humble address of the *low born* of the United States of America, to their fellow slaves scattered throughout the world— greeting.

Whereas it hath been represented unto us that a most dreadful disease hath for these five years last past infected, preyed upon, and almost ruined the government and people of this our country; and of this malady we ourselves have had perfect demonstration, not mentally, but bodily, through every one of the five senses: For although our sensations in regard to the mind be not just so nice as those of the *well born*; yet our feeling, through the medium of the plow, the hoe, and the grubbing axe, is as accute as any nobleman's in the world. And whereas a number of skilful physicians having met together at Philadelphia last summer, for the purpose of exploring, and if possible removing the cause of this direful desease, have, through the assistance of John Adams, Esquire, in the profundity of their great political knowledge, found out and discovered, that nothing but a new government consisting of three different branches, namely, *king, lords,* and *commons,* or in the American language, *president, senate,* and *representatives,* can save this our country from inevitable destruction.—And whereas it hath been reported that several of our *low born* brethren have had the horrid audacity to think for themselves in regard to this new system of government, and, *dreadful thought!* have wickedly began to doubt concerning the perfection of this evangelical constitution, which our political doctors have declared to be a panacea, which (by inspiration) they know will infallibly heal every distemper in the confederation, and finally terminate in the salvation of America.

Now we the *low born,* that is, all the people of the United States except 600 or thereabouts, *well born,* do by this our humble address, declare, and most solemnly engage, that we will allow and admit the said 600 *well born,* immediately to establish and confirm

147

this most noble, most excellent and truely divine constitution: And we further declare that without any equivocation or mental reservation whatever we will support and maintain the same according to the best of our power, and after the manner and custom of all other slaves in foreign countries, namely by the sweat and toil of our body: Nor will we at any future period of time ever attempt to complain of this our *royal* government, let the consequences be what they may.—And although it appears to us that a *standing army,* composed of the purgings of the jails of Great Britain, Ireland and Germany, shall be employed in collecting the *revenue* of this our king and government; yet, we again in the most solemn manner declare, that we will abide by our present determination of non-assistance and passive obedience; so that we shall not dare to molest or disturb those military gentlemen in the service of our royal government. And (which is not improbable,) should any one of those soldiers when employed on duty in collecting the *taxes,* strike off the arm (with his sword,) of one of our *fellow slaves,* we will conceive our case remarkably fortunate if he leaves the other arm on.—And moreover because we are aware that many of our fellow slaves shall be unable to pay their *taxes,* and this incapacity of theirs is a just cause of impeachment of treason; wherefore in such cases we will use our utmost endeavours, in conjunction with the *standing army,* to bring such attrocious offenders before our *federal judges,* who shall have power without *jury* or *trial,* to order the said miscreants for immediate execution; nor will we think their sentence severe unless after being hanged they are also to be both *beheaded* and *quartered.*—And finally we shall henceforth and forever, leave all *power, authority,* and *dominion* over our *persons* and *properties* in the hands of the *well born,* who were designed by Providence to *govern.* And in regard to the *liberty of the press* we renounce all claim to it forever more, Amen; and we shall in future be perfectly contented if our *tongues* be left us to lick the feet of our well born masters.

Done on behalf of three millions of *low born* American slaves.

John Humble, Secretary.

"John Humble" is even more vehement in his opposition to the new Constitution. What is the basis of his opposition?

A New Republic and
the Rise of Parties,
1789–1800

INTRODUCTION

The 1790s were a period of intense partisan conflict. The notion of party politics was anathema to the Framers of the Constitution, who viewed party as a form of factionalism that was incompatible with republican virtue. Nothing better captured the antipathy to party than Washington's decision to include both Jefferson and Hamilton in his cabinet. Ultimately, Hamilton proved more adept at influencing Washington and his agenda to strengthen the new federal government and forced a realignment in politics. With the adoption of the Bill of Rights, former Anti-Federalists shifted their attentions to the dangers posed by Hamilton's program. Anti-Federalists joined forces with an important group of former Federalists who opposed Hamilton to form the Democratic-Republicans. Although many of the most important state leaders of the Democratic-Republican movement were former Anti-Federalists, the most important theorists of the opposition were the former Federalist James Madison and Thomas Jefferson. Many of the issues raised during the debate over ratification of the Constitution resurfaced a scant few years after its adoption. The conflict between the Jeffersonians and the Federalists during the 1790s cut across a broad range of issues including economics, foreign policy, law, and domestic policy.

One of the most important divisions between the Jeffersonians, who were known at the time as Democratic-Republicans, and the Federalists arose over the question of constitutional interpretation. Two key questions resurfaced time and again. What powers had the Constitution granted to the new government? How ought judges, lawmakers, and the executive interpret the text of the Constitution? For Democratic-Republicans the

Constitution was a document intended to provide a limited grant of authority. To preserve this ideal, it was vital to interpret the text of the Constitution in a strict—almost literal—manner. Federalists, by contrast, believed that within its sphere of authority the federal government had broad powers to achieve its objectives.

No issue proved more controversial during the 1790s than conflict over the Alien and Sedition Acts. This debate was not only one of the most important episodes in the struggle to protect freedom of the press, it also was a key moment in the emergence of the notion of states' rights. The material presented below deals with the constitutionality of the Sedition Act and with the political struggle between Jeffersonians and Federalists.

THE FEDERALISTS AND JEFFERSONIANS: THE PROBLEM OF AUTHORITY AND LIBERTY IN THE NEW REPUBLIC

The debate between the Federalists and the Jeffersonians over the Sedition Act has been interpreted in a number of ways by modern scholars. Some historians have focused on this conflict as a political contest between two factions vying for power. While others have focused on the competing political philosophies of the two camps, the problem of constitutional interpretation was clearly central to this conflict. Analyzing the differences between Jeffersonian and Hamiltonian constitutional thought has been a key problem for scholars. For these scholars the debate over the Sedition Act is one example of the difficult task of defining the proper sphere of individual liberty within the context of republican constitutional principles.

The Debate on the Alien and Sedition Acts

The Alien and Sedition Acts prompted the most intense partisan conflict of the 1790s. In this selection, historian James Sharp explores the different perspective of Federalists and Jeffersonians over the necessity of enacting this controversial legislation. The argument between Federalists and Jeffersonians extended beyond the question of the constitutional-

ity of the legislation. In the view of the participants in this conflict, the outcome of this debate would determine the political destiny of America.
Excerpted from James Roger Sharp, American Politics in the Early Republic: The New Nation in Crisis *(New Haven, 1993), 176-80.*

[T]he Federalists moved to consolidate their strength and destroy their political opposition in June and July of 1798 by proposing and passing the Alien and Sedition Laws. As the Federalist minister to Great Britain, Rufus King, was told by a correspondent, the "Spirit of the People is roused" and "ripe for the Support of the most decisive Measures of the Government." And this "spirit of patriotism" could be used, Hamilton suggested, to crush the Republicans so that "there will shortly be *national unanimity*." And if the Republican "leaders of Faction" continued their opposition to the government, he said, the public would revile them much like "the *Tories* of our Revolution."

The three repressive anti-alien acts, including the Act Concerning Aliens, the Naturalization Act, and the Alien Enemies Act, reflected the increasing Federalist concern about the growing number of immigrants coming into the United States. Not only did what were considered dangerous political ideas circulate among these new residents, but also the vast majority of them seemed to support the Republican opposition. The legislation, then, established a registration and surveillance system for foreign nationals in the United States and gave the president extensive powers over them, including the power to deport any whom he considered dangerous to the country's peace and security. These measures, which Jefferson deemed as "worthy of the 8th or 9th century," had "so alarmed the French who are among us," he said, "that they are going off," and a "ship, chartered by themselves for this purpose, will sail within about a fortnight for France, with as many as she can carry."

The Sedition Law, however, was even more ominous and threatening to the Republicans because of its potential to stifle internal dissent. It provided for the punishment of any persons who "unlawfully combine or conspire together, with intent to oppose any measure or measures of the government of the United States . . . or to impede the operation of any law of the United States, or to intimidate . . . any person holding a place or office in or under the government of the United States." The law further prohibited "any false, scandalous and malicious writing or writings against the government . . . or either house of the Congress of the United States; or the President . . . with intent to defame . . . or to bring them . . . into contempt or disrepute; or to excite against them . . . the hatred of the good people of the United States." Infractions could be punished by fines of up to $5,000 and imprisonment for up to five years.

Hamilton had urged that his fellow Federalists use caution in shaping the Alien and Sedition Acts, having been concerned that his colleagues might push too far and cause a reaction that could have considerable political liabilities. "Let us not be cruel or violent," he had warned Timothy Pickering. Also upon reading an earlier and more radical version of the Sedition Act, Hamilton had exhorted his successor, Oliver Wolcott, that the act might "endanger civil War." "Let us not establish a tyranny," he had written, for "energy is a very different thing from violence," and "if we make no false steps we shall be essentially united; but if we push things to an extreme we shall give to faction *body* and solidarity."

The debate within Congress over the measures was acrimonious and accusatory. Federalist Robert Goodloe Harper of South Carolina, one of the most outspoken and zealous supporters of the laws, noted that the same persons who had been against the military measures were now opposing the proposed Alien laws and charged that they did so from the fear that the laws would put "a hook into the nose of persons who are leagued with the enemies of this country." The "zeal shown in this House, and in other places, against this bill," he charged, was evidence of "the deadly hatred of certain people toward . . . [the United States]." Furthermore, Harper saw the efforts of the Republican opposition as treasonable in that the goal was "to completely stop the wheels of Government, and to lay it prostrate at the feet of its external and internal foes."

Although a number of Federalists outdid themselves in conjuring up sinister images of seditious conspiracies, a giant of a man, "Long John" Allen, a six-foot-five-inch, 230-pound Federalist representative from Connecticut, was probably the most passionately and creatively vituperative and paranoid. Accusing Republican newspapers as well as congressmen of treasonable plotting against the government, Allen defended the Sedition Law as essential to the country's well-being. If there ever "was a nation which required a law of this kind," he said, it was the United States. He challenged his colleagues to look at certain newspapers and "ask themselves whether an unwarrantable and dangerous combination does not exist to overturn and ruin the Government by publishing the most shameless falsehoods against the Representatives of the people." These falsehoods and seditious statements, Allen said, included claims that Federalist representatives were "hostile to free Governments and genuine liberty, and of course to the welfare of this country" and should "therefore . . . be displaced" by the people "rais[ing] an *insurrection* against the Government." Allen's apparent equating of Republican efforts to defeat the Federalists at the polls with "an *insurrection* against the Government" reflected a view of the opposition shared by most Federalists.

The Republicans, of course, opposed the Federalist-backed measures. For them there were disquieting parallels between their own government and that of Great Britain in that both governments seemed willing to use almost any means, no matter how arbitrary, to solidify and retain power. For example, in the same year the William Pitt government, fearing a French invasion, suspended habeas corpus and moved against radical clubs in Britain. And indeed, some of the Federalists' arguments during the debate over the Alien and Sedition Laws admitted an admiration for the stringent policies governing internal security in England. Harper maintained that both countries faced similar situations in that their external enemy relied upon "an internal support," which he referred to as being made up of "domestic traitors."

Albert Gallatin was one of the major Republican spokesmen against the Sedition Act. He charged that advocates of the bill had failed to show evidence of any criminal conspiracies or seditious intent. "This bill and its supporters suppose in fact," he concluded, "that whoever dislikes the measures of Administration and of a temporary majority in congress, and shall, either by speaking or writing, express his disapprobation and his want of confidence in men now in power, is seditious, is an enemy, not of Administration, but of the Constitution, and is liable to punishment." Thus, the Sedition bill was no more than a blatant power grab by the Federalists, who hoped to use it to "perpetuate their authority and preserve their present places."

Gallatin's distinction between opposition to the administration and opposition to the Constitution was one that most Americans of both proto-parties of the late eighteenth and early nineteenth centuries were not able to make. The political crisis, coupled with the lack of a tradition of a "loyal opposition," had created a climate of opinion inhospitable to political dissent. Congressman "Long John" Allen, for example, had been so outraged by Gallatin's remarks that he accused the Pennsylvanian of promoting "that spirit which, by preaching up the rights of man, had produced the Western insurrection [Whiskey Rebellion]."

The debate was not confined to Congress. President Adams responded to a large number of petitions from citizens around the country with a series of addresses, some quite inflammatory in their depiction of the dangers posed by the country's external as well as internal foes. He told the citizens in and around Baltimore that while republics were often divided in opinion, these divisions were normally harmless "except when foreign nations interfere, and by their arts and agents excite and foment them into parties and factions." This kind of insidious interference, he said, however, "must be resisted and exterminated" or it would result "in our total destruction as a republican government and independent power."

The Republicans thought that Adams's vehement addresses, which Madison said contained some of "the most abominable and degrading [language] that could fall from the lips of the first magistrate of an independent people," and the scathing attacks being made upon the opposition within Congress and in the Federalist newspapers were just a prelude to war with France, which was being called for by many Federalists. James Lloyd, for instance, author of the Senate version of the Sedition Bill, looked upon a declaration of war as vital to the success of the Federalist program. "I fear that Congress will close the Session" without a declaration of war, he wrote Washington, "which I look upon as necessary to enable us to lay our hands on traitors."

Other Federalists, however, were less enthusiastic. Although Theodore Sedgwick thought that "a wise policy required a declaration of war," he explained to Rufus King, several Federalists were unwilling to go along, fearing that "it would tend to discredit them among their constituents" and that the "opposition would endeavor to create, in the popular estimation, a new denomination of parties–those of peace and war."

The Republicans had expected the declaration of war to coincide with the anniversary of independence, but they later reported to Jefferson that a Federalist caucus had not been able to agree on the timing. The Federalists *were* able, however, to pass the Sedition Act through the Senate on July 4, and a colorful account of the proceedings was given to Jefferson. "The drums, Trumpets and other martial music which surrounded us, drown'd the voices of those who spoke on the question," Jefferson was told, and the "military parades so attracted the attention of the majority that much the greater part of them stood with their bodies out of the windows and could not be kept to order." Finally in the uproar and confusion the bill was passed.

The martial spirit was widespread elsewhere and not just on the Fourth of July. "Our city resembles a camp rather than a commercial port," one of Rufus King's correspondents wrote from New York. "Volunteer companies of horse and infantry are raising; and meetings of the old officers of the army and navy— and of the citizens, in the different wards have been had to concert measures for the defence of our port."

Discuss the difference between Jeffersonian and Hamiltonian views of the Constitution.

THE DEBATE OVER THE SEDITION ACT

Federalist fears about the threat of sedition were intensified by the rising tension between the United States and France. The Jeffersonians were closely identified with the French cause, and Federalists took every opportunity to denounce their opponents as champions of French atheism and anarchism. Suspicion of French influence among the Jeffersonians led the Federalists to pass a strict federal sedition law. The debate between Federalists and Jeffersonians on the legality of the Sedition Act reveals a number of important philosophical differences between these two groups. The conflict over this issue provides an excellent illustration of the profound divisions that arose within a decade of the ratification of the U.S. Constitution.

Jeffersonian Republican Congressman Albert Gallatin Attacks the Sedition Act

Gallatin was a leading spokesman for the Jeffersonian Republican forces in Congress. His speech captures a number of the essential philosophical and constitutional beliefs of the Jeffersonians. His argument seeks to dismantle the Federalist case in favor of the Sedition Act. Excerpted from Annals of Congress, *5th Cong., 2d sess. (July 5 and 10, 1798), 2:2107, 2109, 2159–60, 2162.*

Does the situation of the country, at this time, require that any law of this kind should pass? Do there exist such new and alarming symptoms of sedition, as render it necessary to adopt, in addition to the existing laws, any extraordinary measure for the purpose of suppressing unlawful combinations, and of restricting the freedom of speech and of the press? For such were the objects of the bill, whatever modifications it might hereafter receive. . . .

Was the gentleman afraid, or rather was Administration afraid, that in this instance error could not be successfully opposed by truth? The American Government had heretofore subsisted, it had acquired strength, it had grown on the affection of the people, it had been fully supported without the assistance of laws similar to the bill now on the table. It had been able to repel opposition by the single weapon of argument. And at present, when out of ten presses in the country nine were employed on the side of Administration, such is their want of confidence in the purity of their own views and motives, that they even fear the unequal contest, and require the help of force in order to suppress the limited circulation of the opinions of those who did not approve all their measures. One of the paragraphs says, that it will soon become a question whether there will be more liberty at Philadelphia or Constantinople. . . .

. . . It was in order to remove these fears [that the Constitution could be interpreted to permit the government to suppress free speech], that the amendment, which declares that Congress shall pass no law abridging the freedom of speech or the liberty of the press, was proposed and adopted—an amendment which was intended as an express exception to any supposed general power of *passing laws*, &c., vested in Congress by the other clause. The sense, in which he and his friends understood this amendment, was that Congress could not pass any law to punish any real or supposed abuse of the press. The construction given to it by the supporters of the bill was, that it did not prevent them to punish what they called the licentiousness of the press, but merely forbade their laying any previous restraints upon it. It appeared to him preposterous to say, that to punish a certain act was not an abridgement of the liberty of doing that act. It appeared to him that it was an insulting evasion of the Constitution for gentlemen to say, "We claim no power to abridge the liberty of the press; *that*, you shall enjoy unrestrained. You may write and publish what you please, but if you publish anything against us, we will punish you for it. So long as we do not prevent, but only punish your writings, it is no abridgment of your liberty of writing and printing." Congress were by that amendment prohibited from passing any law abridging, &c.; they were, therefore, prohibited from adding any restraint, either by previous restrictions, or by subsequent punishment, or by any alteration of the proper jurisdiction, or of the mode of trial, which did not exist before; in short, they were under an obligation of leaving that subject where they found it—of passing no law, either directly or indirectly, affecting that liberty. . . .

. . . Whilst, therefore, they [the Federalists] support the bill in its present shape, do they not avow that the true object of the law is to enable one party to oppress the other; that they mean to have the power to punish printers who may publish against them, whilst their opponents will remain alone, and without redress, exposed to the abuse of Ministerial prints? Is it not their object to frighten and suppress all presses which they consider as contrary to their views; to prevent a free circulation of opinion; to suffer the people at large to hear only partial accounts, and but one side of the question; to delude and deceive them by partial information, and, through those means, to perpetuate themselves in power?

What are the main philosophical problems that the Republicans have with the Alien and Sedition Acts?

The Federalists Defend the Sedition Act

Harrison Gray Otis was a leading Federalist politician from Massachusetts. His defense of the constitutionality of the Sedition Act demonstrates the continuing importance of Blackstone to American legal thought. This account of Otis's speech before Congress is taken from Annals of Congress, *5th Cong., 2d sess. (July 10, 1798), 2:2145–48.*

Mr. Otis said the professions of attachment to the Constitution, made by the gentleman from Virginia [Republican John Nicholas, a critic of the sedition bill], are certainly honorable to him; and he could not believe that an attachment so deeply engrafted as he states his to be would be shaken by this bill. The gentleman had caught an alarm on the first suggestion of a sedition bill, which had not yet subsided; and though the present bill is perfectly harmless, and contains no provision which is not practised upon under the laws of the several States in which gentlemen had been educated, and from which they had drawn most of their ideas of jurisprudence, yet the gentleman continues to be dissatisfied with it.

. . . In the first place, had the Constitution given Congress cognizance over the offences described in this bill prior to the adoption of the amendments to the Constitution? and, if Congress had that cognizance before that time, have those amendments taken it away? With respect to the first question, it must be allowed that every independent Government has a right to preserve and defend itself against injuries and outrages which endanger its existence; for, unless it has this power, it is unworthy the name of a free Government, and must either fall or be subordinate to some other protection. Now some of the offences delineated in the bill are of this description. Unlawful combinations to oppose the measures of Government, to intimidate its officers, and to excite insurrections, are acts which tend directly to the destruction of the Constitution, and there could be no doubt that the guardians of that Constitution are bound to provide against them. And if gentlemen would agree that these were acts of a criminal nature, it follows that all means calculated to produce these effects, whether by speaking, writing, or printing, were also criminal. . . .

It was . . . most evident to his mind, that the Constitution of the United States, prior to the amendments that have been added to it, secured to the National Government the cognizance of all the crimes enumerated in the bill, and it only remained to be considered whether those amendments divested it of this power. . . . "Congress shall make no law abridging the freedom of speech and of the press." The terms "freedom of speech and of the press," he supposed, were a phraseology perfectly familiar in the jurisprudence of every State, and of a certain and technical meaning. It was a mode of expression which we had borrowed from the only country in which it had been tolerated. . . . In support of this doctrine, he quoted *Blackstone's Commentaries,* under the head of libels, . . . in several of the State constitutions, the liberty of speech and of the press were guarded by the most express and unequivocal language, the Legislatures and Judicial departments of those States had adopted the definitions of the English law, and provided for the punishment of defamatory and seditious libels.

How does Otis defend the Federalists from charges like Gallatin's?

The Sedition Act

The Constitution details treason as the levying of war against the United States or the giving of aid and comfort to the enemy in time of war. Even though America had not declared war on France, the original version of the Sedition Act defined adherence to the French cause as treason, carrying a penalty of death. The final version of the act, less severe, passed by a slim three-vote majority in the House. The text of the Sedition Act is taken from Public Statutes at Large of the United States of America. . . *(Boston, 1848), 1:596–97.*

SECTION 1. *Be it enacted by the Senate and House of Representatives of the United States of America, in Congress assembled,* That if any persons shall unlawfully combine or conspire together, with intent to oppose any measure or measures of the government of the United States, which are or shall be directed by proper authority, or to impede the operation of any law of the United States, or to intimidate or prevent any person holding a place or office in or under the government of the United States, from undertaking, performing or executing his trust or duty; and if any person or persons, with intent as aforesaid, shall counsel, advise or attempt to procure any insurrection, riot, unlawful assembly, or combination, whether such conspiracy, threatening, counsel, advice, or attempt shall have the proposed effect or not, he or they shall be deemed guilty of a high misdemeanor, and on conviction, before any court of the United States having jurisdiction thereof, shall be punished by a fine not exceeding five thousand dollars, and by imprisonment during a term not less than six months nor exceeding five years; and further, at the discretion of the court may be holden to find sureties for his good behaviour in such sum, and for such time, as the said court may direct.

Sec. 2. *And be it further enacted,* That if any person shall write, print, utter or publish, or shall cause or procure to be written, printed, uttered or published, or shall knowingly and willingly assist or aid in writing, printing, uttering or publishing any false, scandalous and malicious writing or writings against the government of the United States, or either house of the Congress of the United States, or the President of the United States, with intent to defame the said government, or either house of the said Congress, or the said President, or to bring them, or either of them, into contempt or disrepute; or to excite against them, or either or any of them, the hatred of the good people of the United States, or to stir up sedition within the United States, or to excite any unlawful combinations therein, for opposing or resisting any law of the United States, or any act of the President of the United States, done in pursuance of any such law, or of the powers in him vested by the constitution of the United States, or to resist, oppose, or defeat any such law or act, or to aid, encourage or abet any hostile designs of any foreign nation against the United States, their people or government, then such person, being thereof convicted before any court of the United States having jurisdiction thereof, shall be punished by a fine not exceeding two thousand dollars, and by imprisonment not exceeding two years.

Sec. 3. *And be it further enacted and declared,* That if any person shall be prosecuted under this act, for the writing or publishing any libel aforesaid, it shall be lawful for the defendant, upon the trial of the cause, to give in evidence in his defence, the truth of the matter contained in the publication charged as a libel. And the jury who shall try the cause, shall have a right to determine the law and the fact, under the direction of the court, as in other cases.

SEC. 4. *And be it further enacted,* That this act shall continue and be in force until the third day of March, one thousand eight hundred and one, and no longer: *Provided,* that the expiration of the act shall not prevent or defeat a prosecution and punishment of any offence against the law, during the time it shall be in force.

APPROVED, July 14, 1798.

Based on a reading of the Sedition Act, why was the controversy so intense? How does this controversy still manifest itself in American life today?

Jefferson Defends His Vision of Liberty and Republicanism

In his first Inaugural Address (1801), Jefferson sought to heal the nation's political wounds and articulate the essential principles of America's political creed. Excerpted from A Compilation of the Messages and Papers of the Presidents, *comp. James D. Richardson (Washington, 1910), 1:310–12.*

During the contest of opinion through which we have passed the animation of discussions and of exertions has sometimes worn an aspect which might impose on strangers unused to think freely and to speak and to write what they think; but this being now decided by the voice of the nation, announced according to the rules of the Constitution, all will, of course, arrange themselves under the will of the law, and unite in common efforts for the common good. All, too, will bear in mind this sacred principle, that though the will of the majority is in all cases to prevail, that will to be rightful must be reasonable; that the minority possess their equal rights, which equal law must protect, and to violate would be oppression. Let us, then, fellow-citizens, unite with one heart and one mind. Let us restore to social intercourse that harmony and affection without which liberty and even life itself are but dreary things. And let us reflect that, having banished from our land that religious intolerance under which mankind so long bled and suffered, we have yet gained little if we countenance a political intolerance as despotic, as wicked, and capable of as bitter and bloody persecutions. During the throes and convulsions of the ancient world, during the agonizing spasms of infuriated man, seeking through blood and slaughter his long-lost liberty, it was not wonderful that the agitation of the billows should reach even this distant and peaceful shore; that this should be more felt and feared by some and less by others, and should divide opinions as to measures of safety. But every difference of opinion is not a difference of principle. We have called by different names brethren of the same principle. We are all Republicans, we are all Federalists. If there be any among us who would wish to dissolve this Union or to change its republican form, let them stand undisturbed as monuments of the safety with which error of opinion may be tolerated where reason is left free to combat it. I know, indeed, that some honest men fear that a republican government can not be strong, that this Government is not strong enough; but would the honest patriot, in the full tide of successful experiment, abandon a government which has so far kept us free and firm on the theoretic and visionary fear that this Government, the world's best hope, may by possibility want energy to preserve itself? I trust not. I believe this, on the contrary, the strongest Government on earth. I believe it the only one where every man, at the call of the law, would fly to the standard of the law, and would meet invasions of the public order as his own personal concern. Sometimes it is said that man can not be trusted with government of himself. Can he, then, be trusted with the government of others? Or have we found angels in the forms of kings to govern him? Let history answer this question.

Let us, then, with courage and confidence pursue our own Federal and Republican principles, our attachment to union and representative government. . . .

. . . Equal and exact justice to all men, of whatever state or persuasion, religious or political; peace, commerce, and honest friendship with all nations, entangling alliances with none; the support of the State governments in all their rights, as the most competent administrations for our domestic concerns and the surest bulwarks against antirepublican tendencies; the preservation of the General Government in its whole constitutional vigor, as the sheet anchor of our peace at home and safety abroad; a jealous care of the right of election by the people—a mild and safe corrective of abuses which are lopped by the sword of revolution where peaceable remedies are unprovided; absolute acquiescence in the decisions of the majority, the vital principle of republics, from which is no appeal but to force, the vital principle and immediate parent of despotism; a well-disciplined militia, our best reliance in peace and for the first moments of war, till regulars may relieve them; the supremacy of the civil over the military authority; economy in the public expense, that labor may be lightly burthened; the honest payment of our debts and sacred preservation of the public faith; encouragement of agriculture, and of commerce as its handmaid; the diffusion of information and arraignment of all abuses at the bar of the public reason; freedom of religion; freedom of the press, and freedom of person under the protection of the habeas corpus, and trial by juries impartially selected. These principles form the bright constellation which has gone before us and guided our steps through an age of revolution and reformation. The wisdom of our sages and blood of our heroes have been devoted to their attainment. They should be the creed of our political faith, the text of civic instruction, the touchstone by which to try the services of those we trust; and should we wander from them in moments of error or of alarm, let us hasten to retrace our steps and to regain the road which alone leads to peace, liberty, and safety.

Is Jefferson's vision of liberty and republicanism reasonable? Why or why not?

The Triumph and Collapse of Jeffersonian Republicanism, 1800–1824

Introduction

The War of 1812 pitted the young republic of the United States against Great Britain, one of the world's major powers. The origins of the war lay in the legacy of Anglo-American hostility of the American revolutionary era. Tensions mounted after the resumption of Anglo-French war in Europe in 1803. In its quest to defeat France, Britain routinely interfered with the maritime trade of American merchant ships, preventing vessels from transporting cargoes on behalf of its enemy. (France periodically imposed similar restrictions against American ships.) The British Navy also implemented impressment, a practice of forcibly removing from American ships sailors who were naturalized American citizens but deemed by London liable to service in the Royal Navy. Some Americans also concluded that the British military in Canada instigated Native American attacks against settlements along the western frontier. At the same time, U.S. domestic politics divided Republicans, who tended to be pro-French, and Federalists, who were inclined to favor the British.

Republican President Thomas Jefferson (1801–1809) and James Madison (1809–1817) confronted the challenge of balancing the rights of merchant shippers, the fate of citizen sailors, the security of frontierspeople, and the best interests of the republic as a whole. In June 1812, during the Madison presidency, the country declared war against Britain. In a series of battles along America's frontier with Canada, its eastern seaboard, and its southern coastline, U.S. forces neither won nor lost decisively, and the war officially ended when the belligerents signed the Treaty of Ghent on 24 December 1814.

CONTEMPORARY VIEWS
ON THE WAR OF 1812

The documents reprinted below reveal dimensions of the developments that led the United States into the War of 1812. Speeches by Felix Grundy, John Randolph, and James Madison, together with the minutes of the Hartford Convention, display an array of contemporary interpretations about the wisdom and justice of the American decision to wage war.

Felix Grundy Advocates
War against Great Britain

Whether to wage war against Great Britain became a major political issue in the United States in 1810–11. "War Hawks," as advocates of belligerence were known, argued that engaging the British would redress the violations of maritime rights, alleviate the insecurity on the frontier, and perhaps even open British Canada to American conquest. Representative Felix Grundy of Tennessee, elected in 1810 on a prowar platform, delivered the following speech favoring war in Congress in December, 1811. It appeared in The Debates and Proceedings in the Congress of the United States . . . 12th Cong., 1st sess. *(Washington, 1853), 424–26.*

I will now state the reasons which influenced the committee, in recommending the measures now before us.

It is not the carrying trade, properly so called, about which this nation and Great Britain are at present contending. Were this the only question now under consideration, I should feel great unwillingness (however clear our claim might be) to involve the nation in war, for the assertion of a right, in the enjoyment of which the community at large are not more deeply concerned. The true question in controversy, is of a very different character; it involves the interest of the whole nation: It is the right of exporting the productions of our own soil and industry to foreign markets. Sir, our vessels are now captured when destined to the ports of France, and condemned by the British Courts of Admiralty, without even the pretext of having on board contraband of war, enemies' property, or, having in any other respect violated the laws of nations. These depredations on our lawful commerce, under whatever ostensible pretence committed, are not to be traced to any maxims or rules of public law, but to the maritime supremacy, and pride of the British nation. This hostile and unjust policy of that country towards us, is not to be wondered at, when we recollect that the United States are already the second commercial nation in the world. The rapid growth of our commercial importance, has not only awakened the jealousy of the commercial interests of Great Britain, but her statesmen, no doubt, anticipate with deep concern, the maritime greatness of this Republic. . . .

What, Mr. Speaker, are we now called on to decide? It is, whether we will resist by force the attempt, made by that Government, to subject our maritime rights to the arbitrary and capricious rule of her will; for my part I am not prepared to say that this country shall submit to have her commerce interdicted or regulated, by any foreign nation. Sir, I prefer war to submission.

Over and above these unjust pretensions of the British Government, for many years past they have been in the practice of impressing our seamen, from merchant vessels; this unjust and lawless invasion of personal liberty, calls loudly for the interposition of this Government. To those better acquainted with the facts in relation to it, I leave it to fill up the picture. My mind is irresistibly drawn to the West.

Although others may not strongly feel the bearing which the late transactions in that quarter have on this subject, upon my mind they have great influence. It cannot be believed by any man who will reflect, that the savage tribes, uninfluenced by other Powers, would think of making war on the United States. They understand too well their own weakness, and our strength. They have already felt the weight of our arms; they know they hold the very soil on which they live as tenants at sufferance. How, then, sir, are we to account for their late conduct? In one way only; some powerful nation must have intrigued with them, and turned their peaceful disposition towards us into hostilities. Great Britain alone has intercourse with those Northern tribes; I therefore infer, that if British gold has not been employed, their baubles and trinkets, and the promise of support and a place of refuge if necessary, have had their effect.

If I am right in this conjecture, war is not to commence by sea or land, it is already begun; and some of the richest blood of our country has already been shed. . . .

This war, if carried on successfully, will have its advantages. We shall drive the British from our Continent—they will no longer have an apportunity of intriguing with our Indian neighbors, and setting on the ruthless savage to tomahawk our women and children. That nation will lose her Canadian trade, and, by having no resting place in this country, her means of annoying us will be diminished.

Why, according to Grundy, should the United States go to war?

John Randolph Opposes War

In opposition to the War Hawks stood an array of elected officials who opposed war against Britain on various grounds. Some were Federalists who suspected the Republicans of using the conflict to align the country with France; others feared the usurpation of power by the president at the expense of Congress; still others predicted certain defeat at the hands of the British military. One of the most prominent of the antiwar voices belonged to John Randolph of Roanoke, Virginia, who spoke passionately for peace from within the Republican ranks. His speech that appears below was delivered to Congress in December 1811; it is taken from The Debates and Proceedings in the Congress of the United States . . . *12th Cong., 1st sess. (Washington, 1853), 441, 445–47, 450, 454–55.*

An insinuation had fallen from the gentleman from Tennessee, (Mr. Grundy.) that the late massacre of our brethren on the

Wabash had been instigated by the British Government. Has the President given any such information? has the gentleman received any such, even informally, from any officer of this Government? Is it so believed by the Administration? He had cause to think the contrary to be the fact; that such was not their opinion. This insinuation was of the grossest kind—a presumption the most rash, the most unjustifiable. Show but good ground for it, he would give up the question at the threshold—he was ready to march to Canada. It was indeed well calculated to excite the feelings of the Western people particularly, who were not quite so tenderly attached to our red brethren as some modern philosophers; but it was destitute of any foundation, beyond mere surmise and suspicion. . . . Advantage had been taken of the spirit of the Indians, broken by the war which ended in the Treaty of Greenville. Under the ascendency then acquired over them, they had been pent up by subsequent treaties into nooks, straightened in their quarters by a blind cupidity, seeking to extinguish their title to immense wildernesses, for which, (possessing, as we do already, more land than we can sell or use) we shall not have occasion, for half a century to come. It was our own thirst for territory, our own want of moderation, that had driven these sons of nature to desperation, of which we felt the effects. . . .

This war of conquest, a war for the acquisition of territory and subjects, is to be a new commentary on the doctrine that Republics are destitute of ambition—that they are addicted to peace, wedded to the happiness and safety of the great body of their people. But it seems this is to be a holiday campaign—there is to be no expense of blood, or treasure, on our part—Canada is to conquer herself—she is to be subdued by the principles of fraternity. The people of that country are first to be seduced from their allegiance, and converted into traitors, as preparatory to the making them good citizens. Although he must acknowledge that some of our flaming patriots were thus manufactured, he did not think the process would hold good with a whole community. It was a dangerous experiment. . . .

But is war the true remedy? Who will profit by it? Speculators—a few lucky merchants, who draw prizes in the lottery—commissaries and contractors. Who must suffer by it? The people. It is their blood, their taxes, that must flow to support it. . . .

Mr. R. adverted to the defenceless state of our seaports, and particularly of the Chesapeake. A single spot only, on both shores, might be considered in tolerable security—from the nature of the port and the strength of the population—and that spot unhappily governed the whole State of Maryland. His friend, the late Governor of Maryland, (Mr. Lloyd) at the very time he was bringing his warlike resolutions before the Legislature of the State, was liable, on any night, to be taken out of his bed and carried off with his family, by the most contemptible picaroon. Such was the situation of many a family in Maryland and lower Virginia. . . .

He called upon those professing to be Republicans to make good the promises held out by their Republican predecessors when they came into power—promises, which for years afterwards they had honestly, faithfully fulfilled. We had vaunted of paying off the national debt, of retrenching useless establishments; and yet had now become as infatuated with standing armies, loans, taxes, navies, and war, as ever were the Essex Junto. What Republicanism is this?

John Randolph has a very different view. Why does he oppose war? Who gets the better of the argument?

President Madison Asks
Congress to Declare War

War came when the United States declared it on Great Britain in early June 1812. In his message requesting Congress to issue a declaration of war, President Madison listed several reasons for belligerence, aiming most of his barbs at the British. His address, which appears below, was published in Messages of the Presidents of the United States, *comp. Jonathan Phillips (Columbus, Ohio, 1841), 157–58, 160–61.*

I communicate to Congress certain documents, being a continuation of those heretofore laid before them, on the subject of our affairs with Great Britain.

Without going back beyond the renewal, in 1803, of the war in which Great Britain is engaged, and omitting unrepaired wrongs of inferior magnitude, the conduct of her government presents a series of acts, hostile to the United States as an independent and neutral nation.

British cruisers have been in the continued practice of violating the American flag on the great highway of nations, and of seizing and carrying off persons sailing under it; not in the exercise of a belligerent right, founded on the law of nations against an enemy, but of a municipal prerogative over British subjects. . . .

The practice, hence, is so far from affecting British subjects alone, that, under the pretext of searching for these, thousands of American citizens, under the safeguard of public law, and of their national flag, have been torn from their country, and from every thing dear to them; have been dragged on board ships of war of a foreign nation, and exposed, under the severities of their discipline, to be exiled to the most distant and deadly climes, to risk their lives in the battles of their oppressors, and to be the melancholy instruments of taking away those of their own brethren.

Against this crying enormity, which Great Britain would be so prompt to avenge if committed against herself, the United States have in vain exhausted remonstrances and expostulations. And that no proof might be wanting of their conciliatory dispositions, and no pretext left for a continuance of the practice, the British government was formally assured of the readiness of the United States, to enter into arrangements, such as could not be rejected, if the recovery of British subjects were the real and the sole object. The communication passed without effect.

British cruisers have been in the practice, also, of violating the rights and the peace of our coasts. They hover over and harass our entering and departing commerce. To the most insulting pretensions, they have added the most lawless proceedings in our very harbors; and have wantonly spilt American blood within the sanctuary of our territorial jurisdiction. The principles and rules enforced by that nation, when a neutral nation, against armed vessels of belligerents hovering near her coasts, and disturbing her commerce, are well known. When called on, nevertheless, by the United States, to punish the greater offences committed by her own vessels, her government has bestowed on their commanders additional marks of honor and confidence.

Under pretended blockades, without the presence of an adequate force, and sometimes without the practicability of applying one, our commerce has been plundered in every sea; the great staples of our country have been cut off from their legitimate markets; and a destructive blow aimed at our agricultural and maritime interests. . . .

In reviewing the conduct of Great Britain towards the United States, our attention is necessarily drawn to the warfare, just renewed by the savages, on one of our extensive frontiers; a warfare, which is known to spare neither age nor sex, and to be distinguished by features peculiarly shocking to humanity. It is difficult to account for the activity and combinations which have for some time been developing themselves among tribes in constant intercourse with British traders and garrisons, without connecting their hostility with that influence, and without recollecting the authenticated examples of such interpositions, heretofore furnished by the officers and agents of that government.

Such is the spectacle of injuries and indignities, which have been heaped on our country; and such the crisis which its unexampled forbearance and conciliatory efforts, have not been able to avert. . . .

. . . We behold our seafaring citizens still the daily victims of lawless violence committed on the great common and highway of nations, even within sight of the country which owes them protection. We behold our vessels, freighted with the producte of our soil and industry, or returning with the honest preceeds of them, wrested from their lawful destinations, confiscated by prize courts, no longer the organs of public law, but the instruments of arbitrary edicts; and their unfortunate crews dispersed and lost, or forced or inveigled, in British ports, into British fleets, whilst arguments are employed, in support of these aggressions, which have no foundation but in a principle, equally supporting a claim to regulate our external commerce, in all cases whatsoevor.

We behold, in fine, on the side of Great Britain, a state of war against the United States; and on the side of the United States, a state of peace towards Great Britain.

Whether the United States shall continue passive under these progressive usurpations, and these accumulating wrongs; or, opposing force to force in defence of their national rights, shall commit a just cause into the hands of the Almighty Disposer of events; avoiding all connections which might entagle it in the contests or views of other powers, and preserving a constant readines to concur in an honourable re-establishment of peace and friendship, is a solemn question, which the Constitution wisely confides to the legislative department of the government. In recommending it to their early deliberations, I am happy in the assurance, that the decision will be worthy the enlightened and patriotic councils of a virtuous, a free and a powerful nation. . . .

James Madison.
June, 1, 1812.

Is Madison convincing in his request for a declaration of war?

Final Report of the Hartford Convention

Federalist opponents of the war and of wartime policies enacted by the Republican administration voiced their concerns in various ways. Their activism culminated in a wartime convention at Hartford, Connecticut, which passed resolutions censuring Republican practices and suggesting a series of amendments to the U.S. Constitution to safeguard against their recurrence. The final report of the convention, approved in January 1815, appears below. It was printed in Theodore Dwight, History of the Hartford Convention *(New York, 1833), 352–55, 362–63, 365.*

The convention is deeply impressed with a sense of the arduous nature of the commission which they were appointed to execute, of devising the means of defence against dangers, and of relief from oppressions proceeding from the acts of their own government, without violating constitutional principles, or disappointing the hopes of a suffering and injured people. . . . Necessity alone can sanction a resort to this measure; and it should never be extended in duration or degree beyond the exigency, until the people, not merely in the fervour of sudden excitement, but after full deliberation, are determined to change the constitution.

It is a truth, not to be concealed, that a sentiment prevails to no inconsiderable extent, that administration have given such constructions to that instrument, and practised so many abuses under colour of its authority, that the time for a change is at hand. . . .

Although this high state of public happiness has undergone a miserable and afflicting reverse, through the prevalence of a weak and profligate policy, yet the evils and afflictions which have thus been induced upon the country, are not peculiar to any form of government. The lust and caprice of power, the corruption of patronage, the oppression of the weaker interests of the community by the stronger, heavy taxes, wasteful expenditures, and unjust and ruinous wars, are the natural offspring of bad administrations, in all ages and countries. It was indeed to be hoped, that the rulers of these states would not make such disastrous haste to involve their infancy in the embarrassments of old and rotten institutions. Yet all this have they done; and their conduct calls loudly for their dismission and disgrace. But to attempt upon every abuse of power to change the constitution, would be to perpetuate the evils of revolution.

Again, the experiment of the powers of the constitution to regain its vigour, and of the people to recover from their delusions, has been hitherto made under the greatest possible disadvantages arising from the state of the world. The fierce passions which have convulsed the nations of Europe, have passed the ocean, and finding their way to the bosoms of our citizens, have afforded to administration the means of perverting public opinion, in respect to our foreign relations, so as to acquire its aid in the indulgence of their animosities, and the increase of their adherents. Further, a reformation of public opinion, resulting from dear-bought experience, in the southern Atlantic states, at least, is not to be despaired of. They will have felt, that the eastern states cannot be made exclusively the victims of a capricious and impassioned policy. They will have seen that the great and essential interests of the people are common to the south and to the east. They will realize the fatal errors of a system which seeks revenge for commercial injuries in the sacrifice of commerce, and aggravates by needless wars, to an immeasurable extent, the injuries it professes to redress. They may discard the influence of visionary theorists, and recognize the benefits of a practical policy. . . .

In the prosecution of this favourite warfare, administration have left the exposed and vulnerable parts of the country destitute of all the efficient means of defence. The main body of the regular army has been marched to the frontier. The navy has been stripped of a great part of its sailors for the service of the lakes. Meanwhile the enemy scours the sea-coast, blockades our ports, ascends our bays and rivers, makes actual descents in various and distant places, holds some by force, and threatens all that are assailable with fire and sword. The sea-board of four of the New-England states, following its curvatures, presents an extent of more than seven hundred miles, generally occupied by a compact population, and accessible by a naval force, exposing a mass of people and property to the devastation of the enemy, which bears a great proportion to the residue of the maritime frontier of the United States. This extensive shore has been exposed to frequent attacks, repeated contributions, and constant alarms. The regular forces detached by the national government for its defence are mere pretexts for placing officers of high rank in command. They are besides confined to a few places, and are too insignificant in number to be included in any computation. . . .

. . . When a great and brave people shall feel themselves deserted by their government, and reduced to the necessity either of submission to a foreign enemy, or of appropriating to their own use those means of defence which are indispensable to self-preservation, they cannot consent to wait passive spectators of approaching ruin, which it is in their power to avert, and to resign the last remnant of their industrious earnings to be dissipated in support of measures destructive of the best interests of the nation.

This convention will not trust themselves to express their conviction of the catastrophe to which such a state of things inevitably tends. Conscious of their high responsibility to God and their country, solicitous for the continuance of the Union, as well as the sovereignty of the states, unwilling to furnish obstacles to peace—resolute never to submit to a foreign enemy, and confiding in the Divine care and protection, they will, until the last hope shall be extinguished, endeavor to avert such consequences.

According to the Federalists, why are the Republicans fighting this war?

The Jacksonian Era, 1824–1845

INTRODUCTION

In the 1830s, the federal government of the United States forced most of the Native Americans living east of the Mississippi off their homelands. Ostensibly intended to relocate these Indians on sparsely populated and less desirable lands to the west; this massive "removal" resulted in the deaths of many. Because the justification for removal was often framed in terms of savage Indians and civilized whites, the forced migration of the Cherokee people earned the most attention at the time and since. Of the Native American people who were finally forced to leave their lands and migrate across the Mississippi River—Choctaw, Cherokee, Creeks, and others—the Cherokee made the most sustained and successful effort to accommodate to the white man's ways. They aided Andrew Jackson in his victory over the Creeks at the pivotal Battle of Horseshoe Bend, 27 March 1814. They made rapid advancement in agriculture, education, and adoption of the Christian religion. In 1827, the Cherokee adopted a written constitution patterned after the Constitution of the United States and claimed to be a sovereign, independent nation with complete jurisdiction over their territory. Neither the federal nor state governments recognized that claim. Ultimately, their efforts to retain their land and freedom were to no avail.

Soon after the Cherokee adopted their constitution, the states in which they resided, especially Georgia, stepped up efforts to gain control of their land. When Andrew Jackson became president of the United States in 1829, he initiated the first major federal effort to relocate Native American populations. His policy, consonant with that of Georgia and other southern states and reflecting the opinions and desires of most white Americans, was to clear the lands east of the Mississippi River for settlement and exploitation by whites.

Jackson's policy was a success. By the Treaty of New Echota, 29 December 1835, a small group of Cherokee leaders ceded the nation's land east of the Mississippi River to the United States for the sum of $5 million and a promise of sufficient land for their resettlement in the west. The treaty bitterly divided the Cherokee into pro- and anti-removal parties and led to the murder, or execution, of John Ridge, Elias Boudinot, and Major Ridge, who favored the treaty, by members of their own nation.

In 1830, Congress passed the Indian Removal Act, which enabled President Jackson to exchange land west of the Mississippi River for tribal territory in the southeastern states. Almost sixteen thousand Cherokee were forced to emigrate, and, according to one estimate, about one-fourth of them died in concentration camps or along the "Trail of Tears," the Cherokee name for the terrible trek west.

How shall we understand what happened to the Cherokee, and indeed to all Native Americans, following the advent and expansion of Europeans in their land? Andrew Jackson has been accused of genocide, as have, of late, Christopher Columbus and all Europeans who invaded, settled, and conquered the Americas.

What is genocide? Webster's New World Dictionary defines it as: "first applied to the attempted killing or extermination of a whole people or nation." You see the key words: "killing," "extermination," "whole people or nation." Was that Andrew Jackson's intent? Or, if not his intent, was it in any case the result of his policy, abetted by the majority of white Americans? If not, why did what happened happen? Jackson himself believed that what happened was tragic but inevitable. So did many of his contemporaries, and so do many today. Jackson believed the removal and deaths of so many Cherokee was the result of the often-repeated clash between civilization and savagery; between a dynamic, superior culture and a backward, inferior one.

Was there no other, better, way? You decide.

JUDGING JACKSON: PRAGMATIC POLITICIAN OR SCHEMING HYPOCRITE?

Following are two views of Andrew Jackson's removal policy. They present differing, often conflicting interpretations of Jackson as a man and as a political leader, of the complex issues involved in Indian removal, and of the results of Jackson's policy and the related actions of Georgia and other southeastern states in relocating Native Americans west of the Mississippi River.

The first selection is an article written by Francis Paul Prucha, a professor at Marquette University. Perhaps no other scholar has published so extensively on Jackson and Indian removal as Prucha. This early article, published in 1969, clearly explains the position that Prucha has since maintained: that Jackson did not hate Native Americans, that he had no intent to destroy them, that he had the best interests of Native Americans at heart, although he firmly believed that America—the United States—was a white man's country. Edward Pessen, author of the second selection, takes a different view of Jackson's policy. He argues that Jackson zealously worked to bring about removal, regardless of the costs. Pessen questions Jackson's claims to have the best interests of the Cherokee at heart, claims which Prucha accepts at face value.

Jackson as a Pragmatic Statesman

Francis Paul Prucha argues that Jackson's policy toward the Native Americans was dictated primarily by considerations of national security. In the following excerpt Prucha asserts that Jackson actually upheld the rights of Native Americans who lived peaceably with whites. Taken from F.P. Prucha "Andrew Jackson's Indian Policy: A Reassessment," The Journal of American History 56 (December 1969):527–28, 534–36.

A GREAT many persons—not excluding some notable historians—have adopted a "devil theory" of American Indian policy. And in their demonic hierarchy Andrew Jackson has first place. He is depicted primarily, if not exclusively, as a western frontiersman and famous Indian fighter, who was a zealous advocate of dispossessing the Indians and at heart an "Indian-hater." When he became President, the story goes, he made use of his new power, ruthlessly and at the point of a bayonet, to force the Indians from their ancestral homes in the East into desert lands west of the Mississippi, which were considered forever useless to the white man.

This simplistic view of Jackson's Indian policy is unacceptable. It was not Jackson's aim to crush the Indians because, as an old Indian fighter, he hated Indians. Although his years in the West had brought him into frequent contact with the Indians, he by no means developed a doctrinaire anti-Indian attitude. Rather, as a military man, his dominant goal in the decades before he became President was to preserve the security and well-being of the United States and its Indian and white inhabitants. His military experience, indeed, gave him an overriding concern for the safety of the nation from foreign rather than internal enemies, and to some extent the anti-Indian sentiment that has been charged against Jackson in his early career was instead basically anti-British. Jackson, as his first biographer pointed out, had "many private reasons for disliking" Great Britain. "In her, he could trace the efficient cause, why, in early life, he had been left forlorn and wretched, without a single relation in the world." His frontier experience, too, had convinced him that foreign agents were behind the raised tomahawks of the red men. In 1808, after a group of settlers had been killed by the Creeks, Jackson told his militia troops: "[T]his brings to our recollection the horrid barbarity com-

---

"Andrew Jackson's Indian Policy: A Reassessment," by F.P. Prucha, as it appeared in *The Journal of American History* (formerly *The Mississippi Valley Historical Review),* Vol. LVI, No. 3, December 1969. Copyright © 1969 by the Organization of American Historians.

mitted on our frontier in 1777 under the influence of and by the orders of Great Britain, and it is presumeable that the same influence has excited those barbarians to the late and recent acts of butchery and murder. . . ." From that date on there is hardly a statement by Jackson about Indian dangers that does not aim sharp barbs at England. His reaction to the Battle of Tippecanoe was that the Indians had been "excited to war by the secrete agents of Great Britain." . . .

The removal policy, begun long before Jackson's presidency but wholeheartedly adopted by him, was the culmination of these views. Jackson looked upon removal as a means of protecting the process of civilization, as well as of providing land for white settlers, security from foreign invasion, and a quieting of the clamors of Georgia against the federal government. This view is too pervasive in Jackson's thought to be dismissed as polite rationalization for avaricious white aggrandizement. His outlook was essentially Jeffersonian. Jackson envisaged the transition from a hunting society to a settled agricultural society, a process that would make it possible for the Indians to exist with a higher scale of living on less land, and which would make it possible for those who adopted white ways to be quietly absorbed into the white society. Those who wished to preserve their identity in Indian nations could do it only by withdrawing from the economic and political pressures exerted upon their enclaves by the dominant white settlers. West of the Mississippi they might move at their own pace toward civilization.

Evaluation of Jackson's policy must be made in the light of the feasible alternatives available to men of his time. The removal program cannot be judged simply as a land grab to satisfy the President's western and southern constituents. The Indian problem that Jackson faced was complex, and various solutions were proposed. There were, in fact, four possibilities.

First, the Indians could simply have been destroyed. They could have been killed in war, mercilessly hounded out of their settlements, or pushed west off the land by brute force, until they were destroyed by disease or starvation. It is not too harsh a judgment to say that this was implicitly, if not explicitly, the policy of many of the aggressive frontiersmen. But it was not the policy, implicit or explicit, of Jackson and the responsible government officials in his administration or of those preceding or following his. It would be easy to compile an anthology of statements of horror on the part of government officials toward any such approach to the solution of the Indian problem.

Second, the Indians could have been rapidly assimilated into white society. It is now clear that this was not a feasible solution. Indian culture has a viability that continually impresses anthropologists, and to become white men was not the goal of the Indians. But many important and learned men of the day thought that this was a possibility. Some were so sanguine as to hope that within one generation the Indians could be taught the white man's ways and that, once they learned them, they would automatically desire to turn to that sort of life. Thomas Jefferson never tired of telling the Indians of the advantages of farming over hunting, and the chief purpose of schools was to train the Indian children in white ways, thereby making them immediately absorbable into the dominant culture. This solution was at first the hope of humanitarians who had the interest of the Indians at heart, but little by little many came to agree with Jackson that this dream was not going to be fulfilled.

Third, if the Indians were not to be destroyed and if they could not be immediately assimilated, they might be protected in their own culture on their ancestral lands in the East—or, at least, on reasonably large remnants of those lands. They would then be enclaves within the white society and would be protected by their treaty agreements and by military force. This was the alternative demanded by the opponents of Jackson's removal bill—for example, the missionaries of the American Board of Commissioners for Foreign Missions. But this, too, was infeasible, given the political and military conditions of the United States at the time. The federal government could not have provided a standing army of sufficient strength to protect the enclaves of Indian territory from the encroachments of the whites. Jackson could not withstand Georgia's demands for the end of the *imperium in imperio* [an empire within an empire] represented by the Cherokee Nation and its new constitution, not because of some inherent immorality on his part but because the political situation of America would not permit it.

The jurisdictional dispute cannot be easily dismissed. Were the Indian tribes independent nations? The question received its legal answer in John Marshall's decision in *Cherokee Nation v. Georgia*, in which the chief justice defined the Indian tribes as "dependent domestic nations." But aside from the juridical decision, were the Indians, in fact, independent, and could they have maintained their independence without the support—political and military—of the federal government? The answer, clearly, is no, as writers at the time pointed out. The federal government could have stood firm in defense of the Indian nations against Georgia, but this would have brought it into head-on collision with a state, which insisted that its sovereignty was being impinged upon by the Cherokees.

This was not a conflict that anyone in the federal government wanted. President Monroe had been slow to give in to the demands of the Georgians. He had refused to be panicked into hasty action before he had considered all the possibilities. But eventually he became convinced that a stubborn resistance to the southern states would solve nothing, and from that point on he and his successors, John Quincy Adams and Jackson, sought to solve the problem by removing the cause. They wanted the Indians to be placed in some area where the problem of federal versus state jurisdiction would not arise, where the Indians could be granted land in fee simple [permanent transference of land without restrictions] by the federal government and not have to worry about what some state thought were its rights and prerogatives.

The fourth and final possibility, then, was removal. To Jackson this seemed the only answer. Since neither adequate protection nor quick assimilation of the Indians was possible, it seemed reasonable and necessary to move the Indians to some area where they would not be disturbed by federal-state jurisdictional disputes or by encroachments of white settlers, where they could develop on the road to civilization at their own pace, or, if they so desired, preserve their own culture.

Jackson as a Scheming Devil

Edward Pessen contends that Jackson's hypocritical policy toward Indian removal, though couched in pious rhetoric, actually was intended to remove the Native Americans from their homelands at any cost. The following argument is taken from Edward Pessen, Jacksonian America: Society, Personality, and Politics *(Homewood, Illinois, 1978), 296–301.*

Jacksonian Indian policy was a blending of hypocrisy, cant, and rapaciousness, seemingly shot through with contradictions. Inconsistencies however are present only if the language of the presidential state papers is taken seriously. "The language of Indian removal was pious," observes [historian] Michael P. Rogin, "but the hum of destruction is clearly audible underneath." In [historian] Ronald Satz's phrase, such language provided a "convenient humanitarian rationale" for a policy of force. When the lofty rhetoric is discounted and viewed for what it was—sheer rationale for policy based on much more mundane considerations—then an almost frightening consistency becomes apparent. By one means or another the southern tribes had to be driven to the far side of the Mississippi. For as [historian] Mary E. Young has pointed out, by 1830 "east of the Mississippi, white occupancy was limited by Indian tenure of northeastern Georgia, enclaves in western North Carolina and southern Tennessee, eastern Alabama, and the northern two thirds of Mississippi. In this 25-million acre domain lived nearly 60,000 Cherokees, Creeks, Choctaws and Chickasaws." The Jacksonians invoked alleged higher laws of nature to justify removal. Thomas Benton [Senator from Missouri] spoke of a national imperative that the land be turned over to those who would use it "according to the intentions of the creator." Jackson himself referred to the march of progress and civilization, whose American manifestation was "studded with cities, towns and prosperous farms, embellished with all the improvements which art can devise or industry execute, occupied by more than 12 million happy people and filled with all the blessings of liberty, civilization and religion," before which "forests . . . ranged by a few thousand savages" must give ground.

In Miss Young's laconic words, "such a rationalization had one serious weakness as an instrument of policy. The farmer's right of eminent domain over the lands of the savage could be asserted consistently only so long as tribes involved were 'savage.' The southwestern tribes, however, were agriculturists as well as hunters." The obvious proof that the federal government did not take seriously its own justification for removal is the disinterest it displayed in the evidence that Cherokees, Choctaws,

---

and Chickasaws were in fact skilled in the arts of civilization. That "the people it now hoped to displace could by no stretch of dialectic be classed as mere wandering savages," would have given pause to men who sincerely believed in their own professions that it was the Indians' alleged savagery that primarily justified their removal. There is every reason to think that the Jacksonians were fully aware that their doctrine—specious and arrogant at best, with its implication that a people living a "superior" life had the right to take the lands of "inferiors"—was all the more specious because its assumption of Indian savagery was untrue.

White speculators and politicians in the southern states had little interest in *theories* of removal. They wanted removal, however rationalized, and were not fastidious as to the means used to accomplish it. No issue was more important, certainly not in Mississippi, where "to most residents . . . the most salient event of 1833 concerned neither the tariff nor nullification," but the fact that that autumn "the first public auctions of the Choctaw lands were held." According to Edwin Miles, Mississippians were so "grateful to Old Hickory [i.e. Andrew Jackson] for making these lands available to them [that] . . . they were inclined to disregard differences of opinion that he might entertain on issues of less importance." That happy day came to pass in Mississippi and elsewhere only because of the total cooperation shown by the Jackson administration in helping the southern states separate the tribes from their lands. The federal government had to display tact, cunning, guile, cajolery, and more than a hint of coercion. That it proved more than equal to the task was due in no small measure to Andrew Jackson's dedication to it. His performance was not that of responsible government official deferring to the will of constituents but rather that of a zealot who fully shared their biases and rapacity.

Before Jackson became President he had urged that the tribes not be treated as sovereign nations, and when he assumed the highest office he continued to feel that Indians were subjects of the United States, mere hunters who occupied land under its sufferance. A major difference between Jacksonian Indian policy and that of his predecessors lay in this fact. From Jefferson through John Quincy Adams, while national administrations had *desired* the removal of the southwestern tribes and countenanced threats and unlovely inducements to accomplish it, they had continued to treat the tribes "as more or less sovereign nations and to respect their right to remain on their own lands." And where Secretary of War Calhoun, for example, had hoped to accomplish Choctaw removal by "educating" the Indians to see the need for it, Jackson relied on more forceful means certain to work more quickly. In his first inaugural message he promised Indians a humane, just, and liberal policy, based on respect for Indian "rights and wants." A little more than one year later, Secretary of War Eaton induced the highly civilized Choctaws to sign a treaty removing them from their ancient homeland in Mississippi. Eaton succeeded through the use of hypocrisy, bribes, lies, suppression of critics, and intimidation, in securing approval of a treaty that, according to Colonel George Gaines who was present during the negotiations, was "despised by most of the Indians."

Jackson bypassed William Wirt for John Berrien as Attorney-General because he distrusted Wirt on Indian removal. When Wirt subsequently became the lawyer for the Cherokees, Jackson denounced the "wicked" man. He removed the knowledgeable Thomas L. McKenney as head of the Bureau of Indian Affairs because McKenney, as a "warm friend of the Indians," had to be replaced by someone of sounder feelings. (Among McKenney's other flaws, he had been too close to Calhoun and served the Adams Administration too well.) Jackson regarded the practice of negotiating treaties with Indian tribes as an "absurdity" and a "farce." On more than one occasion the President reverted to the practice of his Indian-fighting days, personally dealing with "reluctant tribes" in order to bring about their acquiescence to an agreement detrimental to their interests. He hated [politician William H.] Crawford in part because the latter had exposed the inequity and fraud in the Creek Treaty Jackson had negotiated in 1814. In the judgment of one modern student, Jackson, prior to the Supreme Court decision in the case of *Cherokee Nation* v. *Georgia* in 1831, "threatened the Supreme Court with a refusal to enforce its decree." The Court in that case sidestepped the issue of the constitutionality of Georgia's Indian laws. But when the following year the Court ruled, in *Worcester* v. *Georgia* that the State of Georgia had no right to extend its laws over the Cherokee nation, the Indian tribes being "domestic dependent nations," with limits defined by treaty, the President refused to enforce this decision. Unfortunately for the Cherokee, some of their best friends in

Congress and on the high court now urged them to sign a removal treaty. . . .

The actual procedures used to accomplish the desired end were numerous, ingenious, and effective. Simple force was eschewed, "forbidden by custom, by conscience, and by fear that the administration's opponents would exploit religious sentiment which cherished the rights of the red man." But as Miss Young points out, "within the confines of legality and the formulas of voluntarism it was still possible to acquire the much coveted domain of the civilized tribes." A kind of squeeze was directed against the Indians. On the one hand state governments refused to recognize tribal laws or federally assured rights, bringing Indians under state laws which dealt with them as individuals. Only Indians who chose to become citizens could hold on to what their skill and industry enabled them to accumulate and develop. The federal government continued the earlier policy, begun late in the Madison Administration, of offering reservations or allotments to individual Indians who cultivated their lands and wished to become citizens, while encouraging the trans-Mississippi migration of the others. When a Congressional measure appropriating $500,000 and authorizing the President to negotiate removal treaties with all the eastern tribes was under debate in 1830, even administration critics agreed that the "Indian's moral right to keep his land depended on his actual cultivation of it." In some cases the removal treaties were negotiated after sufficient pressure had been exercised by private individuals or government officials, who resorted to physical threats as well as to more subtle means. Jacksonian emissaries carried money and liquor in ample quantities.

In the case of the Creeks, who refused to agree to emigration, their chiefs were persuaded in March, 1832, to sign an allotment treaty. Ostensibly depriving the tribe of none of its Alabama territories, in fact by allotting most acreage to heads of families, it not only reduced the tribal estate but it made the individual owners prey to thieves and corruptionists in civil or public garb, who took advantage of Indian innocence and ignorance concerning property values and disposal. Advised that speculators were defrauding the Indians, among other ways by simply "borrowing" back the money they had paid for individual allotments without any intention of paying back the "loans," Secretary of War Lewis Cass enunciated the interesting doctrine that the War

Department had no authority to circumscribe the Indian's right to
be defrauded.

The deception practiced by the government in the Creek
Treaty may have been as much self-deception as anything else.
Certainly many federal agents were honest. Nor was the
government's objective profit through fraud. From the Indians'
viewpoint however, as from that of moralistic critics, the federal
purpose was even more terrible. Mere corruptionists could have
been bargained with; zealous believers in their own superiority
and their God-given right to Indian lands, could not. In any case,
"the disposal of Creek reserves exhibited an ironic contrast between the ostensible purposes of the allotment policy and its
actual operation. Instead of giving the tribesmen a more secure
title to their individual holdings, the allotment of their lands
became an entering wedge for those who would drive them from
their eastern domain."

. . . Probably the worst treatment of all was reserved for the
Cherokees. They had balked at moving to a region their own
surveyors described as "nothing but mountains and [a] huge bed
of rocks." In 1838 General Winfield Scott began their systematic
removal, more than 4,000 out of 15,000 of them dying, according
to one estimate, in the course of "the Trail of Tears." One judgment is that "at their worst the forced migrations approached the
horrors created by the Nazi handling of subject peoples."

Men like Edward Everett and [Ralph Waldo] Emerson [nine-
teenth-century writers] recoiled in horror, the New England press
was sickened at the reproach to our national character in this
"abhorrent business." But not Andrew Jackson. In his last message to Congress, he complimented the states on the removal of
"the evil" that had retarded their development. He also expressed
pleasure that "this unhappy race—. . . the original dwellers in our
land—are now placed in a situation where we may well hope that
they will share in the blessings of civilization and be saved from
the degradation and destruction to which they were rapidly hastening while they remained in the states." This bewildering combination of sentiments seemed to mean, as John W. Ward has
observed, that "America would save the Indians for civilization
by rescuing them from civilization." Jackson's certainty that "the
philanthropist will rejoice that the remnant of that ill-fated race
has at length been placed beyond the reach of injury or oppression," may have been warranted although one suspects that this

monument of self-deception might have been chagrined to discover philanthropy's estimate as to the true source of Indian oppression.

Henry Clay and other Whigs opposed particular removal treaties on constitutional and humanitarian grounds. And yet the Whig party position should not be misconstrued. For, as Satz observes, while the Whigs "found it expedient to condemn the Jacksonian removal policy when they were struggling to gain political control of the government," once in power they followed the very same policy. The Harrison and Tyler administration did not allow "Indians still east of the Mississippi River to remain there." In 1842 it was to a Whig Administration that the War Department reported that in the North as in the South, there was no more Indian land "east of the Mississippi, remaining unceded, to be desired by us." As was true too of the "spoils system," a policy begun by the one major party was continued by the other. Individual Whigs may have been more sensitive than their Democratic counterparts but the policies of their parties were at times remarkably similar.

What kinds of evidence and arguments do Prucha and Pessen use to make their cases? Which do you think is the most convincing? Why?

Jackson's Indian policy has been characterized as wrong, ill-conceived and poorly carried out, inevitable, or tragic. If any of these accusations are true, what, according to these writers, explains the shortcomings of the policy?

THE CONTEMPORARY DEBATE

Although a number of historians have used the word "inevitable" to describe the final victory of Jackson's removal policy, it is important to realize that Indian removal was vigorously debated at the time. For over a decade, the white citizens of the United States, the spokespeople for the federal and state governments, and Native Americans bitterly contested every aspect of state and national action regarding removal and every encroachment of whites into territory claimed by Native Americans. The issues involved in this extended debate—among them the status of

Native American nations in the polity of the United States; the constitutional division of power between states and the federal government; the binding nature of treaties between the colonies, states, federal government and Native American peoples; and the moral and ethical nature of removal—remain a focus for often emotional, even violent, disagreement. We who live in the United States of America have not escaped or outlived the consequences of what happened to the Cherokee and their kin. The following selections provide an introduction to the range of opinions, the depth of emotion, and the breadth of significance for this country occasioned by Indian removal in the nineteenth century.

A Benevolent Policy

In his second annual message to Congress, on 6 December 1830, Andrew Jackson explained and defended his policy of Indian removal. Excerpted from A Compilation of the Messages and Papers of the Presidents, 1789–1897, *ed. James D. Richardson (Washington, 1896), 2:519–23.*

It gives me pleasure to announce to Congress that the benevolent policy of the Government, steadily pursued for nearly thirty years, in relation to the removal of the Indians beyond the white settlements is approaching to a happy consummation. Two important tribes have accepted the provision made for their removal at the last session of Congress, and it is believed that their example will induce the remaining tribes also to seek the same obvious advantages.

The consequences of a speedy removal will be important to the United States, to individual States, and to the Indians themselves. The pecuniary advantages which it promises to the Government are the least of its recommendations. It puts an end to all possible danger of collision between the authorities of the General and State Governments on account of the Indians. It will place a dense and civilized population in large tracts of country now occupied by a few savage hunters. By opening the whole territory between Tennessee on the north and Louisiana on the south to the settlement of the whites it will incalculably strengthen the southwestern frontier and render the adjacent States strong enough to repel future invasions without remote aid. It will relieve the whole

State of Mississippi and the western part of Alabama of Indian occupancy, and enable those States to advance rapidly in population, wealth, and power. It will separate the Indians from immediate contact with settlements of whites; free them from the power of the States; enable them to pursue happiness in their own way and under their own rude institutions; will retard the progress of decay, which is lessening their numbers, and perhaps cause them gradually, under the protection of the Government and through the influence of good counsels, to cast off their savage habits and become an interesting, civilized, and Christian community. These consequences, some of them so certain and the rest so probable, make the complete execution of the plan sanctioned by Congress at their last session an object of much solicitude.

Toward the aborigines of the country no one can indulge a more friendly feeling than myself, or would go further in attempting to reclaim them from their wandering habits and make them a happy, prosperous people. I have endeavored to impress upon them my own solemn convictions of the duties and powers of the General Government in relation to the State authorities. For the justice of the laws passed by the States within the scope of their reserved powers they are not responsible to this Government. As individuals we may entertain and express our opinions of their acts, but as a Government we have as little right to control them as we have to prescribe laws for other nations.

With a full understanding of the subject, the Choctaw and the Chickasaw tribes have with great unanimity determined to avail themselves of the liberal offers presented by the act of Congress, and have agreed to remove beyond the Mississippi River. Treaties have been made with them, which in due season will be submitted for consideration. In negotiating these treaties they were made to understand their true condition, and they have preferred maintaining their independence in the Western forests to submitting to the laws of the States in which they now reside. These treaties, being probably the last which will ever be made with them, are characterized by great liberality on the part of the Government. They give the Indians a liberal sum in consideration of their removal, and comfortable subsistence on their arrival at their new homes. If it be their real interest to maintain a separate existence, they will there be at liberty to do so without the inconveniences and vexations to which they would unavoidably have been subject in Alabama and Mississippi.

Humanity has often wept over the fate of the aborigines of this country, and Philanthropy has been long busily employed in devising means to avert it, but its progress has never for a moment been arrested, and one by one have many powerful tribes disappeared from the earth. To follow to the tomb the last of his race and to tread on the graves of extinct nations excite melancholy reflections. But true philanthropy reconciles the mind to these vicissitudes as it does to the extinction of one generation to make room for another. In the monuments and fortresses of an unknown people, spread over the extensive regions of the West, we behold the memorials of a once powerful race, which was exterminated or has disappeared to make room for the existing savage tribes. Nor is there anything in this which, upon a comprehensive view of the general interests of the human race, is to be regretted. Philanthropy could not wish to see this continent restored to the condition in which it was found by our forefathers. What good man would prefer a country covered with forests and ranged by a few thousand savages to our extensive Republic, studded with cities, towns, and prosperous farms, embellished with all the improvements which art can devise or industry execute, occupied by more than 12,000,000 happy people, and filled with all the blessings of liberty, civilization, and religion?

The present policy of the Government is but a continuation of the same progressive change by a milder process. The tribes which occupied the countries now constituting the Eastern States were annihilated or have melted away to make room for the whites. The waves of population and civilization are rolling to the westward, and we now propose to acquire the countries occupied by the red men of the South and West by a fair exchange, and, at the expense of the United States, to send them to a land where their existence may be prolonged and perhaps made perpetual. Doubtless it will be painful to leave the graves of their fathers; but what do they more than our ancestors did or than our children are now doing? To better their condition in an unknown land our forefathers left all that was dear in earthly objects. Our children by thousands yearly leave the land of their birth to seek new homes in distant regions. Does Humanity weep at these painful separations from everything, animate and inanimate, with which the young heart has become entwined? Far from it. It is rather a source of joy that our country affords scope where our young population may range unconstrained in body or in mind, developing the power and faculties of man in their highest perfection. These remove hundreds and almost thousands of miles at their own expense, purchase the lands they occupy, and support themselves at their new homes from the moment of their arrival. Can it be cruel in this Government when, by events which it can not control, the Indian is made discontented in his ancient home to purchase his lands, to give him a new and extensive territory, to pay the expense of his removal, and support him a year in his new abode? How many thousands of our own people would gladly embrace the opportunity of removing to the West on such conditions! If the offers made to the Indians were extended to them, they would be hailed with gratitude and joy.

And is it supposed that the wandering savage has a stronger attachment to his home than the settled, civilized Christian? Is it more afflicting to him to leave the graves of his fathers than it is to our brothers and children? Rightly considered, the policy of the General Government toward the red man is not only liberal, but generous. He is unwilling to submit to the laws of the States and mingle with their population. To save him from this alternative, or perhaps utter annihilation, the General Government kindly offers him a new home, and proposes to pay the whole expense of his removal and settlement. . . .

It is, therefore, a duty which this Government owes to the new States to extinguish as soon as possible the Indian title to all lands which Congress themselves have included within their limits. When this is done the duties of the General Government in relation to the States and the Indians within their limits are at an end. The Indians may leave the State or not, as they choose. The purchase of their lands does not alter in the least their personal relations with the State government. No act of the General Government has ever been deemed necessary to give the States jurisdiction over the persons of the Indians. That they possess by virtue of their sovereign power within their own limits in as full a manner before as after the purchase of the Indian lands; nor can this Government add to or diminish it.

May we not hope, therefore, that all good citizens, and none more zealously than those who think the Indians oppressed by subjection to the laws of the States, will unite in attempting to open the eyes of those children of the forest to their true condition, and by a speedy removal to relieve them from all the evils, real or imaginary, present or prospective, with which they may be supposed to be threatened.

How does Jackson justify his Indian Removal policy? Is he successful?

Tragic Decision

Elias Boudinot was a "civilized" Cherokee who, in terms of education, religion, and aspirations, had come far along the white man's path; or so he believed. He agonized over removal, but finally supported it as a last, desperate means of maintaining the existence of his people. His stand cost him his life. The following selection is from editorials written by Boudinot as editor of the Cherokee Phoenix, *reprinted in* Cherokee Editor: The Writings of Elias Boudinot, *ed. Theda Perdue (Knoxville, 1983), 108–9, 142–43.*

[17 June 1829]
From the documents which we this day lay before our readers, there is not a doubt of the kind of policy, which the present administration of the General Government intends to pursue relative to the Indians. President Jackson has, as a neighboring editor remarks, "recognized the doctrine contended for by Georgia in its full extent." It is to be regretted that we were not undeceived long ago, while we were hunters and in our savage state. It appears now from the communication of the Secretary of War to the Cherokee Delegation, that the illustrious Washington, Jefferson, Madison and Monroe were only tantalizing us, when they encouraged us in the pursuit of agriculture and Government, and when they afforded us the protection of the United States, by which we have been preserved to this present time as a nation. Why were we not told long ago, that we could not be permitted to establish a government within the limits of any state? Then we could have borne disappointment much easier than now. The pretext for

---

Excerpt from the "Memorial and Protest of the Cherokee Nation: Memorial of the Cherokee Representatives," reprinted from House Reports, *24th Cong., 1st sess.*, June 22, 1836, Vol. 7, No. 286.

Georgia to extend her jurisdiction over the Cherokees has always existed. The Cherokees have always had a government of their own. Nothing, however, was said when we were governed by savage laws, when the abominable law of retaliation carried death in our midst, when it was a lawful act to shed the blood of a person charged with witchcraft, when a brother could kill a brother with impunity, or an innocent man suffer for an offending relative. At that time it might have been a matter of charity to have extended over us the mantle of Christian laws & regulations. But how happens it now, after being fostered by the U. States, and advised by great and good men to establish a government of regular law; when the aid and protection of the General Government have been pledged to us; when we, as dutiful "children" of the President, have followed his instructions and advice, and have established for ourselves a government of regular law; when everything looks so promising around us, that a storm is raised by the extension of tyrannical and unchristian laws, which threatens to blast all our rising hopes and expectations?

There is, as would naturally be supposed, a great rejoicing in Georgia. It is a time of "important news"—"gratifying intelligence"—"The Cherokee lands are to be obtained speedily." It is even reported that the Cherokees have come to the conclusion to sell, and move off to the west of the Mississippi—not so fast. We are yet at our homes, at our peaceful firesides, (except those contiguous to Sandtown, Carroll, &c.) attending to our farms and useful occupations. . . .

[12 November 1831]

. . . But alas! no sooner was it made manifest that the Cherokees were becoming strongly attached to the ways and usages of civilized life, than was aroused the opposition of those from whom better things ought to have been expected. No sooner was it known that they had learned the proper use of the earth, and that they were now less likely to dispose of their lands for a mess of pottage, than they came in conflict with the cupidity and self-interest of those who ought to have been their benefactors—Then commenced a series of obstacles hard to overcome, and difficulties intended as a stumbling block, and unthought of before. The "Great Father" of the "red man" has lent his influence to encourage those difficulties. The *guardian* has deprived his *wards* of their rights—The sacred obligations of treaties and laws have been disregarded—The promises of Washington and Jefferson have not been fulfilled. The policy of the United States on Indian affairs has taken a different direction, for no other reason than that the Cherokees have so far become civilized as to appreciate a regular form of Government. They are now deprived of rights they once enjoyed—A neighboring power is now permitted to extend its withering hand over them—Their own laws, intended to regulate their society, to encourage virtue and to suppress vice, must now be abolished, and civilized acts, passed for the purpose of expelling them, must be substituted.—Their intelligent citizens who have been instructed through the means employed by former administrations, and through the efforts of benevolent societies, must be abused and insulted, represented as avaricious, feeding upon the poverty of the common Indians—the hostility of all those who want the Indian lands must be directed against them. That the Cherokees may be kept in ignorance, teachers who had settled among them by the approbation of the Government, for the best of all purposes, have been compelled to leave them by reason of laws unbecoming any civilized nation—Ministers of the Gospel, who might have, at this day of trial, administered to them the consolations of Religion, have been arrested, chained, dragged away before their eyes, tried as felons, and finally immured in prison with thieves and robbers.

Vain Protest

A delegation of Cherokee leaders who opposed the Treaty of New Echota protested to Congress, but in vain. The following excerpt from the "Memorial and Protest of the Cherokee Nation" of 22 June 1836 appears in House Documents, *24th Cong., 1st sess., vol. 7, Doc. no. 286, CIS US Serial no. 292, microprint, 2–5.*

If it be said that the Cherokees have lost their national character and political existence, as a nation or tribe, by State legislation, then the President and Senate can make no treaty with them; but if they have not, then no treaty can be made for them, binding, without and against their will. Such is the fact, in reference to the instrument intered into at New Echota, in December last. If treaties are to be thus made and enforced, deceptive to the Indians and to the world, purporting to be a contract, when, in truth, wanting the assent of one of the pretended parties, what security would there be for any nation or tribe to retain confidence in the United States? If interest or policy require that the Cherokees be removed, without their consent, from their lands, surely the President and Senate have no constitutional power to accomplish that object. They cannot do it under the power to make treaties, which are contracts, not rules prescribed by a superior, and therefore binding only by the assent of the parties. In the present instance, the assent of the Cherokee nation has not been given, but expressly denied. The President and Senate cannot do it under the power to regulate commerce with the Indian tribes, or intercourse with them, because that belongs to Congress, and so declared by the President, in his message to the Senate of February 22, 1831, relative to the execution of the act to regulate trade and intercourse with the Indian tribes, &c. passed 30th of March, 1802. They cannot do it under any subsisting treaty stipulation with the Cherokee nation. Nor does the peculiar situation of the Cherokees, in reference to the States their necessities and distresses, confer any power upon the President and Senate to alienate their legal rights, or to prescribe the manner and time of their removal.

Without a decision of what ought to be done, under existing circumstances, the question recurs, is the instrument under consideration a contract between the United States and the Cherokee nation? It so purports upon its face, and that falsely. Is that statement so sacred and conclusive that the Cherokee people cannot be heard to deny the fact? They have denied it under their own signatures, as the documents herein before referred to will show, and protested against the acts of the unauthorized few, who have arrogated to themselves the right to speak for the nation. The Cherokees have said they will not be bound thereby. The documents submitted to the Senate show, that when the vote was taken upon considering the propositions of the commissioner, there were but seventy-nine for so doing. Then it comes to this: could this small number of persons attending the New Echota meeting, acting in their individual capacity, dispose of the rights and interests of the Cherokee nation, or by any instrument they might sign, confer such power upon the President and Senate?

If the United States are to act as the guardian of the Cherokees, and to treat them as incapable of managing their own affairs, and blind to their true interests, yet this would not furnish power or authority to the President and Senate, as the treaty making power to prescribe the rule for managing their affairs. It may afford a pretence for the legislation of Congress, but none for the ratification of an instrument as a treaty made by a small faction against the protest of the Cherokee people.

That the Cherokees are a distinct people, sovereign to some extent, have a separate political existence as a society, or body politic, and a capability of being contracted with in a national capacity, stands admitted by the uniform practice of the United States from 1785, down to the present day. With them have treaties been made through their chiefs, and distinguished men in primary assemblies, as also with their constituted agents or representatives. That they have not the right to manage their own internal affairs, and to regulate, by treaty, their intercourse with other nations, is a doctrine of modern date. In 1793, Mr. Jefferson said, "I consider our right of pre-emption of the Indian lands, not as amounting to any dominion, or jurisdiction, or paramountship whatever, but merely in the nature of a remainder, after the extinguishment of a present right, which gives us no present right whatever, but of preventing other nations from taking possession, and so defeating our expectancy. That the Indians *have the full, undivided, and independent sovereignty as long as they choose to keep it, and that this may be forever."* This opinion was recognised and practised upon, by the Government of the United States, through several successive administrations, also recognised by the Supreme Court of the United States, and the several States, when the question has arisen. It has not been the opinion only of jurists, but of politicians, as may be seen from various reports of Secretaries of War—beginning with Gen. Knox, also the correspondence between the British and American ministers at Ghent in the year 1814. If the Cherokees have power to judge of their own interests, and to make treaties, which, it is presumed, will be denied by none, then to make a contract valid, the assent of a majority must be had, expressed by themselves or through their representatives, and the President and Senate have no power to say what their will shall be, for from the laws of nations we learn that "though a nation be obliged to promote, as far as lies in its power, the perfection of others, it is not entitled forcibly to obtrude these good offices on them." Such an attempt would be to violate their natural liberty. Those ambitious Europeans who attacked the

American nations, and subjected them to their insatiable avidity of dominion, an order, as they pretended, for civilizing them, and causing them to be instructed in the true religion, (as in the present instance to preserve the Cherokees as a distinct people,) these usurpers grounded themselves on a pretence equally unjust and ridiculous." It is the expressed wish of the Government of the United States to remove the Cherokees to a place west of the Mississippi. That wish is said to be founded in humanity to the Indians. To make their situation more comfortable, and to preserve them as a distinct people. Let facts show how this *benevolent* design has been prosecuted, and how faithful to the spirit and letter has the promise of the President of the United States to the Cherokees been fulfilled—that *"those who remain may be assured of our patronage, our aid, and good neighborhood."* The delegation are not deceived by empty professions, and fear their race is to be destroyed by the mercenary policy of the present day, and their lands wrested from them by physical force; as proof, they will refer to the preamble of an act of the General Assembly of Georgia, in reference to the Cherokees, passed the 2d of December, 1835, where it is said, "from a knowledge of the Indian character, and from the present feelings of these Indians, it is confidently believed, that the right of occupancy of the lands in their possession should be withdrawn, *that it would be a strong inducement to them to treat with the General Government, and consent to a removal to the west;* and whereas, the present Legislature openly avow that their primary object in the measures intended to be pursued *are founded on real humanity to these Indians,* and with a view, in a distant region, to perpetuate them with their old identity of character, *under the paternal care of the Government of the United States;* at the same time frankly disavowing *any selfish or sinister motives towards them in their present legislation."* This is the profession. Let us turn to the practice of *humanity,* to the Cherokees, by the State of Georgia. In violation of the treaties between the United States and the Cherokee nation, that State passed a law requiring all white men, residing in that part of the Cherokee country, in her limits, to take an oath of allegiance to the State of Georgia. For a violation of this law, some of the ministers of Christ, missionaries among the Cherokees, were tried, convicted, and sentenced to hard labor in the penitentiary. Their case may be seen by reference to the records of the Supreme Court of the United States.

Valuable gold mines were discovered upon Cherokee lands, within the chartered limits of Georgia, and the Cherokees commenced working them, and the Legislature of that State interfered by passing an act, making it penal for an Indian to dig for gold within Georgia, no doubt *"frankly disavowing any selfish or sinister motives towards them."* Under this law many Cherokees were arrested, tried, imprisoned, and otherwise abused. Some were even shot in attempting to avoid an arrest; yet the Cherokee people used no violence, but humbly petitioned the Government of the United States for a fulfilment of treaty engagements, to protect them, which was not done, and the answer given that the United States could not interfere. Georgia discovered she was not to be obstructed in carrying out her measures, *"founded on real humanity to these Indians,"* she passed an act directing the Indian country to be surveyed into districts. This excited some alarm, but the Cherokees were quieted with the assurance it would do no harm to survey the country. Another act was shortly after passed, to lay off the country into lots. As yet there was no authority to take possession, but it was not long before a law was made, authorizing a lottery for the lands laid off into lots. In this act the Indians were secured in possession of all the lots touched by their improvements, and the balance of the country allowed to be occupied by white men. This was a direct violation of the 5th article of the treaty of the 27th of February, 1819. The Cherokees made no resistance, still petitioned the United States for protection, and received the same answer that the President could not interpose.

If you were a Cherokee, would you have supported the anti- or pro-removal position among the Cherokee people? Why?

Industrial Change and
Urbanization, 1820–1850

INTRODUCTION

The first half of the nineteenth century witnessed the "take-off" stage of industrialism in America. Efforts to expand production were stimulated by improvements in transportation—better roads, new canals, scheduled shipping, and the rise of the railroad—that enabled an enterprising producer to sell to an expanded market. Technological improvements, like Eli Whitney's cotton gin and his work on techniques to make interchangeable parts for muskets helped increase production. But the "take-off" stage of industrialism was not primarily driven by the invention of new machines. Rather, the most important causes of the initial increase in production were a reorganization of how work was done and a concomitant restructuring of the habits and culture of the people performing that work. The reorganization of work was achieved by pulling the various tasks involved in making a product away from their diverse locations and putting them under a single roof, a "manufactory." The restructuring of values and culture was a more subtle enterprise that activated many of the social reform and religious movements of the antebellum years. At the time of the Civil War, the United States was still an overwhelmingly agrarian nation, yet almost all observers agreed that industrialism and the cultural forces it carried with it were the wave of the future.

FROM "LIBERTINE CULTURE" TO "INDUSTRIAL MORALITY"

The articles that follow focus on the restructuring of work and the efforts to create a new work ethic during the early stages of industrialism in America.

The World of Preindustrial Workers

Historian Bruce Laurie highlights a range of preindustrial behaviors by urban artisans that impeded the efforts of a new manufacturing class to increase production. Abridged from "'Nothing on Impulse': Life Styles of Philadelphia Artisans, 1820–1850," Labor History 15 (1974): 344–48, 350–51.

Fluctuations in trade were not the only determinants of employment. . . . [M]any artisans who lived in the transitional period between the pre-industrial and industrial age adhered to values, customs, and traditions that went against the grain of early industrial discipline. Prizing leisure as well as work, they engaged in a wide spectrum of leisure-time activities, ranging from competitive sport to lounging on street corners. Many of them also belonged to volunteer organizations, which successfully competed with their places of employment for their attention and devotion.

Reprinted from "'Nothing on Impulse': Life Styles of Philadelphia Artisans, 1820–1850," by Bruce Laurie, from Labor History, Milton Cantor, editor, Summer 1974, Vol. 15, No. 3. Copyright © 1974 by The Tamiment Institute.

Traditions die hard, and perhaps none died harder than preindustrial drinking habits. Advances in science and medicine, early industrial change and . . . the advent of revivalism, eroded customary drinking habits among some sectors of the medical profession, the clergy, and the emerging industrial elite. But the old commercial classes and most artisans still clung tenaciously to older ways. They valued alcohol for its own sake and used it as a stimulant or as medicine to combat fatigue, to cool the body in summer or warm it in winter, and to treat common illness.

Numerous contemporaries report that artisans were not particular about where they imbibed. . . . Looking back on his days as a journeyman, [tanner Benjamin] Sewell recalled that young apprentices learned to drink while they learned a trade. Journeymen arrived at work with flasks and appointed an apprentice to make periodic trips to the local pub in order to have them filled, "for which service" he "robs the mail . . . takes a drink before he gets back. . . ." This training ground turned many young wage earners into hardened drinkers, inclined to go on an occasional binge. . . .

Employers winced at such behavior, but one ought not assume that all of them were martinets who enforced regulations against drink. Owners of textile mills could afford to do so because they relied upon a semi-skilled labor force which could be replaced with relative ease. The concentration required by operators of power-driven machinery, moreover, caused some to relinquish drink without much prompting from employers. . . . Smaller employers, on the other hand, were more tolerant of workers who drank. . . . Many, if not most, small employers were former journeymen themselves steeped in preindustrial culture, and those who did custom work anticipated fluctuations in trade and therefore tolerated irregular work habits. These employers "expected" journeymen to shun the shop on holidays—official as well as self-proclaimed—and they endured drinking, as long as their journeymen worked "tolerably regularly" and managed to avoid getting "absolutely drunk."

Most artisans did their drinking in pubs, and pubs probably assumed greater importance in their life after some employers began to prohibit drinking in the shop. Working-class pubs had a style all their own. Signs with piquant inscriptions hung above entranceways and stood in bold contrast to the sedate placards which graced the vestibules of middle-class establishments. . . . Immigrant taverns sometimes advertised popular political causes.

... These taverns offered a wide variety of entertainment, illicit and otherwise. ...

Despite these attractions most workers, we may believe, visited pubs for the sake of camaraderie. At the end of the workday homebound artisans, made detours to their favorite taverns, where they exchanged stories or discussed politics over drams or mugs of a variety of malt liquor. Outworkers broke the boredom of toiling alone by visiting the local pub during the day, and shopworkers probably went there to celebrate the completion of a task or an order. Most observers agree that tavern traffic increased dramatically on Sunday night and in winter when trade slowed. ...

... [A]rtisans especially enjoyed pastimes in which they could participate. They simply loved shooting matches and hunting small game, according to an observer who bemoaned that "every fair day" yielded a "temptation to forsake the shop for the field." The most avid hunters, he contended, were artisans who toiled indoors, for they found a jaunt in the fields especially relaxing. Artisans who resided in the same neighborhood sometimes set aside time for exercise by declaring holidays and staging competitive games. ...

Sport, merrymaking, and drinking were also staples at ethnic gatherings. English, German, and Irish immigrants honored Old World customs and traditions, celebrated weddings and holidays, or gathered simply in order to socialize regardless of the time of day or day of the week. Germans, for instance, set aside Monday as their "principal day for pleasure," and festivities could spill into the middle of the week. ... The Irish were also known to set aside Monday for outings in the suburbs. Their national games, the Donneybrook Fair, traditionally attracted hundreds of enthusiasts and no self-respecting Irish Protestant missed the annual July 12 parade commemorating the glorious victory on the banks of the Boyne in 1690. ...

These pursuits and activities—drinking and gaming, participating in popular sports and in fire companies—characterized a vibrant, preindustrial style of life. A number of factors underpinned this style, the most significant of which were demographic and material. First, as Herbert Gutman notes, it was repeatedly replenished by waves of immigrants and rural-urban migrants, who came from widely divergent sub-cultures but whose values and behavior collided with the imperatives of early industrial discipline. Second, and perhaps more important, at mid-century many wage earners worked in traditional (as against modern) settings which, together with the boom-bust quality of the economy, supported sporadic work habits. Those who know this environment best were outworkers—especially hand-loom weavers, shoemakers, and tailors—who toiled at home without direct supervision of employers and custom workers, who fashioned consumer goods to the taste of individuals and who thereby evaded the more vigorous regimen of workers producing for the mass market.

Outworkers and custom workers displayed traditional forms of behavior in that they made no sharp distinction between work and leisure. Blending leisure with work, they punctuated workdays with the activities sketched above. Nor did they respect the specialization of role and function which normally accompanies modernization. Instead they persisted in assuming the dual role of artisans and firemen in the face of strong opposition from urban reformers who wished to relegate firefighting to paid professionals. It is probable, moreover, that the values, activities, and organizations of this style of life filled the basic needs of its adherents by sanctioning and supplying vehicles for recreation, neighborhood cohesion, ethnic identity, and camaraderie.

At the same time, however, there emerged a competing culture with its own organizations and institutions. Unlike preindustrial culture, it made a sharp distinction between work and leisure and regarded preindustrial culture as wasteful, frivolous and, above all, sinful. Sanctioning a more modern style of life, it originated not among the working class but with the emerging industrial elite and the Presbyterian clergy. This elite was in the process of displacing the old Quaker oligarchy and included manufacturers who represented the most advanced industries, . . . as well as merchants and professionals with investments in industry and transportation.

The Imposition of Industrial Morality

The following essay discusses the efforts of local manufacturers, religious leaders, and their abilities to impose a new value system upon the community's working classes. Excerpted from Paul Faler, "Cultural Aspects of the Industrial Revolution: Lynn, Massachusetts, Shoemakers and Industrial Morality, 1826–1860," Labor History 15 (1974): 367–69, 376–81.

Industrialization is usually described in connection with machinery, factories and workers; or, when considered as a part of labor history, changes in wages, hours, and working conditions. Undeniably, all are crucial aspects. But what of the social and cultural side? The industrial revolution, after all, was more than a series of economic changes in the means of production. It was revolutionary as well in its transformation of traditional society; scarcely any part of the old order escaped its impact. Its cultural dimension is more easily grasped if one keeps in mind an earlier but now seldom used definition of industry—the earnest and constant attention to work. This ethic spills over into the social life of those who took it up.

The cultural aspects of life in Lynn, Massachusetts, is the subject of this study. For Lynn's inhabitants, most of them shoemakers and their families, industrialization meant inner discipline and a tightening up of the moral code through either the abolition or drastic alteration of those customs, traditions, and practices that interfered with productive labor. More than ever before, life became oriented toward work. . . . Citizens would be self-reliant, hard-working, and sober; obedient to their superiors; attentive to their labors; and self-disciplined in all their pursuits. A new morality based on the paramount importance of work was taking shape, an industrial morality that was the cultural expression of the industrial revolution.

Industrial morality was not, as some have suggested, a product of the factory alone. The application of the work ethic in Lynn began long before the 1860s, when machinery and factories first appeared. The shoemakers were handworkers then, not factory operatives. The workplace was the shop or manufactory, not the factory. A cultural apparatus of ideas and institutions outside the work place was chiefly responsible for inculcating the new values. . . .

. . . Efforts to strengthen the new morality formally began in 1826 with the founding of the Society for the Promotion of Industry, Frugality and Temperance. The Society's founders and officers were prominent townfolk, mostly shoe manufacturers and leather dealers, but with a handful of clergymen and lawyers among them as well. Of the ward officials of the Society, the shoe bosses easily made up the largest element. . . . Among the ward representatives were several of Lynn's 700 shoemakers, 60 percent of the town's adult population, whose support would be crucial to the Society's success.

As the Society's name indicated, members sought to promote values that would foster industry and help Lynn prosper as a manufacturing center. Industry required self-discipline, emphasis upon productive labor, and condemnation of wasteful habits. Industry, frugality, and temperance, if conscientiously followed, would result in savings that would bring material reward to the wage earner and well being to the community. Several officers of the Society, not unexpectedly, were also founders and directors of the Lynn Institution for Savings which opened its doors in 1826, the year that the Society itself was founded. . . .

The Society for Industry, Frugality, and Temperance—having 143 members in 1826 and increasing to 450 in 1830—had close ties to Lynn's religious bodies. Its meetings were alternately held at the Methodist and Congregational churches. . . . The churches became vehicles for inculcating the values of this new morality. Preachers pledged themselves to temperance or abstinence and expected their parishioners to do the same. Beginning in the 1840s, thousands of students from the newly-formed Sunday Schools marched under the banner of the cold-water army in monster temperance parades. Some churches established special courts that tried cases of infidelity, drunkenness, or immoral conduct. . . .

Entering a competitive market place that was a continual trial of their shrewdness and steadfastness, the rising entrepreneurs carried with them a conviction of their own personal righteousness. They confidently attributed their success to strength of character, self-discipline and the correctness of the moral code by which they lived. They also recognized an obligation to others: "to whom much is given, of him will much be required." Here was a prescription for social leadership that they exercised with zeal and skill. And in the case of Lynn, they also recognized that success depended not only on their own industry, frugality and temperance but upon like values from those they employed. All were parts of a single social entity. The idle, drunk, and dissolute were a burden upon the industrious wage earners and, unless reformed, would drag all into a "miserable bog or slough." The manufacturers exhibited a mature class consciousness that equated society's interests with their own. Those who gathered in December 1826 to form Lynn's Society for the Promotion of Industry, Frugality, and Temperance intended nothing less than a moral reformation in the culture of an entire city.

Lynn's poor were among the first to attract the Society's attention. That indifference which characterized the eighteenth century view of paupers and poor relief quickly came to an end in the 1820s. No longer would reformers fatalistically accept the view that "the poor ye always have with you." They attacked the causes of poverty which they identified as idleness, intemperance, and lax self-discipline. In the case of idleness, they would "banish it from the world" with a mandatory work regiment. For inmates of the poor house, confinement would become "a punishment and a terror to the intemperate and idle," and would instill a "strong sense of fear accompanied by absolute humility and contrition." Although reformers sometimes made a distinction between the worthy and unworthy poor, the distinction rapidly crumbled in their eagerness to deal with "willful" offenders.

Lynn's poor fell roughly into two groups: those who were completely dependent upon the town for food and shelter, and who resided at the Alms House which the community had built in 1819; and those who were partly dependent and who lived at home but received some support from the town. Aid to the first group was in-the-house relief; aid to the second was out-of-the-house relief. The reformers proposed measures that significantly affected each group.

The slack discipline that permitted Alms House residents to wander the streets and converse with ordinary townsfolk ended in 1828. The town meeting, at the Society's urging, established regular visiting hours; at all other times the inmates would be isolated from the outside world. To enforce its order, the town appropriated $100 to construct a ten foot wooden fence topped with iron spikes. . . . Overseers of the Poor transferred male inmates from farm work to shoe-making with materials furnished by Isaiah Breed, himself an Overseer, shoe manufacturer, and owner of the store that supplied commodities to the indigent shoemakers. In 1828, the town deprived the poor of liquor; $120 had been spent on alcoholic beverages for the poor in the previous year. Although rejecting the recommendation of one reformer who proposed a diet of bread and water for able-bodied males on relief, the Overseers did apply sound business principles, and effectively reduced Poor House maintenance costs to a minimum. All three Overseers responsible for implementing the new policy were Quakers, and two were officers in the Society for the Promotion of Industry, Frugality, and Temperance. Their control over poor relief gave them a splendid opportunity to put their reforms into practice. But without approval of the town meetings that elected them, the changes could not have been made.

Reformers also changed the method of dispensing goods to the poor living outside the Alms House, many of them unemployed shoemakers whom depression periodically reduced to want. Overseers in the past gave needy citizens orders or credits drawn on local stores, allowing the recipient free choice in selecting those items he most needed. But a special committee reported that the poor did not choose wisely. They might buy meat instead of fish, flour instead of Indian meal, coffee instead of potatoes. The town therefore abolished the order system and directed the Overseers to stock staple commodities at the Alms House, doling these out in the amount they deemed sufficient. . . .

The emerging code of industrial morality gave work paramount place in life. Whatever distracted from this duty of work became objectionable. Lebbeus Armstrong, an early temperance advocate in New York, reported that "the effect of intoxicants on labour efficiency was the strongest argument that could be presented in support of temperance." Temperance must be viewed as an integral part of the larger process of social disciplining and not merely as a "symbolic crusade." It's connection with other reforms is especially close in the early years, for drinking seemed conducive to every vice—poverty, debauchery, crime, idleness, brawling, civil disturbances—that frustrated the new order. . . .

In the vanguard of the temperance movement, Lynn was one of the first towns in Massachusetts to request a prohibition on the sale of spirituous liquors. . . . To encourage temperance, reformers used both moral suasion and legal coercion, as well as methods that fell somewhere in between. Some shoe manufacturers employed no worker who drank. . . . Some doctors renounced the use of liquor for medicinal purposes and adopted the cold-water theories of Vincenz Preisnitz (1790–1851), the German doctor who, for good health, prescribed cold baths and a diet that included copious amounts of cold water (20–25 glasses per day) and cold, unseasoned food. Young ladies were urged to rebuff courting young men who drank.

The principal coercive agents here were the law and the police. Temperance reformers succeeded in converting the new moral values into a binding legal code enforced by Lynn's constables. In the past, the main task of the police had been to canvass Lynn before the town meeting and read the warrant explaining the business agenda to each citizen. Chosen annually by the selectmen, the constables were not professionals. They received no regular pay, wore no uniforms, and carried no weapons. Their badge of office was a long staff ringed at the top with alternating bands of colored stripes. But their function and composition changed as they were called upon to enforce the new code of industrial morality. In the late 1840s, the traditional staff was cut into pieces to make billy clubs. At about the same time, some constables became permanent members of the force. A survey of arrests in Lynn during the late 1850s shows that the majority were for the illegal sale of liquor, drunkenness, and disorderly conduct, and not for serious crimes against persons or property. . . .

Lynn shoemakers, like New Englanders generally, were also citizen soldiers. In the years following the war of 1812, they converted militia training days into occasions for boisterous fun. . . . Proponents of industrial morality were understandably hostile. "Scenes of riot and drunkenness" were "disgusting and harmful." "Men and boys in a brutal state of intoxication, and even large numbers of females were to be observed mixing with the motley crowd." . . .

The abolition of compulsory militia training aided the cause of morality, but the volunteer fire companies that replaced the militia also offended reformers. Each unit, which numbered sixty men, was made up primarily of the neighborhood's shoemakers who supplied the muscle to operate the hand-pumped apparatus. The companies frequently engaged in competitive musters that tested their speed, strength, and accuracy. But the fire houses also became important social and political centers in which the enginemen met for discussions generally well-lubricated by liquor. . . . The muster was the nineteenth-century equivalent of modern spectator sport. An 1846 contest, for example, drew 2,000 spectators; another in 1848 attracted 2,500. The temperance movement made inroads among the shoemaker-enginemen. Some units became temperate; others remained drinkers. Those converted provide another indication of success of industrial morality among shoemakers, altering their lives outside the shop. . . .

Lynn's schools, as might be expected, helped to inculcate the new values, becoming an important instrument in shaping good character. Indeed, the annual reports of its school officials often read like the proceedings of the Society for the Promotion of Industry, Frugality, and Temperance. No longer could children be ignored or allowed to be initiated into society through the public house or neighborhood gang. Bad habits or dangerous opinions, once formed, would be difficult to change. Schools were a strong antidote. They were "the very places for cultivating self-restraint, order, decency and a regard for all the proprieties of life." In addition to useful knowledge, educators would teach "morals and manners," particularly "sobriety, industry and frugality, chastity, moderation and temperance." They also had to foster "habits of application, respect to superiors, and obedience to law." One such habit was punctuality, "a habit invaluable to individual credit, successful business, and general tranquility." The importance of "having a place, time and order for everything, and everything in its order, time and place" was the all-encompassing maxim to be taught.

Control over education shifted from the neighborhood prudential committee to the town school committee with enlargement of the administrative unit from the neighborhood to the town. This administrative change led to the accession to office of Lynn's prominent and wealthy rather than the obscure and middling townsfolk. The school committee stripped the prudential committees of the power to hire and fire teachers, to set the curriculum, and to prescribe a code of student conduct. . . . Emphasis upon "moral character" occurred simultaneously with the assignment to women of the primary responsibility for child rearing and for the defense of a stern moral code. Partly for this reason perhaps, a shift from male to female teachers took place in the elementary schools.

Reformers often encountered indifference to their efforts to tighten school discipline. Truancy was a major problem. In 1838, one third of those enrolled in Massachusetts' public schools were absent during the winter months. In the summer, this figure increased to 40 percent. The situation was worse in Lynn. Of the 1,430 town children in 1830 between four and fourteen years of age, 1,130 were enrolled in the common schools. Average attendance was about 650. If the minds of the young were to be shaped properly, a way was needed to compel enrollment and attendance. Beginning in 1851, Massachusetts passed the first compulsory attendance laws. In subsequent years truant officers tracked down the runaways.

Reformers also encountered the obstinate cultural legacy of the eighteenth century, an age that had been indifferent to self-discipline, obedience to authority, and self-imposed restraints on natural impulses, or that had encouraged their opposites. The clash between the new nineteenth-century morality and the earlier immorality produced conflict in the schools. . . .

Compliance to rules of behavior that students had not acquired in the home was the goal of Lynn's reformers and the teachers they hired. . . . To gain student compliance to the new rigorous code, teachers and school officials employed both persuasion and coercion. They preferred a "kind and paternal discipline," but used the whip and stick when paternalism failed. . . .

Massachusetts school reformers also began to segregate the sexes in the public schools. Floor plans for "model" schools provided for separate playgrounds, entrances, stairways, and halls. Boys and girls would be together in the classroom, to be sure, but always under the watchful eye of an instructor of sound moral character.

The clash within the schools between the loose morality of the past and the more rigorous industrial morality was part of a broader struggle, one which encompassed such issues as poor relief, drinking habits, forms of recreation, leisure activities, sexual practices, and work habits. Advocates of industrial morality made significant gains over two decades, but complete success eluded them. Many townsfolk, though vulnerable to hardship and poverty, struggled mightily to avoid becoming public charges. Yet the number of inmates in the Alms House increased and relief rolls grew—not proportionate to population growth, to be sure, but upward nonetheless. Some of Lynn's inhabitants renounced drink in favor of cold water, but others persisted in heavy and frequent tippling. The boisterous brawling and earthiness of the eighteenth century disappeared from many public places but continued in a moral underground, away from the scrutiny and censure of respectable opinion.

What were some of the main features of preindustrial urban artisan culture, and how did they interfere with efforts to expand production? What are the main features of industrial morality?

Historian Herbert Gutman has argued that one of the major themes of American history is the continuous introduction of people holding preindustrial values into our industrial culture, which generates tensions between those already possessed of industrial morality and the newcomers with other ways. What groups can you identify in the more recent past whose values resembled those of "libertine culture" and how did mainstream society respond to them?

TRANSITION TO
INDUSTRIAL DISCIPLINE

The documents that follow present various aspects of the transition that occurred in working-class life and work during the early stages of industrialism. The letter from "A Mechanic" points out how lifestyles were restructured as a result of the transportation revolution. The work regulations lay out the new behavior standards expected of workers in the industrial age. Collectively, these documents hint at a fundamental transition in American culture in the decades prior to the Civil War. To native-born artisans this transition was sharply apparent, but the thousands of immigrating laborers from Great Britain put conditions in industrializing America into a different context. The last two documents present the impressions of an English and an Irish traveller to America, and suggest why so many Europeans thought life in the United States would be so much better.

Railroads and Competition

The following letter from "A Mechanic" in Georgia explains how the transportation revolution widened market opportunities for manufacturers and increased the competitive pressures on local artisans. This letter is taken from A Documentary History of American Industrial Society, *ed. John R. Commons et al. (Cleveland, 1910), 2:336–37.*

Brother Mechanics of Georgia, and Especially of our own Village: The Mechanics of all kinds in this country are injured by rail roads to some extent. They are brought single handed to compete with those large manufacturing establishments in the northern States and foreign countries, where labor is worth comparatively nothing, brought in opposition by the aid of steam and the rail roads as it were in your own village, by the transportation of the manufactured articles of all kinds, and sold at your own shop doors at reduced prices by your own merchants, and bought by your own farmers, from whom you expected patronage. Is not this one of the main causes why your villages are not flourishing, the houses vacant, and in a dilapidated condition, your academies destitute of teachers, or if teachers, destitute of pupils? It certainly is one of the main causes why Mechanics are reduced to poverty, not being able to build up our towns and cities or to educate their children so as to make them respectable members of society. Brother mechanics, this is not as it should be   then rouse up from your lethargy, go drooped down and depressed no longer, come forth in your might and power, and at once, as it were, you will be able to correct the evil. —You should form yourselves into large and permanent manufacturing companies. With your skill and enterprise you may soon rear up in your midst, manufacturing establishments of various kinds to manufacture those very articles that afford a considerable item in the commerce of the country, make your towns and villages soon become flourishing, affording a great market for surplus products, raised by the farmers in our own midst—and as all classes will feel the benefit in a short time it will be but a little while before your business will be profitable to yourselves and the country in which you live. I might be asked to suggest some plan to give the above suggestions a permanent and practical notice to the community at large. One that I would mention is that it should be the business of every mechanic of every branch of business, to apply himself closely to his business. Let that be his daily employment, instead of, as is too often the case, quitting his shop, taking the streets, becoming a street politician, a dandy, or a drunkard. Remedy those three evils and the work is half accomplished.

A MECHANIC.

What is the impact of railroads on American economic life for "a Mechanic"?

Factory Regulations in Lowell

The regulations imposed by the Hamilton Manufacturing Company of Lowell, Massachusetts went beyond controlling behavior on the shop floor and invaded the worker's personal life. The following document is from A Documentary History of American Industrial Society, *ed. John R. Commons et al. (Cleveland, 1910), 7:135–36.*

REGULATIONS TO BE OBSERVED by all persons employed in the factories of the Hamilton Manufacturing Company. The overseers are to be always in their rooms at the starting of the mill, and not absent unnecessarily during working hours. They are to see that all those employed in their rooms, are in their places in due season, and keep a correct account of their time and work. They may grant leave of absence to those employed under them, when they have spare hands to supply their places, and not otherwise, except in cases of absolute necessity.

All persons in the employ of the Hamilton Manufacturing Company, are to observe the regulations of the room where they are employed. They are not to be absent from their work without the consent of the overseer, except in cases of sickness, and then they are to send him word of the cause of their absence. They are to board in one of the houses of the company and give information at the counting room, where they board, when they begin, or, whenever they change their boarding place; and are to observe the regulations of their boarding-house,

Those intending to leave the employment of the company, are to give at least two weeks' notice thereof to their overseer.

All persons entering into the employment of the company, are considered as engaged for twelve months, and those who leave sooner, or do not comply with all these regulations, will not be entitled to a regular discharge.

The company will not employ any one who is habitually absent from public worship on the Sabbath, or known to be guilty of immorality.

A physician will attend once in every month at the counting-room, to vaccinate all who may need it, free of expense.

Any one who shall take from the mills or the yard, any yarn, cloth or other article belonging to the company, will be considered guilty of stealing and be liable to prosecution.

Payment will be made monthly, including board and wages. The accounts will be made up to the last Saturday but one in every month, and paid in the course of the following week.

These regulations are considered part of the contract, with which all persons entering into the employment of the Hamilton Manufacturing Company, engage to comply.

JOHN AVERY, Agent.

Could such a contract or set of regulations exist today? Why or why not?

Two Foreign Travellers' Observations

While American-born artisans were troubled by the changes they experienced in the workplace and community, European-born travelers to America saw the industrial transformation in a different light. In the following documents, an Englishman in 1843 and an Irishman in 1850 offer diverse observations about working-class life in America as compared to their homelands. Taken from A Documentary History of the American Industrial Society, *ed. John R. Commons et al. (Cleveland, 1910), 7:47–56, 71–73, 75–76.*

[An Englishman's View]

It is much easier to obtain employment, at present, in the United States than in England; but in this respect they are getting into a worse and worse condition. The manufacturers, in the East, have introduced all our improvements in machinery, (and the effects are the same as in this country) they are making very large quantities of goods; competition is increasing, prices are very much reduced, and the wages of labour, generally, throughout the States and Canada, have been reduced from thirty to fifty per cent within the last four years, and wages are still reducing in some parts of the country, in spite of their trades' unions and democratic institutions; and, if competition continue, no parties can prevent wages from falling as low there as they are in England, and this within a comparatively short period. Wages in America are not much higher, even now, than they are with us. Agricultural labourers can be hired, in Illinois and other states, for from eight to twelve dollars per month. Smiths and mechanics for from twelve to eighteen dollars per month, with board. The boarding of labourers of all kinds is almost universal in the small towns and villages in the agricultural districts. . . .

The price of fuel, and the rents of houses for labourers are very high in all the eastern states; food is also much higher there than in the west. It is highest at Boston and New York, but even there, food is from 25 to 50 per cent cheaper than in Liverpool. Rents are high in all parts of the Union, and clothing is higher than it is with us. Wood fuel can be had for merely the expense of cutting and preparing in most parts of the west. . . .

One of the greatest evils the working classes have to contend with in the United States and in Canada, for it is generally practised in both countries, is the abominable cheating truck system, which is carried on with more barefaced impudence there, and to a greater extent than it ever was practised in this country. The following is a verbatim copy of a printed notice given by Ben. Cozzens, a large manufacturer, who has two large cotton factories and a print work, and employs from a thousand to fifteen hundred pair of hands, at Crompton mills in Rhode Island. Single men at board, who cannot take goods, have ten per cent deducted from their wages in lieu of it.

NOTICE. Those employed at these mills and works will take notice, that a store is kept for their accommodation, where they

can purchase the best of goods at fair prices, and it is expected that all will draw their goods from said store. Those who do not are informed, that there are plenty of others who would be glad to take their places at less wages.   BENJ. COZZENS.
Crompton Mills, February, 1843.

One of the printed notices, from which this was copied, was put into my hands by a man who lately worked for Benjamin Cozzens, and who has returned home, tired of America, in the Roscius. Five colliers returned home by the same vessel, who had been working at Pittsville, in Pennsylvania, where the same vile truck system is carried on to the greatest extent. They declared that when their American wages were turned into cash, they could earn as much, and were as well off, in their own country. I know the general prevalence of this system, by information from masters as well as men. The average of loss to the workmen by this system is not less than twenty-five per cent of their wages, and in many cases it is attended with a loss of fifty per cent. When masters have no shops of their own, they give notes to the men to get their goods at other shops, who supply them with inferior articles at high prices, and out of the money the workmen are cheated of, they allow a per centage to the master. In many places the shopkeepers will not give flour and groceries for these notes; they tell them these are cash articles only, in which case the men are compelled to take other goods which they do not want, and then have to submit to a still greater loss in disposing of them for cash to get absolute necessaries. . . .

. . . In judging of their condition, you must take into account the length and severity of their winters, and the excessive heat of their summers, in the northern states and in Canada. Their winters commence in November, and continue till the end of April—about six months in the year—during which period all building operations, and all agricultural employments, except the felling of timber and preparing fuel, are suspended; and, being all frozen up, navigation on their rivers and canals, and all employments dependent on these, are stopped, and many other employments, depending on water power, are also stopped; the cold is so excessive that the thermometer is frequently twenty degrees below zero; they are obliged to keep large fires in their dwellings, and to have a large quantity of extra warm clothing to prevent them from perishing; it is often dangerous to go out of doors for any length of time, in winter, without completely covering every part of the body; parties sometimes have their nose, or some other part of their face, frozen, without being aware of it themselves; a friend meets them, and tells them that they are frozen, the remedy is immediately to rub the part affected with snow, which restores it; but many perish from cold, particularly the blacks in Canada. As goods cannot be brought to the ports, commerce is also in a great degree prevented. The consequence is, that unless workmen get good wages and plenty of work in summer, to enable them to lay in a good supply for winter; their condition is and must be much more wretched than the labourers in England. Indeed, for several winters past, and especially last winter, great numbers out of employment in Boston, Salem, Providence, New York, and other places, were supplied with soup, bread, fuel, and other articles, by charitable contributions. . . .

In the middle of summer, on the contrary, the weather is so excessively hot, (frequently ninety to a hundred degrees), that it is very difficult to do a day's work at hard labour, beside which, in the western states, you are much annoyed by the bite of mosquitoes, and, in those parts, fever and ague are very prevalent in summer. . . .

I was talking with some of the workmen, spinners, in the largest jean manufactory in Steubenville, in the state of Ohio, who were telling me of the recent reductions in their wages, and of the rascally truck system, which is universally practised in that town and neighborhood—the workmen are generally paid by notes on the shops, by which they lose at least 25 per cent, in price and quality; but, they are frequently paid in pieces of jean of their own make, charged at high prices, by which they often lose 50 per cent, which reduces their actual wages to about 2s. per day, English money. I asked why they submitted to these impositions, why they did not leave it and go to the land, &c. They replied—"The land in Ohio is dear, generally, and we could not travel to the west without money, and we cannot save money; it is as much as we can do to provide our families with necessaries. We should want money to travel, then money would be wanted to buy the land, to buy agricultural implements, to buy seed, and then we should want more to support us till we could dispose of part of our crops, and we have no money at all. But, suppose we had all these means, we know nothing about the cultivation of land—we have all our lives worked in a factory, and know no other employment, and how is it likely that we should succeed? besides which, we have always been used to live in a town, where we can get what little things we want if we have money, and it is only those who have lived in the wilderness, who know what the horrors of a wilderness-life are."

From what has been said it must be evident to our readers:

First. That the wages of labour are everywhere falling in the United States and in Canada, and that the condition of the working population is getting worse and worse, in spite of their high protective duties upon foreign goods, and every other means they have adopted to prevent these reductions.

Second. That the vile truck system is carried on in these countries to a greater extent than it was ever practised in our own, in spite of annual parliaments, universal suffrage, and vote by ballot.

Third. That going upon the land, on the most favourable terms, under a system of society based upon competition, would afford no remedy for these evils, but would in the end only increase them, even though there were neither rent, tithes, nor taxes to be paid.

Fourth. That American labourers, being necessarily idle nearly half the year, during the winter, ought to receive double our English wages in summer, to place them on equal terms with English labourers, which is not the case, as their wages are nominally very little higher than they are here. The only advantages they have are more employment, freedom from taxes, and the cheapness of provisions. But we have seen that even the cheapness of food is a great injury to the mass of the people, the agricultural population.

Fifth. That the causes of those evils are the same in America as in England, the vast extension of scientific and mechanical power, and the consequent great increase of manufactured goods, and the great and rapid extension of agricultural operations; by which means an immense surplus is produced, whilst competition reduces everything to so low a price that no parties are able to get a remuneration for producing them; and that all that is wanted, either in America or in England, is, rational arrangements to distribute the wealth produced in a just and equitable manner for the benefit of all classes.

[An Irishman's View]

Nor do they content themselves with learning one trade only. Most young mechanics learn two trades, and that in half the time usually devoted to acquire trades in Ireland; two to three years is about the measure of time devoted to the study of a mechanical branch in America. They labour hard in the day, and they attend all kinds of lectures, instruction, and amusements in the evening. The young girls who work in factories, or at trades in their own homes, pay superior teachers for instruction in the light and more elegant female accomplishments, such as singing, music, dancing, drawing and languages.

The necessity imposed upon every one to obtain by his or her own exertions a living, begets that industry which pervades every American family. Every member of the family will do something to contribute to the family commonwealth: though the father may hold a public office, the boys are ready and willing to do any work which they know how to do to obtain money. . . .

A great share of the light manufacture of America, is done by women in the farm-houses, especially in the New England states. For instance, straw bonnets. There are large straw bonnet establishments in New York and Boston, which have their agents continually travelling among the farm-houses. This agent drives a sort of van or omnibus, and brings round bunches of straw plait, and models of bonnets of the newest fashion. These he leaves with the farmers' wives and daughters, all round the country, who work up into bonnets, according to the peculiar model, the plait so left. In due season the agent returns with some more plait, and distributes it to the straw-sewers as before, and receives up the bonnets, for the making of which he pays. All the females of an entire district, including the doctors' and ministers' wives, are engaged in this work. . . . Nor is it all work and no play with these republicans. On the contrary, the boys and girls, of a family have plenty of money of their own saving, and no people of the world enjoy more public amusement. Lectures, concerts, balls, pictorial exhibitions, theatricals, circuses, are to be met with in every village and hamlet. Every swarming village has its reading room and "lyceum," in which a course of public lectures is delivered during the winter. Those lectures embrace all that is interesting to the people, from the constitution of man to that of steam engines. The people are passionately fond of music and dancing, and all such amusements. They dress gaily, and wear out their clothes very fast; but they have a perpetual income from their industry, on which they rely in full confidence to replenish their wardrobes and their pockets. They keep their persons very neat, very cleanly, and study much the art of dress. I think they are the best dressed population in the world, though it must be admitted that streaks of absurdity are sometimes visible in their sumptual economy. . .

The food of the American farmer, mechanic, or labourer, is the best I believe enjoyed by any similar classes in the whole world. At every meal there is meat, or fish, or both; indeed, I think the women, children, and sedentary classes, eat too much meat for their own good health. However, it is an error on the right side, easily cured when discovered. The breakfast of the common people is made up of coffee or tea, fish meat, butter, bread, potatoes, all on the table. Dinner: meat and fish, potatoes, bread, pies made of apples or berries of all sorts, indian pudding. Supper: tea, meat, bread, hot cakes, &c.

This kind of diet, or "board," with lodging and washing, can be had in the "mechanics' boarding houses" in any of the cities of America (except those in the south) at two and a half dollars a week (11s. British) for men, and one dollar and a half (6s. 6d. British) for women. In the western states the same board and lodging can be had by the same classes for two dollars (8s. 6d. British) a week for men, and one dollar for women. In the southern cities board is nearly double these rates.

From all these causes the value of common manual labour is higher in the United States than in any other part of the world. The average value of a common uneducated labourer is 80 cents (3s. 4d.) a day. Of educated or mechanical labour, 125 to 200 cents (5s. to 8s.) a day; of female labour, 40 cents (1s. 8d.) a day. Against meat, flour, vegetables, and groceries at one-third less than they rate in Great Britain and Ireland; against clothing, house rent and fuel, at about equal; against public taxes at about three-fourths less; and a certainty of employment, and the facility of acquiring houses and lands, and education for children, a hundred to one greater. The farther you penetrate into the country, Patrick, the higher in general will you find the value of labour, and the cheaper the price of all kinds of living.

How does life in America compare to life in Britain during the start of the industrial era? What is the value of such a comparison?

The Way West

INTRODUCTION

During the 1840s, the United States acquired control over vast tracts of land in Texas, the southwest, including California, and the Oregon Territory. Some of the land was acquired by diplomacy and some by force; all of it has remained an integral part of the country. Some Americans advocated and celebrated such enormous territorial growth by rallying behind a sense of national mission and exceptionalism called "Manifest Destiny" and supporting war against Mexico as a means to continental empire. Others opposed this expansionism on political, economic, strategic, and moral grounds. Such controversy over expansionism has persisted since the 1840s.

THE CONTEMPORARY DEBATE OVER CONTINENTAL EXPANSION

The following documents reveal many aspects of the debate on expansionism that began in the 1830s and persisted into the 1840s. The first two documents offer contrasting views of the general question of expansionism. The remaining documents reveal the parameters of debate as it focused on specific issues: whether to annex Texas in 1844, whether to wage war on Mexico in 1846–1848, and whether to permit slavery to spread into the territories acquired. Collectively, these records demonstrate that the American people reached no consensus either in favor of, or in opposition to, the expansionism that occurred.

John L. O'Sullivan
Advocates Manifest Destiny

An intellectual atmosphere conducive to expansionism stood behind the United States's drive across the continent in the 1840s. Some of the strongest advocates of expansion and conquest were writers of editorials in the popular press, and of these perhaps the most famous was John L. O'Sullivan, editor of The United States Magazine and Democratic Review. *The selection printed below, comprised of parts of two O'Sullivan editorials published in 1839 and 1845, conveys the themes and tone of O'Sullivan's advocacy. The editorials originally appeared in* The United States Magazine and Democratic Review, 6 *(November 1839):426–27, 429–30; and 17 (July 1845):5, 7–8.*
[1839]

chapter 12

The American people having derived their origin from many other nations, and the Declaration of National Independence being entirely based on the great principle of human equality, these facts demonstrate at once our disconnected position as regards any other nation; that we have, in reality, but little connection with the past history of any of them, and still less with all antiquity, its glories, or its crimes. On the contrary, our national birth was the beginning of a new history, the formation and progress of an untried political system, which separates us from the past and connects us with the future only; and so far as regards the entire development of the natural rights of man, in moral, political, and national life, we may confidently assume that our country is destined to be *the great nation* of futurity. . . .

We have no interest in the scenes of antiquity, only as lessons of avoidance of nearly all their examples. The expansive future is our arena, and for our history. We are entering on its untrodden space, with the truths of God in our minds, beneficent objects in our hearts, and with a clear conscience unsullied by the past. We are the nation of human progress, and who will, what can, set limits to our onward march? Providence is with us, and no earthly power can. We point to the everlasting truth on the first page of our national declaration, and we proclaim to the millions of other lands, that "the gates of hell"—the powers of aristocracy and monarchy—"shall not prevail against it."

The far-reaching, the boundless future will be the era of American greatness. In its magnificent domain of space and time, the nation of many nations is destined to manifest to mankind the excellence of divine principles; to establish on earth the noblest temple ever dedicated to the worship of the Most High—the Sacred and the True. Its floor shall be a hemisphere—its roof the firmament of the star-studded heavens, and its congregation an Union of many Republics, comprising hundreds of happy millions, calling, owning no man master, but governed by God's natural and moral law of equality, the law of brotherhood—of "peace and good will amongst men.". . .

Yes, we are the nation of progress, of individual freedom, of universal enfranchisement. Equality of rights is the cynosure of our union of States, the grand exemplar of the correlative equality of individuals; and while truth sheds its effulgence, we cannot retrograde, without dissolving the one and subverting the other. We must onward to the fulfilment of our mission—to the entire

232

development of the principle of our organization—freedom of conscience, freedom of person, freedom of trade and business pursuits, universality of freedom and equality. This is our high destiny, and in nature's eternal, inevitable decree of cause and effect we must accomplish it. All this will be our future history, to establish on earth the moral dignity and salvation of man—the immutable truth and beneficence of God. For this blessed mission to the nations of the world, which are shut out from the life-giving light of truth, has America been chosen; and her high example shall smite unto death the tyranny of kings, hierarchs, and oligarchs, and carry the glad tidings of peace and good will where myriads now endure an existence scarcely more enviable than that of beasts of the field. Who, then, can doubt that our country is destined to be *the great nation* of futurity?

[1845]

It is time now for opposition to the Annexation of Texas to cease, all further agitation of the waters of bitterness and strife, at least in connexion with this question,—even though it may perhaps be required of us as a necessary condition of the freedom of our institutions, that we must live on for ever in a state of unpausing struggle and excitement upon some subject of party division or other. But, in regard to Texas, enough has now been given to Party. It is time for the common duty of Patriotism to the Country to succeed;—or if this claim will not be recognized, it is at least time for common sense to acquiesce with decent grace in the inevitable and the irrevocable.

Texas is now ours. Already, before these words are written, her Convention has undoubtedly ratified the acceptance, by her Congress, of our proffered invitation into the Union; and made the requisite changes in her already republican form of constitution to adopt it to its future federal relations. Her star and her stripe may already be said to have taken their place in the glorious blazon of our common nationality; and the sweep of our eagle's wing already includes within its circuit the wide extent of her fair and fertile land. She is no longer to us a mere geographical space—a certain combination of coast, plain, mountain, valley, forest and stream. She is no longer to us a mere country on the map. She comes within the dear and sacred designation of Our Country; no longer a *"pays,"* [country] she is part of *"lu putrie;"* [the nation] and that which is at once a sentiment and a virtue,

Patriotism, already begins to thrill for her too within the national heart. . . .

Why, were other reasoning wanting, in favor of now elevating this question of the reception of Texas into the Union, out of the lower region of our past party dissensions, up to its proper level of a high and broad nationality, it surely is to be found, found abundantly, in the manner in which other nations have undertaken to intrude themselves into it, between us and the proper parties to the case, in a spirit of hostile interference against us, for the avowed object of thwarting our policy and hampering our power, limiting our greatness and checking the fulfilment of our manifest destiny to overspread the continent allotted by Providence for the free development of our yearly multiplying millions. This we have seen done by England, our old rival and enemy; and by France. . . .

. . . Texas has been absorbed into the Union in the inevitable fulfilment of the general law which is rolling our population westward; the connexion of which with that ratio of growth in population which is destined within a hundred years to swell our numbers to the enormous population of *two hundred and fifty millions* (if not more), is too evident to leave us in doubt of the manifest design of Providence in regard to the occupation of this continent. It was disintegrated from Mexico in the natural course of events, by a process perfectly legitimate on its own part, blameless on ours; and in which all the censures due to wrong, perfidy and folly, rest on Mexico alone. And possessed as it was by a population which was in truth but a colonial detachment from our own, and which was still bound by myriad ties of the very heartstrings to its old relations, domestic and political, their incorporation into the Union was not only inevitable, but the most natural, right and proper thing in the world—and it is only astonishing that there should be any among ourselves to say it nay.

W. E. Channing Denounces Expansion

Of course, not all Americans endorsed the annexation of Texas or the general pattern of continental expansion. Many Americans opposed this territorial growth on the grounds that it would undermine democratic institutions at home, estrange relations with foreign states, encourage the spread of slavery, and violate the country's deepest values, such as peace and the rule of law. Boston minister William Ellery Channing emerged as a leading anti-expansionist spokesman during the national debate on the Republic of Texas's request for annexation in 1837, a request that, at first, was denied. The selection below is taken from Channing's letter of August 1837 to Henry Clay. Excerpted from The Works of William E. Channing, D.D., *6th edition, (Boston, 1846), 2:183–87, 204–8, 210, 217–18, 220, 231–32, 240.*

MY DEAR SIR,

. . . It is with great reluctance that I enter on the topic of this letter. . . . I desire nothing so much as to devote what remains of life to the study and exposition of great principles and universal truths. But the subject of Texas weighs heavily on my mind, and I cannot shake it off. To me, it is more than a political question. It belongs eminently to morals and religion. . . . Should Texas be annexed to our country, I feel that I could not forgive myself, if, with my deep, solemn impressions, I should do nothing to avert the evil. I cannot easily believe, that this disastrous measure is to be adopted, especially at the present moment. The annexation of Texas, under existing circumstances, would be more than rashness; it would be madness. That opposition to it must exist at the South, as well as at the North, I cannot doubt. Still, there is a general impression, that great efforts will be made to accomplish this object at the approaching session of Congress, and that nothing but strenuous resistance can prevent their success. I must write, therefore, as if the danger were real and imminent; and if any should think that I am betrayed into undue earnestness by a false alarm, they will remember that there are circumstances, in which excess of vigilance is a virtue. . . .

We have a strong argument against annexing Texas to the United States, in the Criminality of the revolt which threatens to sever that country from Mexico. On this point our citizens need light. The Texan insurrection is seriously regarded by many among us as a struggle of the oppressed for freedom. The Texan revolution is thought to resemble our own. Our own is contaminated by being brought into such relationship, and we owe to our fathers and ourselves a disclaimer of affinity with this new republic. The Texan revolt, if regarded in its causes and its means of success, is criminal; and we ought in no way to become partakers in its guilt. . . .

Having unfolded the argument against the annexation of Texas from the criminality of the revolt, I proceed to a second very solemn consideration, namely, that by this act our country will enter on a career of encroachment, war, and crime, and will merit and incur the punishment and woe of aggravated wrong-doing. The seizure of Texas will not stand alone. It will darken our future history. It will be linked by an iron necessity to long-continued deeds of rapine and blood. Ages may not see the catastrophe of the tragedy, the first scene of which we are so ready to enact. It is strange that nations should be so much more rash than individuals; and this, in the face of experience, which has been teaching, from the beginning of society, that, of all precipitate and criminal deeds, those perpetrated by nations are the most fruitful of misery.

Did this country know itself, or were it disposed to profit by self-knowledge, it would feel the necessity of laying an immediate curb on its passion for extended territory. It would not trust itself to new acquisitions. It would shrink from the temptation to conquest. We are a restless people, prone to encroachment, impatient of the ordinary laws of progress, less anxious to consolidate and perfect than to extend our institutions, more ambitious of spreading ourselves over a wide space than of diffusing beauty and fruitfulness over a narrower field. We boast of our rapid growth, forgetting that, throughout nature, noble growths are slow. Our people throw themselves beyond the bounds of civilization, and expose themselves to relapses into a semi-barbarous state, under the impulse of wild imagination, and for the name of great possessions. . . .

It is full time, that we should lay on ourselves serious, resolute restraint. Possessed of a domain, vast enough for the growth of ages, it is time for us to stop in the career of acquisition and conquest. Already endangered by our greatness, we cannot advance without imminent peril to our institutions, union, prosperity, virtue, and peace. . . .

Even were the dispositions of our government most pacific and opposed to encroachment, the annexation of Texas would almost certainly embroil us with Mexico. This territory would be overrun by adventurers; and the most unprincipled of these, the proscribed, the disgraced, the outcasts of society, would, of course, keep always in advance of the better population. These would represent our republic on the borders of the Mexican States. The history of the connexion of such men with the Indians, forewarns us of the outrages which would attend their contact with the border inhabitants of our southern neighbour. . . .

Hitherto I have spoken of the annexation of Texas as embroiling us with Mexico; but it will not stop here. It will bring us into collision with other states. It will, almost of necessity, involve us in hostility with European powers. . . .

I proceed now to a consideration of what is to me the strongest argument against annexing Texas to the United States. . . . The annexation of Texas, I have said, will extend and perpetuate slavery. It is fitted, and, still more, intended to do so. On this point there can be no doubt. . . .

I now ask, whether, as a people, we are prepared to seize on a neighbouring territory for the end of extending slavery? I ask, whether, as a people, we can stand forth in the sight of God, in the sight of the nations, and adopt this atrocious policy? Sooner perish! Sooner be our name blotted out from the record of nations! . . .

I now proceed to another important argument against the annexation of Texas to our country, the argument drawn from the bearings of the measure on our National Union. Next to liberty, union is our great political interest, and this cannot but be loosened, it may be dissolved, by the proposed extension of our territory. . . .

I proceed now to the last head of this communication. I observe, that the cause of Liberty, of free institutions, a cause more sacred than union, forbids the annexation of Texas. It is plain from the whole preceding discussion, that this measure will exert a disastrous influence on the moral sentiments and principles of this country, by sanctioning plunder, by inflaming cupidity, by encouraging lawless speculation, by bringing into the confederacy a community whose whole history and circumstances are adverse to moral order and wholesome restraint, by violating national faith, by proposing immoral and inhuman ends, by placing us as a people in opposition to the efforts of philanthropy, and the advancing movements of the civilized world. It will spread a moral corruption, already too rife among us, and, in so doing, it will shake the foundations of freedom at home, and bring reproach on it abroad. It will be treachery to the great cause which has been confided to this above all nations.

Polk Asks for War on Mexico

Nine months after the Senate rejected the annexation treaty, lame-duck President John Tyler pushed through Congress a joint resolution authorizing the admission of Texas into the Union. That move provoked tension between the United States and Mexico, a country that felt cheated by the annexation of Texas and that contested American claims regarding Texas's border. Perhaps eager to provoke a war of conquest, President James K. Polk ordered the U.S. Army deep into the contested land. Fighting erupted between U.S. and Mexican soldiers in April 1846, and in early May, Polk asked Congress, in the message printed below, to issue a declaration of war. The message is taken from A Compilation of the Messages and Papers of the Presidents. . ., *ed.* James D. Richardson *(New York, 1897), 6:2287, 2291–93.*

WASHINGTON, May 11, 1846.

To the Senate and House of Representatives:

The existing state of the relations between the United States and Mexico renders it proper that I should bring the subject to the consideration of Congress. . . .

The Army moved from Corpus Christi on the 11th of March, and on the 28th of that month arrived on the left bank of the Del Norte opposite to Matamoras, where it encamped on a commanding position, which has since been strengthened by the erection of field works. . . .

The Mexican forces at Matamoras assumed a belligerent attitude, and on the 12th of April General Ampudia, then in command, notified General Taylor to break up his camp within twenty-four hours and to retire beyond the Nueces River, and in the event of his failure to comply with these demands announced that arms, and arms alone, must decide the question. . . .

The grievous wrongs perpetrated by Mexico upon our citizens throughout a long period of years remain unredressed, and solemn treaties pledging her public faith for this redress have been disregarded. A government either unable or unwilling to enforce the execution of such treaties fails to perform one of its plainest duties.

. . . Our forbearance has gone to such an extreme as to be mistaken in its character. Had we acted with vigor in repelling the insults and redressing the injuries inflicted by Mexico at the commencement, we should doubtless have escaped all the difficulties in which we are now involved.

Instead of this, however, we have been exerting our best efforts to propitiate her good will. Upon the pretext that Texas, a nation as independent as herself, thought proper to unite its destinies with our own, she has affected to believe that we have severed her rightful territory, and in official proclamations and manifestoes has repeatedly threatened to make war upon us for the purpose of reconquering Texas. In the meantime we have tried every effort at reconciliation. The cup of forbearance had been exhausted even before the recent information from the frontier of the Del Norte. But now, after reiterated menaces, Mexico has passed the boundary of the United States, has invaded our territory and shed American blood upon the American soil. She has proclaimed that hostilities have commenced, and that the two nations are now at war.

As war exists, and, notwithstanding all our efforts to avoid it, exists by the act of Mexico herself, we are called upon by every consideration of duty and patriotism to vindicate with decision the honor, the rights, and the interests of our country....

In further vindication of our rights and defense of our territory, I invoke the prompt action of Congress to recognize the existence of the war, and to place at the disposition of the Executive the means of prosecuting the war with vigor, and thus hastening the restoration of peace.

JAMES K. POLK

Abraham Lincoln
Challenges Polk's Justification for War

The war against Mexico went well for the United States, which eventually occupied Mexico City and forced Mexico to cede approximately one-third of its land. Yet from the earliest days of fighting, many in the United States questioned the legal and moral grounds for conducting what they viewed as an aggressive war of conquest. The following address, delivered by Representative Abraham Lincoln, Whig of Illinois, in Congress on 12 January 1848, raised such concerns. The speech is reprinted from Complete Works of Abraham Lincoln, *ed. John G. Nicolay and John Hay (New York, 1905), 1:329–30, 338–41.*

[T]aking for true all the President states as facts, he falls far short of proving his justification. . . . The President, in his first war message of May, 1846, declares that the soil was ours on which hostilities were commenced by Mexico, and he repeats that declaration almost in the same language in each successive annual message, thus showing that he deems that point a highly essential one. In the importance of that point I entirely agree with the President. To my judgment it is the very point upon which he should be justified, or condemned. . . .

. . . I propose to state my understanding of the true rule for ascertaining the boundary between Texas and Mexico. It is that wherever Texas was exercising jurisdiction was hers; and wherever Mexico was exercising jurisdiction was hers; and that whatever separated the actual exercise of jurisdiction of the one from that of the other was the true boundary between them. . . . The extent of our territory in that region depended not on any treaty-fixed boundary (for no treaty had attempted it), but on revolution. . . .

. . . In my view, just so far as she carried her resolution by obtaining the actual, willing or unwilling, submission of the people, so far the country was hers, and no farther. Now, sir, for the purpose of obtaining the very best evidence as to whether Texas had actually carried her revolution to the place where the hostilities of the present war commenced, let the President answer the interrogatories I proposed, as before mentioned, or some other similar ones. Let him answer fully, fairly, and candidly. . . . And if, so answering, he can show that the soil was ours where the first blood of the war was shed,—that it was not within an inhabited country, or, if within such, that the inhabitants had submitted themselves to the civil authority of Texas or of the United States, and that the same is true of the site of Fort Brown,—then I am with him for his justification. . . . But if he can not or will not do this,— if on any pretense or no pretense he shall refuse or omit it—then I shall be fully convinced of what I more than suspect already—that he is deeply conscious of being in the wrong; that he feels the blood of this war, like the blood of Abel, is crying to Heaven against him; that originally having some strong motive—what, I will not stop now to give my opinion concerning—to involve the two countries in a war, and trusting to escape scrutiny by fixing the public gaze upon the exceeding brightness of military glory,—that attractive rainbow that arises in showers of blood—that serpent's eye that charms to destroy,—he plunged into it, and has swept on and on till, disappointed in his calculation of the ease with which Mexico might be subdued, he now finds himself he knows not where. How like the half-insane mumbling of a fever dream is the whole war part of his late message!

The Expansion of Slavery Justified

The acquisition of vast territory in the southwest raised the question of whether slavery would be permitted to expand there. Representative David Wilmot, a Pennsylvania Democrat, provoked furious debate by proposing in August 1846 a prohibition against slavery in lands acquired in the war. The so-called Wilmot Proviso repeatedly passed the House, where northerners enjoyed a majority, but died in the Senate, where southerners and other Democrats blocked it. The document that follows, an editorial condemning the Wilmot Proviso, first appeared in The United States Magazine and Democratic Review *(October 1847), 21:292.*

All the territory of the Union is the common property of all the states—every member, new or old, of the Union, admitted to partnership under the constitution, has a perfect right to enjoy the territory, which is the common property of all. Some of the territory was acquired by treaty from England—much of it by cession from the older states; yet more by treaties with Indians, and still greater quantities by purchase from Spain and France;—large tracts again by the annexation of Texas—and the present war will add still more to the quantity yet to be entered by citizens of the United States, or of those of any of the countries of Europe that choose to migrate thither. All this land, no matter whence it was derived, belongs to all the states jointly. . . . [N]o citizen of the United States can be debarred from moving thither with his property, and enjoying the liberties guaranteed by the constitution. . . . Any law or regulation which interrupts, limits, delays or postpones the rights of the owner to the immediate command of his service or labor, operates a discharge of the slave from service, and is a violation of the constitution. . . . To set up therefore a pretence that if they adhere to the property they possess, they shall be deprived of their rights in the states to be formed in any acquired territory, is an unprincipled violation of a solemn treaty, an attack upon the constitution, and a gross injustice to the rights of neighboring states. If the constitution is respected, then the rights of no member in the common property can be impaired, because it is possessed of other property distasteful to other members.

The Expansion of Slavery Condemned

Among the most strident supporters of the Wilmot Proviso stood the noted abolitionist Charles Sumner of Massachusetts. In this treatise, written for the Massachusetts legislature in April 1847, Sumner criticizes the war against Mexico on anti-slavery and other grounds. Taken from "Report on the War with Mexico," in Old South Leaflets, *no. 132 (Boston, n.d.), 150–53, 155–56 [separately paginated as 14–17, 19–20].*

It can no longer be doubted that this is a war of conquest. . . .

A war of conquest is bad; but the present war has darker shadows. It is a war for the extension of slavery over a territory which has already been purged, by Mexican authority, from this stain and curse. Fresh markets of human beings are to be established; further opportunities for this hateful traffic are to be opened; the lash of the overseer is to be quickened in new regions; and the wretched slave is to be hurried to unaccustomed fields of toil. It can hardly be believed that now, more than eighteen hundred years since the dawn of the Christian era, a government, professing the law of charity and justice, should be employed in war to extend an institution which exists in defiance of these sacred principles.

It has already been shown that the annexation of Texas was consummated for this purpose. The Mexican war is a continuance, a prolongation, of the same efforts; and the success which crowned the first emboldens the partisans of the latter, who now, as before, profess to extend the area of freedom, while they are establishing a new sphere for slavery. . . . But it is not merely proposed to open new markets for slavery: it is also designed to confirm and fortify the "Slave Power.". . . Regarding it as a war to strengthen the "Slave Power," we are conducted to a natural conclusion, that it is virtually, and in its consequences, a war against the free States of the Union. . . . Nor should we be indifferent to the enormous expenditures which have already been lavished upon the war, and the accumulating debt which will hold in mortgage the future resources of the country. It is impossible to estimate the exact amount of these. At this moment the cost of the war cannot be less than seventy millions. It may be a hundred millions.

This sum is so vast as to be beyond easy comprehension. It may be estimated, partly, by reference to the cost of other objects of interest. It is far more than all the funds for common schools throughout the United States. It is ample for the endowment of three or more institutions like Harvard College in every State. It would plant churches in all the neglected valleys of the land. It would bind and interlace every part of the country by new railroads. It would make our broad and rude soil blossom like a garden. . . .

. . . The war is a crime, and all who have partaken in the blood of its well-fought fields have aided in its perpetration. It is a principle of military law that the soldier shall not question the orders of his superior. If this shall exonerate the army from blame, it will be only to press with accumulated weight upon the government, which has set in motion this terrible and irresponsible machine.

On what grounds did some Americans advocate expansion into Texas, Oregon, and other regions? Why did other Americans oppose such steps? In your judgment, which side made the most compelling arguments on political, legal, and moral grounds?

Was the U.S. war against Mexico justified?

How did slavery and the emerging sectional dispute influence the debate over expansion? How did the acquisition of territory, in turn, aggravate the sectional conflict?

Slavery and the Old South, 1800–1860

INTRODUCTION

For nearly two and a half centuries, Africans were enslaved on the North American continent. The system of racial slavery that developed in colonial America and the United States had a distinct impact on the nation's development. It helped shape the unique social and economic system of the South; it was a significant force propelling westward expansion; it was the underlying factor leading to the trauma of the Civil War; it generated the ideology of Black inferiority that led to Jim Crowism and African American economic impoverishment for well over a century after emancipation; and it established the racial tensions and divisions under which our nation still suffers.

Generations of enslavement also had a profound impact on African American culture. The practice of slavery in North America, it must be remembered, lasted for more years than the United States has yet been in existence. During this time of enslavement, Blacks shaped a distinctive culture by combining their African heritage with acquired European practices in a manner that allowed them to enjoy meaningful lives within the confines of bondage. The culture that emerged was one that not only enabled the enslaved Africans to survive but one that gave them a sense of dignity, self-worth, and hope under the most bleak of circumstances.

The world the slaves made continues to influence African American life in the present, although developments since emancipation have caused a continual evolution of Black culture. One of the most important of these developments was the mass movement of African Americans from the rural, agrarian South to the urban, industrial North during the great migration that began at the end of the nineteenth century. Another critical development has been the more recent struggle for Black equality, with its diverse themes of integration, Black Power, and Afrocentrism. Yet despite ongoing historical developments, scholars can still discern that the world the slaves made—the attitudes and practices developed while enslaved—still carries great meaning for all Americans.

THE ORIGINS OF BLACK CULTURE

During the last part of the nineteenth century and the first half of the twentieth, scholars and publicists alike perpetuated the myth that the slave experience relieved American Blacks from their "inferior" African heritage and acculturated them to the "higher" values of European American civilization. It was only in the 1970s that the academic community started to pay serious attention to how contemporary Black culture, and American culture in general, was significantly influenced by African values adapted to life under slavery. Today, historians recognize that colonial and antebellum America was an outpost of West African culture, just as it was for the culture of Northern Europe.

Africa, Slavery, and the Roots of Contemporary Black Culture

Two of the scholars pioneering the rediscovery of the world the slaves made are Mary F. Berry and John W. Blassingame, who introduce some of their findings in the section below. Excerpted from "Africa, Slavery, & the Roots of Contemporary Black Culture" in Chant of Saints: A Gathering of Afro-American Literature, Art, and Scholarship, *ed. Michael S. Harper and Robert B. Stepto (Urbana, Illinois, 1979), 241–44, 246–56.*

"It is of consequence," America's premier folklorist, William Wells Newell, declared in 1894, "for the American Negro to retain the recollection of his African origin, and of his American servitude." This was necessary, Newell said, because "for the sake of the honor of his race, he should have a clear picture of the mental condition out of which he has emerged: this picture is not now complete, nor will [it] be made so without a record of song, tales, beliefs, which belong to the stage of culture through which he has passed." The collection of the data noted by Newell had reached a point by the middle of the twentieth century that scholars could begin to answer the question of the origin of black culture. There is, however, no unanimity. The debate on origins has centered on the folktale.

Richard M. Dorson, in his *Negro Folktales in Michigan* (1956) argued that an overwhelming majority of Afro-American folktales came originally from Europe. Since Dorson compiled his tales in the 1950's, his theory may be correct for the latter half of the twentieth century. Obviously, the spread of literacy, radio and television sets in the twentieth century led to the diffusion of European folklore in the black community. Just as obvious, however, is the fact that the widespread illiteracy of slaves and the absence of mass communications media in the nineteenth century severely limited the diffusion of the folklore of European immigrants in the slave community.

Given the degree of isolation between antebellum whites and blacks and differences in languages and roles, it is inconceivable that European sailors—when transporting Africans to the Americas—or that white plantation owners and overseers—while the slaves were at work or rest—regaled the blacks with European folktales, proverbs, and riddles. Most of the diffusion of folklore in the nineteenth century involved whites borrowing from blacks: slaves customarily entertained their master's children with tales, white folklorists regularly visited the quarters and recorded them, and large segments of the white community read the stories compiled by Joel Chandler Harris, Charles C. Jones, Jr., Alcée Fortier, and others.

Whatever the situation in the twentieth century, about 65% of the folktales of slaves in the American South in the nineteenth century came from Africa. The 200 slave tales recorded by Abigail

---

"Africa, Slavery, and the Roots of Contemporary Black Culture," by Mary F. Berry and John W. Blassingame, reprinted by permission from *Chant of Saints: A Gathering of Afro-American Literature, Art, and Scholarship,* Michael S. Harper and Robert B. Stepto, editors, published by University of Illinois Press, 1979. Copyright © 1979 by the Board of Trustees of the University of Illinois.

Christensen in South Carolina, Joel Chandler Harris and Charles C. Jones, Jr. in Georgia, Alcée Fortier in Louisiana, and Hampton Institute's black folklorists all over the South between 1872 and 1900 were generally identical in structure, detail, function, motif, attitudes, and thought patterns to African ones. Rarely did the slave's tales show any trace of the sentimentality and romanticism characteristic of European folklore.

The African origin of nineteenth-century black folktales has long been recognized by the collectors of African folklore. In 1892, A. Gerber compared Afro-American and African folklore and asserted that "not only the plots of the majority of the stories, but even the principal actors, are of African origin." African scholars found striking parallels between the Uncle Remus stories collected by Harris and West African folktales. According to Alta Jablow, the traditional West African animal stories "served as the prototype of the well-known Uncle Remus stories." And in 1966, H. A. S. Johnston, after studying more than 1,000 traditional Hausa and Fulani folktales in Nigeria, asserted: "Brer Rabbit is undoubtedly the direct descendant of the hare of African folktales. Not only are his characteristics exactly the same as those of the Hausa Zomo but the plots in at least thirteen of the Uncle Remus stories are parallels of those in Hausa stories."

A number of the nineteenth-century collectors of slave folktales also recognized their African origin. William Owen, in one of the first analyses of black folklore, wrote in 1877 that the slave's tales were "as purely African as are their faces or their own plaintive melodies . . . the same wild stories of Buh Rabbit, Buh Wolf, and other *Buhs* . . . are to be heard to this day in Africa, differing only in the drapery necessary to the change of scene." Although Joel Chandler Harris knew very little about African folklore, one of the scholars (Herbert H. Smith) he contacted about the origin of his first series of Uncle Remus stories wrote: "One thing is certain. The animal stories told by the negroes in our Southern States and in Brazil were brought by them from Africa." Christensen pointed out that the ancestors of her South Carolina informants had "brought parts of the legends from African forests." In fact, one of her informants, Prince Baskins, told Christensen that he had first heard the tales from his grandfather, a native African. Many of the tales collected by Christensen, Joel Chandler Harris, and Fortier even contained African words in them.

The folktale served some of the same functions in the slave quarters as it had in Africa. It was a means of entertainment, inculcating morality in the young, teaching the value of cooperation, and explaining animal behavior. Like the Africans, the slaves were preoccupied with "pourquoi" stories, or why animals got to be the way they were. The why stories constituted 29.5% of the tales recorded by Hampton Institute collectors and 23.5% of those collected by Christensen in the nineteenth century.

Among the slaves the folktale was also a means of training young blacks to cope with bondage. By modelling their behavior on that of the rabbit or tortoise, the slaves learned to use their cunning to overcome the strength of the master, to hide their anger behind a mask of humility, to laugh in the face of adversity, to retain hope in spite of almost insuperable odds, to create their own heroes, and to violate plantation rules while escaping punishment. In many of the tales a slave used his wits to escape from work and punishment or to trick his master into emancipating him. . . .

"A proverb," say the Yoruba, "is the horse of conversation." Before the arrival of European invaders, West Africans relied on proverbs more than any other people. They were used as greetings, played on drums, included in songs, provided the ending for folktales, and applied as nicknames. Until the last decades of the twentieth century, proverbs served as precedents in reaching judicial decisions. The scholar George Herzog, writing in the 1930's, said that in Liberian "legal proceedings it may happen that at a certain stage most of the discussion narrows down to quoting proverbs." Among the Ashanti, when a master called his slave's name, the bondsman always answered with a proverb. As a revelation of the philosophy of a people and as a way of utilizing the past to cope with a new situation, the West African proverb differed little from those found among Europeans. But West African proverbs had greater flexibility of imagery and application, symmetrical balance, poetic structure, and rhythmic quality than European ones. The correct use of proverbs in African society often involved an intricate and artistic portrayal of abstract ideas.

The primary objective of the proverb was to teach modes of conduct, religious beliefs, hospitality, respect for elders, caution, bravery, humility, and cooperation by drawing on the lessons learned from history, mythology, and the observation of flora, fauna, and human behavior. The proverb survived the coming of the Europeans. One of the major reasons for this was that the moral of a tale was stated as a proverb; often the proverb remained when the tale was forgotten. Through the fables of Aesop, the slave trade, and the writings of travellers, many African proverbs were incorporated into the sayings of Europeans, Arabs, and Asians. It is not surprising, therefore, to find that many of them appeared in the language of nineteenth-century slaves in the southern United States.

Largely banned from acquiring literacy, the slaves remained, like their African ancestors, an oral people. They resorted to proverbs to teach morality and behavioral skills to their children. A comparison of the 382 proverbs contained in the folklore collections of J. Mason Brewer and Hampton Institute with 7,000 proverbs from West Africa shows that 122 or 31% of them were brought by the blacks directly from Africa. Many of the proverbs are identical in form and meaning to West African ones, but often reflect the impact of slavery and the American environment.

About 50% of the proverbs the slaves used reflected the plantation experience. They borrowed less than 20% of them from their white masters. These plantation proverbs contained advice about how much labor the slave should perform, how to avoid punishment, and frequently referred to such activities as ploughing and harvesting cotton, corn, and wheat, religious meetings, corn shuckings and singing. They included such sayings as the following: "The overseer regulates the daybreak. Don't fling all your power into a small job. Don't say more with your mouth than your back can stand (be cautious in talking to the master). . . . "

It is a testament to the wisdom of the slaves that many of their proverbs (or variants) were still being used by Americans, black and white, in the last decades of the twentieth century. They included: "The sun shines in every man's door once (fortune changes). If you can't stand the hot grease, get out of the kitchen. . . . "

The place the witch, ghost, and medicine man had in traditional African society was occupied by hags, hants, and conjurors in the slave quarters. They shared many identical characteristics. Although similar in many ways to its European counterpart, the traditional African witch was a more malevolent and frightful reality. Possessing the ability to turn people into animals, ride, kill, and eat them, the witch caused sores, incurable diseases, sterility, impotence, adultery, stillbirths, and robbed a person of his money or food. Since witches were persons inhabited by demons, they could change into any animal form or become invisible and enter a dwelling through the smallest opening. The African detected witches by spreading pepper around or through dreams. Amulets, rings, chains, and bags of powder worn on the body or placed in dwellings offered some protection, as did objects placed under pillows, the blood of fowls, effigies, and shrines. Persons proven to be witches were killed.

Ghosts play a prominent role in African religions and cosmology. Viewed as the indwelling spirit or soul of a man which departs his body on his death, the ghosts retain an interest in the affairs of the living and punish or frighten them for misdeeds, aid descendants, remain in the vicinity of their graves, and sometimes inhabit the body of newly born infants. The African's belief in ghosts is part of the process of honoring ancestors and functions to preserve social order.

The African medicine man or priest was a mediator between the living and the dead, a discoverer of witchcraft, and a physician. He could prepare poisons to be placed in the food of or on a path frequented by an intended victim. He sold powders and charms to insure success in love, war, planting, hunting and other activities.

There were some inversions and combinations of roles in the transfer of witches, ghosts, and medicine men from Africa to America. The witch, or hag, for example, lost some of its malevolence. Even so, the slaves continued to believe that witches met as a group, took the shape of animals, and rode a person at night. They were invisible, entered a dwelling through a keyhole, and sometimes caused death. If one cut off the limb of a hag while in the shape of an animal, that limb would be missing when the witch returned to its human form. Protection against hags included sticks, sifters, horseshoes, and bottles of salt over the door, or Bibles, forks, and needles under the pillow. Salt and pepper burned the skin of the witch.

Many features of African cosmology regarding ghosts were retained in the Americas. The slaves believed that a person's soul remained on earth three days after death, visiting friends and enemies, and that ghosts remained near graveyards, communicated with and could harm or help the living, and might return to claim property which had belonged to them. The main function of the ghost in the quarters was, as in Africa, to engender respect for the dead. The slaves universally believed, according to many nineteenth-century observers, that if "the living neglect in any way their duty to the dead, they may be haunted by them."

The conjurer, claiming to have received his power from God and believed by many to be in league with the devil, combined the malevolence of the witch with the benevolence of the African medicine man and priest. In the slave's world the conjurer was the medium for redressing wrongs committed by his master or fellows and served as his druggist, physician, faith healer, psychologist, and fortune teller. Bondsmen believed the conjurer could prevent floggings, guarantee successful rebellions or flights for freedom, cast and remove spells, and cause and cure illness. He was the source of love potions, poisons, and "trick bags." Spells resulted from the ingestion of his potions or simply from walking over ground containing a trick bag. Like the Africans, slaves believed that the conjurer used items of personal property or hair and nail clippings to cast spells. In removing spells and curing illnesses he used what was tantamount to autosuggestion or hypnotism and his knowledge of herbs. Mixing teas made from boiling sassafrass, nutmeg, asafoetida, or wild cherry, oak, dogwood, and poplar bark with vinegar, cider, whiskey, turpentine, quinine, calomel, molasses, and honey, the conjurer was remarkably successful in curing the slaves of colds, fevers, chills, etc.

It would take several volumes to describe all of the cultural elements the slaves brought with them from Africa. Some indication of the extent of the African survivals in Afro-American culture appears in a study of Georgia blacks in the 1930's, *Drums and Shadows* (1940). The Georgia investigators found 70 elements of African culture in the region. In addition to the things noted above, they included funeral rites, spirit possession, decoration of graves, taboos, woodcarving, and weaving. Other scholars have noted that the rhythmic complexity and call and response pattern of black music, children's games, religious practices and some dances of American blacks have their origin in Africa.

According to most scholars, the most obvious African retentions in black American culture have been in music and dance. The melody, harmony, rhythm, form, emphasis on percussion, and aesthetics of slave music were all African. In West Africa and among blacks in the antebellum South music was an intimate part of life, of play, religion, and work. Harold Courlander in *Negro Folk Music, USA* (1963) wrote that the black work song "particularly the kind sung by railroad gangs, roustabouts (stevedores), woodcutters, fishermen, and prison road gangs, is an old and deeply rooted tradition. Few Negro musical activities come closer than gang singing does to what we think of as an African style . . . the overall effect instantly calls to mind the group labor songs of Jamaica, Haiti, and West Africa."

The ring games and songs of slave children also originated in Africa. A Nigerian scholar, Lazarus Ekwueme, concluded from his study of African and Afro-American forms: "A black Louisiana housewife sings to her crying baby not too differently from the way a Jamaican mother does or an Ewe woman in Ghana. The children's games, 'Ring around the Rosie' or 'Bob a needle,' each with its accompanying song, have counterparts in Africa, such as the 'Akpakolo' of Igbo children in West Africa or the funny game-song of the Kikuyu of Kenya called 'R-r-r-r-r-na ngubiro,' which is a special East African follow-your-leader version of 'Ring around the Rosie.'"

In contrast to the music and games, few of the slaves' omens and signs appear to have come from Africa. The major reason for this was that there was such a difference in the flora, fauna, and weather in Africa and America. The correct interpretation of signs and omens was extremely important in the slave quarters. By carefully observing the habits of animals, the slaves developed (as did most rural people) skill in predicting changes in the weather. Although this was the primary function of signs, the slaves used them for many other reasons. First, they utilized them as taboos in an effort to teach good manners to children. Young slaves were taught that bad luck followed when they stepped over grown-ups, washed in water used by someone else, tore their clothes, beat cats and dogs, swore, kept their hats on when entering the cabin, or made fun of a cross-eyed person. Second, the slaves insisted that slovenly housekeeping habits (sweeping the floor or cleaning the table after dark) lead to bad luck and death in the family. Third, they used taboos to promote good work habits: "Don't skip a row in planting or someone in your family will die." A fourth function of the signs, omens, and taboos was to inculcate morality in the young. In an effort to prevent girls from being promiscuous, for example, the slaves said: "If you kiss a boy before you marry, you'll never care much for him."

One of the major functions of signs was to enable the slave to deal with the ever present and always unpredictable specter of death. The actions of owls, killdeer, roosters, dogs, cats, hogs, and rabbits were the most frequent signs of an impending death. Every sign called for a corresponding action to prevent death. Typical ways for stopping the screeching of an owl, for instance, were to put an iron poker, horseshoe, or salt in the fire, or to turn your pockets wrong side out.

Seeking control over a harsh world where masters and overseers were capricious and irrational, the slaves developed an unshakable belief in the infallibility of dreams and signs as predictors of future events on the plantation. Primarily an effort to determine when whippings and separations were going to occur, these signs reflect the major fears of the slaves: "If your left eye twitches, you will soon receive a whipping. If you dream of your owner counting money, some slave is going to be sold. If you mock an owl, you'll get a whipping. . . . "

The slaves transmitted many elements of their culture to twentieth-century blacks. The clearest example of this, of course, is the spiritual; many of those religious songs of the slaves could still be heard in black churches in the last decades of the twentieth century. What is less obvious is the slave's contribution to another distinctive genre of American music—the blues. Practically all of the motifs and patterns of the blues were present in the non-religious or secular songs of the slaves. . . .

The oppression of whites, bouts with patrollers, floggings, and conflicts with masters and overseers represented major themes in the slaves' secular songs. In their ironic and humorous twists these songs became the prototypes for similar characteristics in the blues. The slaves approached artistry when they commented on the hypocrisy of their owners:

My old missus promise me
When she die she set me free
She live so long her head git bald
She give up de idea of dyin' a-tall.

When the slaves sang of love and courting, they probably came closest to the blues. References to unfaithful partners were frequent in both types. According to the slave, "When I'se here you call me honey, when I'se gone, you honies everybody." Metaphoric references to sexual intercourse were often identical in the slave songs and in the blues. For example, the blues singer often uses the word "rocking" to refer to sexual intercourse. In one blues song a woman sang in the 1920's:

> Looked at the clock, clock struck one,
> Come on daddy, lets have some fun.
> Looked at the clock, clock struck two,
> Believe to my soul you aint half through.
> Looked at the clock, clock struck three,
> Believe to my soul, you gonna kill poor me.
> Looked at the clock, clock struck four,
> If the bed breaks down we'll finish on the floor.
> My daddy rocks me with one steady roll,
> Dere ain't no slippin' when he once takes hold. . . .

The slaves also resorted to the double meanings and veiled messages of the blues in other sexual references: "cake" and "chicken" meant a woman and "shake" and "pushing" signified sexual intercourse in both types.

One characteristic of the blues frequently noted by musicologists is boasting. The slave singers boasted of their ability to trick their masters:

> I fooled old Mastah seven years
> Fooled the overseer three;
> Hand me down my banjo
> And I'll tickle you bellee (belly).

They emphasized their ability to fight, "to get drunk agin," and their sexual conquests: "When I was young and in my prime, I'se a courtin' them gals, most all de time."

Like the blues men, the slaves were always looking for a "do right" woman. They asked "what make de young girls so deceivin? so deceivin, so deceivin"; warned other men "don't steal my sugar"; lamented "When I got back my chicken was gone"; made the query, "Whose been here since I been gone?"; scorned former lovers who'd gotten pregnant by another man ("her apron strings wouldn't tie,") or observed that "Many a man is rocking another man's son when he thinks he's rocking his own."

The women boasted of their ability to steal someone else's lover: "You steal my partner, and I steal yours." They enjoined their mates to treat them "good" or suffer the consequences: "If you treat me good, I'll stay till de Judgement Day. But if you treat me bad, I'll sho' to run away." Another distinctive feature of the blues is a preoccupation with getting revenge on a lover who has "done you wrong." . . .

Twentieth-century blacks obviously inherited what folklorists call "skill in the verbal arts" from the slaves. Precursors of those most distinctive features of twentieth-century black culture—the dozens, toasts, prayers, sermons, slang, and signifying—appear in collections of slave folklore. The slave was the quintessential folk poet. In his courtship rituals, toasts, and greetings he demonstrated those rhythmical patterns characteristic of twentieth-century black speech. The sources permit, however, only slight glimpses of some of these forms in the quarters. The practice of playing the dozens and signifying, for example, involves the use of so much profanity and so many explicit references to copulation that Victorian nineteenth-century folklorists refused to record them. Even so, some elements of signifying and the dozens (parody, taunts, verbal dueling by indirection, allusion and innuendo, and metaphoric references) can be found in slave speech.

In Harlem in the 1940's, the typical answer to the greeting "whatcha know ole man?" was "I'm like the bear, just ain't getting nowhere." The formalized greetings of the slaves were similar; they would answer the question "How do you do" or such variants as "How is all?" or "How do you shine?" in one of the following ways: "I'm kicking, but not high. I'm barking, but I won't bite. White folks calculating to keep me behind, but I have to keep on gwine (going). I'm fat, but don't show it. . . ."

The verbal "put down" of a protagonist characteristic of the dozens also appeared in slave responses to verbal boasts and threats: "You can saddle me, but you can't ride me. I was never run out of a pond by a tadpole yet. No use clouding up, you can't rain."

Similarities in the verbal art of the bondsmen and twentieth-century blacks are clearly apparent in their courtship practices. According to the folklorist William Ferris, twentieth-century blacks in the rural South have a highly formalized courtship ritual involving the propounding of a series of questions to determine one's availability as a sexual partner. Called "high pro" by the blacks, the practice is a verbal duel.

The prototype of "high pro" was created in the slave quarters where old men taught the young the art of courtship. In order to win a mate, a young man or woman had to "know how to talk." The courtship ritual consisted of riddles, poetic boasting, innuendos, put downs, figurative speech, repartee, circumlocution, and a test of wit. In an effort to determine whether a young lady was free to go courting a young man would typically ask: "Are you a rag on the bush or a rag off the bush? (Answer—If a rag on the bush, free, if off, engaged)." . . . To show that she accepted her suitor, the young girl had to frame a suitably clever response: "I hears dat you is a dove flyin' from lim' to lim' wid no where to res' your weary wings. I's in de same condition an' hopes you kin fin' a place to res' your heart."

Having found someone to "eat out of the dish" with him, the young man would begin boasting of his prowess and proclaiming, through poetic allusions, his love for her: "Dear miss, ef I was starving and had jes one ginger-cake, I would give you half, an' dat would be the bigges' half." . . .

According to the former slave Frank D. Banks, "on the plantation the ability to understand and answer the figurative speeches of her lover was the test of wit and culture by which the slave girl was judged in the society of the quarters." The blacks interviewed by Ferris in the 1970's felt that through a courtship formula remarkably similar to that of the slaves, "you can test a lady out to see what she is and what she stands for and who she really are."

The more religious slaves displayed their verbal skills in church. The chief medium for this was the prayer. Reduced to formulas, taught to young converts, the prayers were intoned in a musical rhythmic chant with frequent pauses for audience responses (usually moans). The power of the prayers came from their method of delivery and the vivid word pictures, fervid imagery, metaphors, and imaginative flights. The bondsman began his prayer by expressing his humility and then called on God to "come sin-killing, soul-reviving" to "the low grounds of sorrow and sin" and confront sinners and "Hammer hard on their hard rock hearts with the hammer of Jeremiah and break their hearts in ten thousand pieces." . . .

The slave's religious beliefs differed from those of his master in a number of ways. First, most black Christians believed in conjurers, and according to one observer, they talked "freely at their religious gatherings of 'tricking' and 'conjuring' and tell marvelous tales of the power of those endowed with supernatural gifts." Second, many of the death and burial customs differed from those of whites, with funerals held long after burials and graves being decorated with articles belonging to the deceased. Third, music was more important in black than white churches and had a more complicated rhythmical structure. The conversion experience was a long one and had to end with a definite sign that one had been saved. Blacks considered dreams as messages from God, signs of conversion or of being called to preach.

Among other unique features of the theology of the slave was his belief that it was no sin to steal from masters, that "no white people went to Heaven," and that faith, not acts, was all-important. In contrast to the staid services in most *white* churches, the slave's service was a blur of motion with constant shouting, clapping of hands, and stamping of feet.

Although the first slaves learned of Christianity from white missionaries, they quickly fused it with West African beliefs to create their own religion. The "frenzied shouting" frequently noted by white observers was, for example, a variant of African spirit possession. So was the ring shout, the call-and-response pattern of sermons, prayers and songs, the unrestrained joy, and predilection for total immersion. Ekwueme asserted that religion was an "area in which Africans share a common heritage with their brothers in the New World, as evidenced in the similarity of modes of worship. . . . The music, dances, and occult rites associated with Voodoo have equivalents in most parts of Africa. The concomitant ecstasy and quasi-psychical entranced upliftment capturing the minds and physique of participants, achieved more through the medium of music than by any other means, have been adopted by black Christian churches in the United States to the point that they are now a *sine qua non* in religious worship for all black people."

The interpreter of black theology was the slave preacher. Since white ministers were always calling upon the slaves to obey their masters, the bondsmen naturally turned to those men who could discover a promise of their salvation and freedom in the Bible. Possessing a memory bordering on the photographic, the black preacher created his sermon from a few details of white church services, verses read to him by whites, or, when literate, his own reading of the Bible, and a close attention to the troubles and dreams of his congregation. Delivered in a musical recitation with pauses for audience response, the antebellum sermon was a model of folk poetry unmatched in its metaphors, figures of speech, and vivid word pictures. The black preacher told his flock that as with the Israelites, God was on the side of the blacks. The historian Eugene Genovese declared that the slaves "guided by their preachers, resisted slavery's psychological assault manfully; they learned to love each other and have faith in their deliverance." In uplifting and guiding the bondsmen, the slave preacher created a style which would later be imitated in evangelical white churches and remained unchanged in its essential ingredients in most black churches in the twentieth century.

In religion, as in other aspects of their lives, the slaves left a legacy to Americans, black and white, which is still evident. However much debate there is regarding the extent of African survivals, many scholars accept the veracity of the Ashanti proverb, "Ancient things remain in the ears." Although fewer of the ancient African practices and beliefs remained in the ears of American blacks than in the ears of those in Latin America, it was the African memory which made the Afro-Americans a distinctive people. Without Africa and slavery, American folklore, speech, music, literature, cooking, and religion would be unimpressive replicas of European ones, barren and somewhat sterile. Without Africa and slavery, America would not have created spirituals, blues, jazz, or rock and roll. Nor would European immigrants in the Americas ever have escaped from the constricting tentacles of the sexual repression they inherited from the Middle Ages. In short, Africa and the slave experience are central to an understanding of the American past and present.

What factors make it highly unlikely that "the overwhelming majority of African American folktales came originally from Europe"?

What role did signs and omens play in the way that slaves dealt with their day-to-day existence?

What appear to be the major themes of the secular folksongs composed by the slaves? What elements of the institution of slavery may have led to the emphasis that the slaves placed upon these themes?

What made Black theology different and more meaningful for the African American slave than the theology of the white Christian missionary or slaveholder?

Based upon your reading of this article, how much of what most Americans consider to be "American culture" would it be fair to say has its origins and development rooted with the African American slave experience?

THE CULTURE OF THE ENSLAVED

While they shared a common heritage, slaves' experiences varied widely. Throughout the South, Blacks toiled on large plantations, small farms, and in urban areas. For a fortunate few, the opportunity for education and perhaps manumission existed. Most, however, were doomed to a life of bondage, in which old age set in before age fifty. All slaves, however, contributed to the development of a culture that allowed them to survive and find meaning for their life in servitude, and also provided a foundation for acts of resistance, both small and large.

The Voices of the Enslaved

Much of what scholars know about slavery is derived from the records and letters that have survived from the white slave owners, their family members, the local governments and courts that they controlled, or from northern or European whites touring the South and writing on their observations. The institution of slavery created major barriers to slaves generating sources that could later inform historians. Foremost among these barriers was a general prohibition against teaching enslaved Africans to read or write, which limited their ability to create a record for posterity. Fortunately, during the Depression-plagued 1930s, as part of the New Deal's relief work efforts, the Federal Writers' Project employed a number of interviewers to seek out and question the few thousand aged African Americans who had been born into slavery and had subsequently been freed at the close of the Civil War. These "slave narratives," while somewhat tinted by the passage of six decades from the events being described, nonetheless have proved to be an invaluable source for understanding what the "peculiar institution" of slavery meant to those enslaved, how it influenced their attitudes and behavior, and how they built a culture of dignity while under its yoke. These passages are written in

263

Black dialect, itself a heritage of generations of bondage without access to formal education. Many of the interviewers of the former slaves, moreover, were particularly interested in speech patterns and went out of their way to transcribe their subject phonetically. These excerpts are taken from Bullwhip Days: The Slaves Remember, An Oral History *(New York, 1988), 42, 47–48, 92–93, 197–98.*

Anna Wright

You wants ter know 'bout some ole slavery foods? Well, I'll tell you what I knows.

Did you ever hear of kush? Kush wus corn bread cooked on de big griddle in de fireplace, mashed up with raw onions an' ham gravy poured over it. You might think dat hit ain't good, but hit am.

Fried chicken wus seasoned, drapped in flour, an' den simmered in a big pan of ham gravy wid de lid on hit, till hit wus tender. Den, de lid wus tuck off, an' de chicken wus fried a golden brown, as quick as possible.

De griddle cakes wus flour an' meal mixed, put on a big ole iron griddle in de fireplace an' flipped over two times.

Ash cake wus made of either meal or flour, wrapped in a damp cloth an' cooked in de hot ashes on de ha'th. Taters wus cooked in de ashes, too, an' dey wus good like dat.

Fish, dem days, wus dipped in meal 'fore dey wus cooked, 'cept catfish, an' dey wus stewed wid onions.

Cornmeal dumplin's wus biled in de turnip greens, collards, cabbages, an' so on, even ter snap beans, an' at supper de pot-licker wus eat wid de dumplin's. Dat's why de folks wus so healthy.

Speakin' 'bout sweets de blackberry or other kind of pie wus cooked in a big pan wid two crusts. Dat made more an' wus better to boot. Cakes wus mostly plain or had jelly fillin', 'cept fer special company.

Excerpts from "Interviews with Former Slaves," reprinted from *Bullwhip Days: The Slaves Remember, An Oral History,* James Mellon, editor. Published by Avon Books by arrangement with Weidenfeld & Nicholson.

Annie Reed

Way back in de old days, when de creatures was all people, Br'er Fox give a log-rollin' and invite all de neighborhood. Br'er Possum was dere, and Br'er Rabbit, and all de rest. Old Sis' Fox and some de neighbor women was fixin' de dinner. Dey done de churnin' too, and Sis' Fox go sat de bucket of butter in de spring where it be good and cool for de big dinner.

Br'er Rabbit, he keep cuttin' he eye roun' all de time, and he see Sis' Fox put de butter in de spring. At dat, he grin to hisse'f and lick his mouf. When dey start rollin' de logs, Br'er Rabbit was right dar wid he shoulder down, jest a-gruntin'. But he ain't do no wuk.

'Long up in de mornin', when de sun get hot, Br'er Rabbit, he let out a big holler: "Hooee, Br'er Fox got to run back home a li'l while!"

"What de matta now, Br'er Rabbit?"

"My wife gwine bring me a new heir."

Den, Br'er Rabbit, he run over in de woods like he takin' de shawtcut home. But he jest creep roun' to de spring and take up dat bucket of butter and eat it all. Den, he wipe he mouf and he hands and lay down in de shade to take a nap.

Jest 'fore dinner time, he git up and come out of de woods walkin' slow and proud.

Br'er Fox see him and holler, "Well, has you got de new heir, Br'er Rabbit?"

Br'er Rabbit say, "Uhuh, got a new heir."

Br'er Fox say, " What you name dis-un?"

Br'er Rabbit say, "He name 'Lickbottom.'" Br'er Rabbit tole dat 'cause he done lick de bottom of de butter bucket.

Br'er Fox say, "Well, dat sho' is fine; sho' hope he does well. And now, it's 'bout de middle of de day, so le's knock off and git dinner."

So dey all go up to de house, and Br'er Fox, he go down to de spring to git de butter. When he git dere, he find all de butter gone.

Br'er Fox, he go back to de house and he say, "Somebody done been to de spring and et all de butter. Any of you-all de one what done it?"

Dey all say dey ain't seen no butter. Den, Br'er Fox, he say, "Well, ain't nobody else been roun' heah, so somebody tole a lie. On'y way we kin find out is to hold ever'body up to de fiah [fire] and make de butter run out de one what done it."

Dey all 'greed to dat, and den dey start holdin' one 'nother up to de fiah, startin' off wid Br'er Possum. So dey keep on till dey git to Br'er Rabbit, and when dey hold him up, here come all de butter runnin' out.

Den, dey all say, "Uhuh, Br'er Rabbit got de butter. What us gwine do wid him?"

Some say to th'ow him in de fiah, and some say th'ow him in de brierpatch. Br'er Rabbit, he don't say nothin'.

Den, Br'er Fox, say, "Br'er Rabbit, which one you ruther us do?"

Br'er Rabbit, he say, "Th'ow me in de fiah, please, Br'er Fox; dem ole briers jest tear my eyes out, if you th'ow me in de brierpatch."

So dey tuk him and th'owed him in de brierpatch. And Br'er Rabbit, he shook he'se'f and jump 'way up on de hill and laugh and say, "Thank you, Br'er Fox. I was bred and born in a brierpatch."

Henry Lewis

One time, dey was two boys what went out to git hick'ry nuts. Some of 'em was white—dem dat had de hulls off—and dem what had de hulls on was black. When dey gwine back home, dey drap a couple out de bag by de gate of de graveyard. Warn't long befo' a nigger come by, and he hear 'em sortin' out de nuts, jis' inside de gate. He ain't see 'em, but he hear 'em say, "You tek de black ones and I'll tek de white ones." He t'ink it were de Lord and de Debil tekin' de souls of the white folks and cullud folks what been bury dere, and he lit out and run home and tell de marster.

Marster, he say he gwine see 'bout dat, and if dat nigger lyin' he gwine give him hundred lashes. So he go back wid de nigger, and when dey git to de gate de boys inside was done 'vidin' up deir nuts. Den, one say, "How 'bout dem two at de gate?" And de other say, "You tek de white one and I tek de black one." Wid dat, de white marster say, "I'm damned iffen you kin tek me. Tek de nigger. I'm gone." And he lit out. But when he git where he gwine de nigger git dere jis' a leedle bit ahead of him.

Sarah Wilson

I's larned to read de Bible, an' my chillun larned to read an' write, but our white folks didn't believe in niggers larnin' anything. Dey thought hit would make de niggers harder to keep slaves, an' to make dem wuk. All de slaves dat I knowed couldn't read nor write.

Mandy Jones

De slaves would run away, sometimes, an' hide out in de big woods. Dey would dig pits an' kivver de spot wid bushes an' vines, an' mebbe lay out fer a whole year. An' dey had pit schools, in slave days, too—way out in de woods. Dey *was* woods den, an' de slaves would slip out o' de quarters at night an' go to dese pits, an' some niggah dat had some learnin' would have a school.

De way de cullud folks would learn to read was from de white chillun. De white chillun thought a heap of de cullud chillun, an' when dey come out o' school wid deir books in deir han's, dey take de cullud chillun, an' slip off somewhere, an' learns de cullud chillun deir lessons what deir teacher has jus' learned dem.

Culture and Resistance to Slavery

While the distinctive culture that African American slaves created helped them endure the hardships and brutality of slavery, it also helped them actively resist their mistreatment. Frederick Douglass, perhaps the most famous of all antebellum African Americans, was born a slave in 1818 on the Eastern Shore of Maryland. Over the course of the next twenty years, Douglass's life was filled with experiences that were both typical and atypical for most slaves during this time. One of the more uncommon was his being taught to read by his master's wife and children, eventually figuring out the meaning of "abolition," and hearing of slaves running away to the North. By the mid-1830s, Douglass reached a point in his life where he decided to rebel against his oppressors. In 1834 Douglass was hired out by his master, Thomas Auld, to Edward Covey, a farmer with a reputation for "breaking" unruly slaves. The following passage vividly describes the blending of black culture and resistance. Taken from his autobiography, Narrative of the Life of Frederick Douglass, An American Slave, Written by Himself, *ed. David W. Blight (Boston, 1993), 75–79.*

I have already intimated that my condition was much worse, during the first six months of my stay at Mr. Covey's, than in the last six. The circumstances leading to the change in Mr. Covey's course toward me form an epoch in my humble history. You have seen how a man was made a slave; you shall see how a slave was made a man. On one of the hottest days of the month of August, 1833, Bill Smith, William Hughes, a slave named Eli, and myself, were engaged in fanning wheat. Hughes was clearing the fanned wheat from before the fan, Eli was turning, Smith was feeding, and I was carrying wheat to the fan. The work was simple, requiring strength rather than intellect; yet, to one entirely unused to such work, it came very hard. About three o'clock of that day, I broke down; my strength failed me; I was seized with a violent aching of the head, attended with extreme dizziness; I trembled in every limb. Finding what was coming, I nerved myself up, feeling it would never do to stop work. I stood as long as I could stagger to the hopper with grain. When I could stand no longer, I fell, and felt as if held down by an immense weight. The fan of course stopped; every one had his own work to do; and no one could do the work of the other, and have his own go on at the same time.

Mr. Covey was at the house, about one hundred yards from the treading-yard where we were fanning. On hearing the fan stop, he left immediately, and came to the spot where we were. He hastily inquired what the matter was. Bill answered that I was sick, and there was no one to bring wheat to the fan. I had by this time crawled away under the side of the post and rail-fence by which the yard was enclosed, hoping to find relief by getting out of the sun. He then asked where I was. He was told by one of the hands. He came to the spot, and, after looking at me awhile, asked me what was the matter. I told him as well as I could, for I scarce had strength to speak. He then gave me a savage kick in the side, and told me to get up. I tried to do so, but fell back in the attempt. He gave me another kick, and again told me to rise. I again tried, and succeeded in gaining my feet; but, stooping to get the tub with which I was feeding the fan, I again staggered and fell. While down in this situation, Mr. Covey took up the hickory slat with which Hughes had been striking off the half-bushel measure, and with it gave me a heavy blow upon the head, making a large wound, and the blood ran freely; and with this again told me to get up. I made no effort to comply, having now made up my mind to let him do his worst. In a short time after receiving this blow, my head grew better. Mr. Covey had now left me to my fate. At this moment I resolved, for the first time, to go to my master, enter a complaint, and ask his protection. In order to [do] this, I must that afternoon walk seven miles; and this, under the circumstances, was truly a severe undertaking. . . . [A]fter a journey of about seven miles, occupying some five hours to perform it, I arrived at master's store. I then presented an appearance enough to affect any but a heart of iron. From the crown of my head to my feet, I was covered with blood. My hair was all clotted with dust and blood; my shirt was stiff with blood. My legs and feet were torn in sundry places with briers and thorns, and were also covered with blood. I suppose I looked like a man who had escaped a den of wild beasts, and barely escaped them. In this state I appeared before my master, humbly entreating him to interpose his authority for my protection. I told him all the circumstances as well as I could, and it seemed, as I spoke, at times to affect him. He would then walk the floor, and seek to justify Covey by saying he expected I deserved it. He asked me what I wanted. I told him, to let me get a new home; that as sure as I lived with Mr. Covey again, I should live with but to die with him; that Covey would surely kill me; he was in a fair way for it. Master Thomas ridiculed the idea that there was any danger of Mr. Covey's killing me, and said that he knew Mr. Covey; that he was a good man, and that he could not think of taking me from him; that, should he do so, he would lose the whole year's wages; that I belonged to Mr. Covey for one year, and that I must go back to him, come what might; and that I must not trouble him with any more stories, or that he would himself *get hold of me*. After threatening me thus, he gave me a very large dose of salts, telling me that I might remain in St. Michael's [town] that night, (it being quite late,) but that I must be off back to Mr. Covey's early in the morning; and that if I did not, he would *get hold of me*, which meant that he would whip me. I remained all night, and, according to his orders, I started off to Covey's in the morning, (Saturday morning,) wearied in body and broken in spirit. I got no supper that night, or breakfast that morning. I reached Covey's about nine o'clock; and just as I was getting over the fence that divided Mrs. Kemp's fields from ours, out ran Covey with his cowskin [bullwhip], to give me another whipping. Before he could reach me, I succeeded in getting to the cornfield; and as the corn was very high, it afforded me the means of hiding. He seemed very angry, and searched for me a long time. My behavior was altogether unaccountable. He finally gave up the chase, thinking, I suppose, that I must come home for something to eat; he would give himself no further trouble in looking for me. I spent that day mostly in the woods, having the alternative before me,—to go home and be whipped to death, or stay in the woods and be starved to death. That night, I fell in with Sandy Jenkins, a slave with whom I was somewhat acquainted. Sandy had a free wife who lived about four miles from Mr. Covey's; and it being Saturday, he was on his way to see her. I told him my circumstances, and he very kindly invited me to go home with him. I went home with him, and talked this whole matter over, and got his advice as to what course it was best for me to pursue. I found Sandy an old adviser. He told me, with great solemnity, I must go back to Covey; but that before I went, I must go with him into another part of the woods, where there was a certain *root*, which, if I would take some of it with me, carrying it *always on my right side*, would render it impossible for Mr. Covey, or any other white man, to whip me. He said he had carried it for years; and since he had done so, he had never received a blow, and never expected to while he carried it. I at first rejected the idea, that the simple carrying of a root in my pocket would have any such effect as he had said, and was not disposed to take it; but Sandy impressed the necessity with much earnestness, telling me it could do no harm, if it did no good. To please him, I at length took the root, and, according to his direction, carried it upon my right side. This was Sunday morning. I immediately started for home; and upon entering the yard gate, out came Mr. Covey on his way to meeting. He spoke to me very kindly, made me drive the pigs from a lot near by, and passed on towards the church. Now, this singular conduct of Mr. Covey really made me begin to think that there was something in the root which Sandy had given me; and had it been on any other day than Sunday, I could have attributed the conduct to no other cause than the influence of that root; and as it was, I was half inclined to think the root to be something more than I at first had taken it to be. All went well till Monday morning. On this morning, the virtue of the *root* was fully tested.

Long before daylight, I was called to go and rub, curry, and feed, the horses. I obeyed, and was glad to obey. But whilst thus engaged, whilst in the act of throwing down some blades from the loft, Mr. Covey entered the stable with a long rope; and just as I was half out of the loft, he caught hold of my legs, and was about tying me. As soon as I found what he was up to, I gave a sudden spring, and as I did so, he holding to my legs, I was brought sprawling on the stable floor. Mr. Covey seemed now to think he had me, and could do what he pleased; but at this moment—from whence came the spirit I don't know—I resolved to fight; and, suiting my action to the resolution, I seized Covey hard by the throat; and as I did so, I rose. He held on to me, and I to him. My resistance was so entirely unexpected, that Covey seemed taken all aback. He trembled like a leaf. This gave me assurance, and I held him uneasy, causing the blood to run where I touched him with the ends of my fingers. Mr. Covey soon called out to Hughes for help. Hughes came, and, while Covey held me, attempting to tie my right hand. While he was in the act of doing so, I watched my chance, and gave him a heavy kick close under the ribs. This kick fairly sickened Hughes, so that he left me in the hands of Mr. Covey. This kick had the effect of not only weakening Hughes, but Covey also. When he saw Hughes bending over with pain, his courage quailed. He asked me if I meant to persist in my resistance. I told him I did, come what might; that he had used me like a brute for six months, and that I was determined to be used so no longer. With that, he strove to drag me to a stick that was lying just out of the stable door. He meant to knock me down. But just as he was leaning over to get the stick, I seized him with both hands by his collar, and brought him by a sudden snatch to the ground. By this time, Bill came. Covey called upon him for assistance. Bill wanted to know what he could do. Covey said, "Take hold of him, take hold of him!" Bill said his master hired him out to work, and not to help to whip me; so he left Covey and myself to fight our own battle out. We were at it for nearly two hours. Covey at length let me go, puffing and blowing at a great rate, saying that if I had not resisted, he would not have whipped me half so much. The truth was, that he had not whipped me at all. I considered him as getting entirely the worst end of the bargain; for he had drawn no blood from me, but I had from him. The whole six months afterwards, that I spent with Mr. Covey, he never laid the weight of his finger upon me in anger. He would occasionally say, he didn't want to get hold of me again. "No," thought I, "you need not; for you will come off worse than you did before."

This battle with Mr. Covey was the turning-point in my career as a slave. It rekindled the few expiring embers of freedom, and revived within me a sense of my own manhood. It recalled the departed self-confidence, and inspired me again with a determination to be free. The gratification afforded by the triumph was a full compensation for whatever else might follow, even death itself. He only can understand the deep satisfaction which I experienced, who has himself repelled by force the bloody arm of slavery. I felt as I never felt before. It was a glorious resurrection, from the tomb of slavery, to the heaven of freedom. My long-crushed spirit rose, cowardice departed, bold defiance took its place; and I now resolved that, however long I might remain a slave in form, the day had passed forever when I could be a slave in fact. I did not hesitate to let it be known of me, that the white man who expected to succeed in whipping, must also succeed in killing me.

How can the folktales by Annie Reed and Henry Lewis be interpreted as "tales of personal empowerment"?

What functions did conjuring and spells have in a slave's life? In particular, how did conjuring aid Frederick Douglass in his resistance to slavery?

How were the pit schools described by Mandy Jones and the case of Sarah Wilson teaching her children to read and write everyday forms of resistance?

Thomas R. Dew's Defense of Slavery (1832)

Thomas R. Dew, a young professor at William and Mary College in Virginia, was one of the earliest defenders of the institution of slavery. In the following excerpts from his Review of the Debate in the Virginia Legislature of 1831 and 1832, *published in 1832, Dew denied that slavery was unchristian, immoral, or undemocratic. In the years to*

*follow his arguments were supplemented by almost everyone of impor-
tance in the South. As you read Dew's review, think about the following
questions:*

1. *In your opinion, how convincing are each of Dew's arguments?*
2. *How might an abolitionist have challenged his arguments?*

. . . . It is said slavery is wrong . . . and contrary to the spirit of
Christianity . . . we . . . deny most positively, that there is anything
in the Old or New testament, which would go to show that
slavery, when once introduced, ought at all events to be abrogated
(abolished), or that the master commits any offense in holding
slaves. The children of Israel themselves were slaveholders, and
were not condemned for it . . . they were permitted expressly to
purchase slaves of the heathen, and keep them as an inheritance
for their posterity; and even the children of Israel might be
inslaved for six years. When we turn to the New Testament, we
find not one single passage at all calculated to disturb the conscience of an honest slaveholder. No one can read it without
seeing and admiring that the meek and humble Savior of the
World in no instance meddled with the established institutions of
mankind; he came to save a fallen world, and not to excite the
black passions of men and array them in deadly hostility against
each other . . .

But it is further said that the moral effects of slavery are of the
most deleterious and hurtful kind; . . . Look to the slaveholding
population of our country, and you every where find them characterized by noble and elevated sentiments, by humane and virtuous feelings . . . It is not a fact, known to every man in the south,
that the most cruel masters are those who have been unaccustomed to slavery, It is well known that northern gentlemen who
marry southern heiresses, are much severer masters than southern gentleman . . .

. . . a merrier being does not exist on the face of the globe, than
the negro slave . . . When then, since the slave is happy. . . . should
we endeavor to disturb his contentment by infusing into his mind
a vain and indefinite desire for liberty—a something which he
cannot comprehend, and which must inevitable dry up the very
sources of his happiness. . . ?

Thomas R. Dew, *Review of the Debate in the Virginia Legislature of 1831 and
1832* (1832), pp. 106–13.

It has been contended that slavery is unfavorable to a republican spirit; . . .

. . . (a) cause of this (southern spirit of liberty) is the perfect spirit of equality so prevalent among the whites of all the slaveholding states . . . The menial and low offices being all performed by the blacks, there is at once taken away the greatest cause of distinction, the true mark of aristocracy, and all who are white are equal in spite of the variety of occupation . . .

John C. Calhoun Sees Slavery as a "Positive Good" (1837)

Senator John C. Calhoun made the following remarks in the United States Senate on February 6, 1837. As you read then, determine why Calhoun believed slavery was a "positive good."

I believe when two races come together which have different origins, colors, and physical and intellectual characteristics, that slavery is, instead of an evil, a good,—a positive good. I must freely upon the subject, for the honor and interests of those I represent are involved. I maintain then, that a wealthy and civilized society has never existed in which one part of the community did not, in fact, live on the labor of others. Broad and general as this assertion is, history supports it. It would be easy to trace the various ways by which the wealth of all civilized communities has been divided unequally. It would also be easy to show how a small share has been allotted to those by whose labor it was produced and a large share given to the nonproducing classes. Innumerable methods have been used to distribute wealth unequally. In ancient times, brute force was used; in modern times, various financial contrivance (schemes) are used.

I will now compare the position of the African laborer in the South with that of the European worker. I may say with truth that in few countries has so much been left to the laborer's share, and so little expected from him, or where more kind attention is paid

Richard K. Cralle (ed.), *Works of John C. Calhoun* (1856). pp. 631–32.

to him when he is sick or old. Compare the slaves' condition with that of the tenants of the poorhouse in the more civilized parts of Europe.

I will not dwell on this aspect of the question; rather I will turn to the political issue. Here I fearlessly assert that the existing relationship between the two races in the South, against which these blind fanatics (abolitionists) are waging war, forms the most solid and durable foundation on which to build free and stable political institutions. The fact cannot be disguised that there is and always has been, in an advanced stage of wealth and civilization; a conflict between labor and capital. Slavery exempts Southern society from the disorders and dangers resulting from this conflict. This explains why the political condition of the slaveholding States has been so much more stable and quiet than that of the North.

Reforming Antebellum Society, 1815–1850

INTRODUCTION

Opposition to slavery in North America was as old as the institution itself. Africans—after being transported forcibly from their homes—resisted their enslavement from the day they reached American shores. At an early date, a few sympathetic whites joined them in condemning bondage. A religiously inspired movement aimed at abolishing slavery began in the middle of the eighteenth century when Quakers made opposition to slavery a condition of membership in their sect. Soon after, during the revolutionary period, a new concern for Natural Rights helped end slavery in the northern states. Some southerners also freed their slaves at that time, but antislavery sentiment in the South never became general enough to lead any southern state to abolish the institution.

Most early opponents of slavery assumed that it would be ended gradually by state legislative action, and that abolition would be accompanied by colonization—the removal of at least some of the freed men and women from the United States. But around 1830 a younger, more determined, more spirited group of abolitionists rejected each of these assumptions. Their demand for the immediate end of slavery and the abandonment of all plans for the expatriation of African Americans ushered in a new, exceedingly contentious phase of the antislavery movement. African Americans heartily endorsed the new "immediatist" program and joined in promoting it. They focused on the plight of their race in the northern states more consistently than did most of their white colleagues and were more intent than were most whites on working against such evidences of prejudice as segregated schools and discriminatory laws. Nonetheless, from beginning to end, the

278

antislavery movement was a partnership, albeit an unequal one, of white and African American abolitionists.

Abolitionists condemned slavery as a cruel and sinful institution that ought to be ended at once. They argued, first, that it violated the principles set forth in the Declaration of Independence upon which the nation was founded, and, second, that it conflicted with such fundamental biblical teachings as the Golden Rule.

The majority of Americans at the time, patriotic and religious though they may have been, did not find these arguments persuasive. Abolitionists always comprised only a minority in the northern population and typically were both scorned and feared as dangerous fanatics. Their campaign to end slavery aroused fierce opposition throughout the north as well as the south. Abolitionist lecturers were regularly mobbed, their printing presses were wrecked, and one abolitionist editor, Elijah P. Lovejoy, was murdered.

A later generation may find such resistance to a call for freedom, justice, and equality hard to understand because the abolitionists' program and their point of view now form part of the American consensus: They are taken for granted. But we should remember that this achievement came only at the cost of a horrendous civil war and, a century later, the painful social and political upheaval incident to the civil rights struggles of the1960s.

ABOLITIONISM:
ACTION AND RESPONSE

Abolitionists tried to publicize their program through lectures, newspapers, and pamphlets. Opposition to this effort by a resistant and sometimes enraged public (one abolitionist was mobbed two hundred times) inevitably raised the issue of civil rights for white Americans as well as for blacks and brought in to the open this important question: Should public opinion be allowed to stifle the rights of free speech, free assembly, and free press simply because a majority finds certain ideas or expressions objectionable or judges them dangerous? Abolitionist activism and rhetoric highlighted the debate on the proper limits of free speech, including the extent to which a community is obliged to tolerate speech that it deems offensive.

In order to consider these issues with respect to the abolitionists, it is necessary to examine their program, their rhetoric, and their mode of agitation, as well as the opposition to them.

The American Anti-Slavery Society Declares its Sentiments

At its founding in 1833, the American Anti-Slavery Society adopted this Declaration of Sentiments. In his characteristically impassioned rhetoric, William Lloyd Garrison condemned slavery and set forth the new organization's principles and proposed activities. Excerpted from William Lloyd Garrison, Selections from the Writings and Speeches of William Lloyd Garrison *(Boston, 1852), 66-71.*

More than fifty-seven years have elapsed, since a band of patriots convened in this place, to devise measures for the deliverance of this country from a foreign yoke. The corner-stone upon which they founded the Temple of Freedom was broadly this—'that all men are created equal; that they are endowed by their Creator with certain inalienable rights; that among these are life, LIBERTY, and the pursuit of happiness.' At the sound of their trumpet-call, three millions of people rose up as from the sleep of death, and rushed to the strife of blood; deeming it more glorious to die instantly as freemen, than desirable to live one hour as slaves. They were few in number—poor in resources; but the honest conviction that Truth, Justice and Right were on their side, made them invincible.

We have met together for the achievement of an enterprise, without which that of our fathers is incomplete; and which, for its magnitude, solemnity, and probable results upon the destiny of the world, as far transcends theirs as moral truth does physical force. . . .

Their principles led them to wage war against their oppressors, and to spill human blood like water, in order to be free. Ours forbid the doing of evil that good may come, and lead us to reject, and to entreat the oppressed to reject, the use of all carnal weapons for deliverance from bondage; relying solely upon those which are spiritual, and mighty through God to the pulling down of strong holds.

Their measures were physical resistance—the marshalling in arms—the hostile array—the mortal encounter. Ours shall be such only as the opposition of moral purity to moral corruption—the destruction of error by the potency of truth—the overthrow of prejudice by the power of love—and the abolition of slavery by the spirit of repentance.

Their grievances, great as they were, were trifling in comparison with the wrongs and sufferings of those for whom we plead. Our fathers were never slaves—never bought and sold like cattle—never shut out from the light of knowledge and religion—never subjected to the lash of brutal taskmasters.

But those, for whose emancipation we are striving—constituting at the present time at least one-sixth part of our countrymen—are recognized by law, and treated by their fellow-beings, as marketable commodities, as goods and chattels, as brute beasts; are plundered daily of the fruits of their toil without redress;

really enjoy no constitutional nor legal protection from licentious and murderous outrages upon their persons; and are ruthlessly torn asunder—the tender babe from the arms of its frantic mother—the heart-broken wife from her weeping husband—at the caprice or pleasure of irresponsible tyrants. For the crime of having a dark complexion, they suffer the pangs of hunger, the infliction of stripes, the ignominy of brutal servitude. They are kept in heathenish darkness by laws expressly enacted to make their instruction a criminal offence.

These are the prominent circumstances in the condition of more than two millions of our people, the proof of which may be found in thousands of indisputable facts, and in the laws of the slaveholding States.

Hence we maintain—that, in view of the civil and religious privileges of this nation, the guilt of its oppression is unequalled by any other on the face of the earth; and, therefore, that it is bound to repent instantly, to undo the heavy burdens, and to let the oppressed go free.

We further maintain—that no man has a right to enslave or imbrute his brother—to hold or acknowledge him, for one moment, as a piece of merchandize—to keep back his hire by fraud—or to brutalize his mind, by denying him the means of intellectual, social and moral improvement.

The right to enjoy liberty is inalienable. To invade it is to usurp the prerogative of Jehovah. Every man has a right to his own body—to the products of his own labor—to the protection of law—and to the common advantages of society. It is piracy to buy or steal a native African, and subject him to servitude. Surely, the sin is as great to enslave an American as an African.

Therefore we believe and affirm—that there is no difference, in principle, between the African slave trade and American slavery:

That every American citizen, who detains a human being in involuntary bondage as his property, is, according to Scripture, (Ex. xxi. 16,) a man-stealer:

That the slaves ought instantly to be set free, and brought under the protection of law:

That if they had lived from the time of Pharaoh down to the present period, and had been entailed through successive generations, their right to be free could never have been alienated, but their claims would have constantly risen in solemnity:

chapter 14

That all those laws which are now in force, admitting the right of slavery, are therefore, before God, utterly null and void . . .

We further believe and affirm—that all persons of color, who possess the qualifications which are demanded of others, ought to be admitted forthwith to the enjoyment of the same privileges, and the exercise of the same prerogatives, as others; and that the paths of preferment, of wealth, and of intelligence, should be opened as widely to them as to persons of a white complexion.

We maintain that no compensation should be given to the planters emancipating their slaves:

Because it would be a surrender of the great fundamental principle, that man cannot hold property in man:

Because slavery is a crime, and therefore is not an article to be sold:

Because the holders of slaves are not the just proprietors of what they claim; freeing the slave is not depriving them of property, but restoring it to its rightful owner; it is not wronging the master, but righting the slave—restoring him to himself:

Because immediate and general emancipation would only destroy nominal, not real property; it would not amputate a limb or break a bone of the slaves, but by infusing motives into their breasts, would make them doubly valuable to the masters as free laborers; and

Because, if compensation is to be given at all, it should be given to the outraged and guiltless slaves, and not to those who have plundered and abused them.

We regard as delusive, cruel and dangerous, any scheme of expatriation which pretends to aid, either directly or indirectly, in the emancipation of the slaves or to be a substitute for the immediate and total abolition of slavery.

We fully and unanimously recognise the sovereignty of each State, to legislate exclusively on the subject of the slavery which is tolerated within its limits; we concede that Congress, under the present national compact, has no right to interfere with any of the slave States, in relation to this momentous subject:

But we maintain that Congress has a right, and is solemnly bound, to suppress the domestic slave trade between the several States, and to abolish slavery in those portions of our territory which the Constitution has placed under its exclusive jurisdiction. . . .

These are our views and principles—these our designs and measures. With entire confidence in the overruling justice of God, we plant ourselves upon the Declaration of our Independence and the truths of Divine Revelation, as upon the Everlasting Rock.

We shall organize Anti-Slavery Societies, if possible, in every city, town and village in our land.

We shall send forth agents to lift up the voice of remonstrance, of warning, of entreaty, and of rebuke.

We shall circulate, unsparingly and extensively, anti-slavery tracts and periodicals.

We shall enlist the pulpit and the press in the cause of the suffering and the dumb.

We shall aim at a purification of the churches from all participation in the guilt of slavery.

We shall encourage the labor of freemen [free African Americans] rather than that of slaves, by giving a preference to their productions: and

We shall spare no exertions nor means to bring the whole nation to speedy repentance.

Our trust for victory is solely in God. We may be personally defeated, but our principles never! Truth, Justice, Reason, Humanity, must and will gloriously triumph. Already a host is coming up to the help of the Lord against the mighty, and the prospect before us is full of encouragement.

Why does Garrison begin with a comparison to the founding generation? Do you think his rejection of compensation for slave holders is practical?

A Call for Women to Become Abolitionists

Women helped organize the American Anti-Slavery Society, held fundraising antislavery bazaars, circulated antislavery petitions, and otherwise promoted the abolitionist cause. This essay is one of the earliest appeals to women. It also shows that women's participation in the movement was sometimes opposed even by women themselves. This excerpt is a response to a woman who objected to other women publicly advocating emancipation. Taken from Elizabeth Margaret Chandler, The Poetical Works of Elizabeth Margaret Chandler *(Philadelphia, 1836), 21-23.*

We have been so long accustomed to consider the duty of the female sex, with regard to slavery, as entirely plain, that we had almost imagined it must be equally so to any unprejudiced thinker upon the subject. Not that we expected to find no difference of feeling, or contrariety of sentiment; apathy and prejudices we were prepared for; but we certainly had not thought that the interference of woman in behalf of suffering humanity, could be seriously objected to, as improper, and at variance with right principles. Yet this we are sorry to find is the light in which it is regarded by one of our own sex—a lady, whose talents and character we respect very highly, and whose approbation of the course we are pursuing, we should be proud to have obtained. But as this is withheld, and it is probable she may not be singular in her opinions, we have taken the liberty of quoting some of her sentiments, and appending to them a statement of our own ideas on the same subject.

"Should you inquire why I do not devote myself more sedulously to promote the cause of emancipation?—I would tell you, that I think it is a work which requires the energies of *men*."

And so it does; but it requires also the *influence of woman*. She was given to man 'to be a helpmeet [helpmate] for him;' and it is therefore her duty, whenever she can do so, to lend him her aid in every great work of philanthropy. In *this* her cooperation may be of essential service, without leading her one step beyond her own proper sphere. . . .

"It is a subject so connected with those of government, of law and politics, that I should fear the direct or even apparent interference of my own sex, would be a departure from that propriety of character which nature, as well as society, imposes on woman."

It is true that it is a question of government and politics, but it also rests upon the broader basis of humanity and justice; and it is on *this* ground only, that we advocate the interference of women. We have not the least desire to see our own sex transformed into a race of politicians; but we do not think that in this case such consequences are in the least to be apprehended. To plead for the miserable, to endeavour to alleviate the bitterness of their destiny, and to soften the stern bosoms of their oppressors into gentleness and mercy, can never be unfeminine or unbefitting the delicacy of woman! She does not advocate Emancipation because slavery is at variance with the political interests of the state, but because it is an outrage against *humanity* and *morality* and *religion;* because it is *criminal,* and because her own supineness makes her a *sharer in the crime;* and because a great number of *her own sex* are among its victims. It is therefore, that she should steadily and conscientiously rank among the number of its opponents, and refuse to be benefited by its advantages. She does not by this become a partizan of any system of policy—she seeks only to shield from outrage all that is most holy in her religion! She does not seek to direct, or share with men, the government of the state; but she entreats them to lift the iron foot of despotism from the neck of her sisterhood; and this we consider not only quite within the sphere of her privileges, but also of her positive duties.

Does the author call on women to take greater responsibility in government? What are the practical results for women's rights in her call for women's involvement in the abolitionist movement?

An Abolitionist Lecturer's Instructions

In 1834 the American Anti-Slavery Society commissioned Theodore Dwight Weld to serve as an abolitionist agent in Ohio. These are his instructions. Abridged from Letters of Theodore Dwight Weld, Angelina Grimké Weld and Sarah Grimké, 1822-1844, vol. 1, ed. Gilbert H. Barnes and Dwight L. Dumond *(New York, 1934), 125-27.*

Dear Sir—You have been appointed an Agent of the American Anti-Slavery Society; and will receive the following instructions from the Executive Committee. . . .

The general principles of the Society are set forth in the Declaration, signed by the members of the Convention which formed it at Philadelphia, Dec. 7, 1833. Our object is, the overthrow of American slavery, the most atrocious and oppressive system of bondage that has ever existed in any country. We expect to accomplish this, mainly by showing to the public its true character and legitimate fruits, its contrariety to the first principles of religion, morals, and humanity, and its special inconsistency with our pretensions, as a free, humane, and enlightened people. In this way, by the force of truth, we expect to correct the common errors that prevail respecting slavery, and to produce a just public sentiment, which shall appeal both to the conscience and love of character, of our slave-holding fellow-citizens, and convince them that both their duty and their welfare require the immediate abolition of slavery.

You will inculcate every where, the great fundamental principle of IMMEDIATE ABOLITION, as the duty of all masters, on the ground that slavery is both unjust and unprofitable. Insist principally on the SIN OF SLAVERY, because our main hope is in the consciences of men, and it requires little logic to prove that it is always safe to do right. To question this, is to impeach the superintending Providence of God.

We reprobate the idea of compensation to slave holders, because it implies the right of slavery. It is also unnecessary, because the abolition of slavery will be an advantage, as free labor is found to be more profitable than the labor of slaves. We also reprobate all plans of expatriation, by whatever specious pretences covered, as a remedy for slavery, for they all proceed from prejudice against color; and we hold that the duty of the whites in regard to this cruel prejudice is not to indulge it, but to repent and overcome it.

The people of color ought at once to be emancipated and recognized as citizens, and their rights secured as such, equal in all respects to others, according to the cardinal principle laid down in the American Declaration of Independence. . . .

Do not allow yourself to be drawn away from the main object, to exhibit a detailed PLAN of abolition; for men's consciences will be greatly relieved from the feeling of present duty, by any objections or difficulties which they can find or fancy in your plan. Let the *principle* be decided on, of immediate abolition, and the plans will easily present themselves. What ought to be done can be done. . . .

You will make yourself familiar with FACTS, for they chiefly influence reflecting minds. Be careful to use only facts that are well authenticated, and always state them with the precision of a witness under oath. You cannot do our cause a greater injury than by overstating facts. . . .

In traversing your field, you will generally find it wise to visit first several prominent places in it, particularly those where it is known our cause has friends. In going to a place, you will naturally call upon those who are friendly to our objects, and take advice from them. Also call on ministers of the gospel and other leading characters, and labor specially to enlighten them and secure their favor and influence. Ministers are the hinges of community, and ought to be moved, if possible. If they can be gained, much is gained. . . .

Form Auxiliary Societies, both male and female, in every place where it is practicable. Even if such societies are very small at the outset, they may do much good as centres of light, and means of future access to the people. Encourage them to raise funds and apply them in purchasing and circulating anti-slavery publications gratuitously. . . .

You are not to take up collections in your public meetings, as the practice often prevents persons from attending, whom it might be desirable to reach.

What is the method employed by the American Anti-Slavery Society?

ASPECTS OF THE MOVEMENT FOR ABOLITION

If abolitionists imagined that their program would be welcomed and easily achieve success, they quickly learned otherwise. Hostility met their every effort. Mobs assailed antislavery lecturers in the north; legislatures in the south offered rewards to anyone who would deliver them for trial. What explains such intense resistance? Since the majority apparently found the abolitionists' program utterly unacceptable, how and why was slavery ended? The following readings suggest answers to these perplexing questions.

Abolitionism as Revolution

Abolitionism is customarily listed as one of the many reform movements that pervaded antebellum America. Historian Herbert Aptheker argues that abolitionists should be thought of as revolutionaries, not reformers. Abridged from Herbert Aptheker, Abolitionism: A Revolutionary Movement *(Boston, 1989), xi-xiii.*

In the first six decades of the nineteenth century, the malignancy of slavery affected every facet of life in the United States. Constant ferment marked its existence; countervailing forces were finally sufficiently potent to overcome it, but only after a fierce war had taken hundreds of thousands of lives and the survival of the Republic had been in doubt.

Leading the momentous struggle against slavery, informing it, inspiring it, was the Abolitionist movement—the second successful revolutionary movement in the history of the United States.

The bulk of the vast literature on Abolitionism treats it as simply one of numerous reform movements of the pre-Civil War era; in this sense the literature ignores the question of its revolutionary character. . . .

The fact is that many, perhaps most, of the Abolitionists were revolutionists in their own minds, and the movement as a whole was a revolutionary one in every respect. . . .

The term *revolutionary movement* is used in this work in its precise sense. That is, the Abolitionists sought the uncompensated emancipation, at once, of the slaves. This meant the confiscation of billions of dollars worth of private property, the ownership of which constituted the power of, and defined the nature of, the slave-owning class, which predominated in the South and nationally, in the latter case until the mid-1850s. It was the ruling class. In its ownership of the slaves, the best land, the animals and tools to make that land productive, and the crops thereby realized, the slaveholding class possessed wealth far in excess of any other property-owning class prior to the Civil War. Fundamentally because of this economic dominance, slaveholders controlled both political parties—usually favoring one, but dominating the other, too. It also controlled thereby the executive, legislative, and judicial arms of the federal government and so dominated its domestic and foreign policy. This economic and political predominance assured the slaveholding class effective control, too, over the ideological structure of the society. The slaveholding influence was decisive in publishing—books, periodicals, and newspapers; in education—texts, faculties, and administrators; and in religion—preferred texts and personnel.

The Abolitionists led a movement whose basic aim was the termination of the base of this power, the slaveholding system. It meant the overthrow of the propertied ruling class in the only way such a class can be overthrown—by the elimination of the property upon which its power rests. . . .

Given its fundamental aim, one would expect this second revolution to be more truly democratic than was the first American Revolution, with its less profound property challenge and its less ambitious transformation of society. Indeed it was more democratic: it was a black-white movement much more fully than its predecessor; it was a male-female movement much more fully than its predecessor; it was more fully conscious of its challenge to property rights. Moreover, that challenge was a fundamental characteristic of the second revolution, whereas it was only at the fringes of the first. . . .

Although a salient feature of the Abolitionist movement was its black-white character, it is important to emphasize the overwhelming consequence of its black component. Slavery was the unique experience of black people in the United States. . . . They alone endured it, survived it, and combated it. They were the first and most lasting Abolitionists. Their conspiracies and insurrections, individual struggles, systematic flights, maroon [runaway slave] communities, efforts to buy freedom, cultural solidity, creation of antislavery organizations and publications—all preceded the black-white united efforts. They developed a convention movement, with delegates from many states meeting annually from 1830 to the Civil War and collectively deciding on priorities and strategies for their people. They rejected colonizationism. Without the initiative of the Afro-American people, without their illumination of the nature of slavery, without their persistent struggle to be free, there would have been no national Abolitionist movement.

Would Garrison see himself as a revolutionary? What is the difference between a reformer and a revolutionary?

The Failure of the Abolitionists

The following essay discusses the abolitionists' program and tactics and argues that they did not achieve their original goals. Abridged from Merton L. Dillon, "The Failure of the American Abolitionists," Journal of Southern History 25 (May 1959): 160, 163-76.

The success of any historical movement, it would seem, ought to be judged by its own terms and values; the extent of its accomplishments ought to be measured against its professed aims and methods. Viewed in such fashion, the antislavery movement must be ranked not as a triumph but as one of the major failures of our history. This is not to depreciate either the sincerity and nobility of the abolitionists or their ultimate effect upon the course of events. It is to say, however, that they failed to carry out their announced mission. The abolitionists—from the gentle Benjamin Lundy to the fanatical John Brown—had much to do with establishing emotional commitments in both North and South. By their remorseless agitation they sharpened sectional antagonisms; by their insistence upon viewing all issues in terms of principle, they transmuted sectional controversies into titanic moral struggles, thus rendering compromise unlikely if not impossible. Southerners, reacting to their verbal attacks, defended slavery and "Southern Rights" more stubbornly. Northerners, accepting at least part of the abolitionist indictment of slavery and slaveholders, thereby became more willing to fight an intersectional war. That the abolitionists in such fashion helped to bring about the Civil War and thus to end slavery few can doubt. But this is by no means the same thing as saying that they succeeded in accomplishing their program. . . .

Surveying the nation in 1830, the reformers saw (as reformers have always been able to see) vast numbers of people ignoring the ordinary imperatives of morality. This seemed to be true in whichever quarter they looked but in no place quite so flagrantly as the South. There, they concluded, a proud and powerful section of the country flourished in wickedness, quite beyond the pale of New England's moral influence. The Southern practice of slavery provided salient evidence of this fact, the abolitionists believed. For they had pronounced slavery a sin—it was not merely bad policy, it was not merely evil (theologians would understand the distinction), it was a positive sin. The abolitionists, in their role as the dedicated instruments of God, set themselves to destroy this palpable violation of God's law. . . .

. . . No calamity that might have befallen America could have taken the abolitionists by surprise. They thoroughly expected God momentarily to wreak His awful vengeance upon both the North and the South for their persistence in maintaining slavery, the nation's most conspicuous sin. "Look at the manner in which our sister state, Louisiana, is treating her slaves!" commanded the indignant antislavery editor Elijah P. Lovejoy. "Why, as surely as there is a thunderbolt in Heaven and strength in God's right arm to launch it, so surely will it strike the authors of such cruel oppression." If the holocaust of the Civil War proved such predictions at least circumstantially correct, it also measured the extent of abolitionist failure, for judgment—whether from God or not—came in the form of war, and abolitionist efforts had been powerless to end slavery and thus to avert war.

The abolitionists' apocalyptic view was by no means a casual or an incidental thing; indeed it came to be generally accepted. The pervasiveness of their interpretation of the Civil War as Divine retribution may be gauged in the vivid conceits of Julia Ward Howe's "Battle Hymn of the Republic," in which God is pictured amidst the carnage of war "trampling out the vintage where the grapes of wrath are stored." The idea appears with equal clarity in the solemn sentences of the penultimate paragraph of Abraham Lincoln's second inaugural address, which are informed by echoes of Lovejoy's prophecy written thirty years before. . . .

Thus with motives grand and obligations solemn, the abolitionists inaugurated their crusade to banish slavery from the land. . . . By speeches and publications they would attempt to persuade all Americans—but especially slaveholders—that slavery was a heinous sin calling for immediate repentance. Since slaveholders, however misdirected, were assumed to be reasonable creatures whose better natures when properly enlightened could be trusted to govern them, the abolitionists hoped they would repent and free their slaves as soon as the incontrovertible fact of their sin had been laid before them.

The abolitionists soon realized, however, that the process of enlightenment was not likely, by itself, to end slavery. A formidable obstacle, they concluded, blocked the success of their program. This was the conviction held by most people, North and South, of the Negro's anthropological inferiority. That belief, more than anything else, caused even many Northerners who otherwise accepted the abolitionists' view of slavery to hesitate to espouse their program for ending it. . . . Unless racial prejudice might in some way be destroyed, the antislavery crusade could hardly succeed, for adherence to the idea of the Negro's inferiority, the abolitionists discovered, tended to produce not ardent crusaders but half-hearted antislavery "men who would abolish slavery only in the abstract, and somewhere about the middle of the future."

Most Americans in the early nineteenth century considered the presence of large numbers of free Negroes within the community so dangerous to society as to be intolerable. How, then, could prudent men contemplate freeing the slaves, it was often asked, unless some way were found to transport the freedmen out of the country? And that had proved to be a physical impossibility. The American Colonization Society, the major national organization concerned with slavery before 1833, had long worked to send free Negroes to Africa, but it had accomplished little. Few of the objects of its philanthropy desired to leave their homes in order to move to Africa, nor did the society ever have available enough ships or money to transport in significant numbers even that minority of Negroes willing to emigrate. The abolitionists, unlike the colonizationists, denied both the necessity and the morality of attempting expatriation. The slaves, abolitionists insisted, must be freed at once and the freedmen allowed to remain in the United States. The abolitionists made no concessions whatever to the prevailing racial prejudice, which had served as one of the main bulwarks of the American Colonization Society, nor did they become discouraged when they found that prejudice was nearly universal. While readily granting the fact that racial prejudice existed, the abolitionists denied its inevitability. As radical reformers they refused to recognize any view or any institution as unmalleable under the blows of heaven-inspired emotion and logic. "They contended," as Henry B. Stanton, an official of the American Anti-Slavery Society, explained, "that this prejudice was visible; that being a sin it could be repented of, being a folly it could be cured." . . .

The abolitionists' two goals—(1) to spread the doctrine of the sin of slavery and (2) to eradicate the nearly universal prejudice—

once accomplished would, they supposed, work a moral revolution in the country. They viewed the two goals as inseparable. Indeed, so intertwined were they in abolitionist thought that it is quite impossible to imagine their acceptance of the one without the other. If anything, they believed the ending of prejudice must precede, not follow, the abolition of slavery. As soon as the Negro is "felt to be in *fact* and in *right* our own countryman, the benevolence of the country will be emancipated from its bondage," predicted an early abolitionist. "It will flow out to meet the colored man . . . it will proclaim his rights—and the fetters of the slave will fall asunder." In such a spirit of optimism the reformers began their work, assuming that with the Negro recognized as an equal and slaveholders convinced of their sin, the slaves would be freed. The entire nation would accept this event, the abolitionists supposed, and the freedmen would be welcomed by their fellow countrymen. Thus the caste system would end, justice and harmony prevail, and God's will be done on earth. . . .

The abolitionists directed their program of moral suasion with equal vigor toward both the North and the South, and it was rejected with almost equal vehemence by the people of both sections. The abolitionists perhaps asked too much—and it was no doubt simple-minded to ask it at all—when they pleaded with Southerners to relinquish their valuable slave property. In any event, after 1830 Southerners managed largely to stifle abolitionist efforts to persuade them of their sin. Southern states passed laws imposing severe punishment on those who circulated antislavery literature or uttered antislavery sentiments. Abolitionists who ventured into the South were threatened with punishment so extreme that few dared enter the area, and most of those native Southerners who opposed slavery either kept their views to themselves or fled to the North. . . .

Meanwhile the abolitionists attempted to carry out their program to end racial prejudice in areas and among groups more easily accessible to them. In the Northern states, especially in the cities bordering the Ohio and Mississippi Rivers, lived thousands of free Negroes—most of them social outcasts, economically depressed, and suffering the pressures of legal and extra-legal discrimination. They were living proof, some thought, of the fact of racial inferiority and the dangers inherent in emancipation. The abolitionists, on the other hand, saw in the miseries of the free people of color an opportunity and a challenge. If they could improve the condition of these people, Northern skeptics and perhaps Southerners, too, would be compelled to discard their racial prejudices and admit the feasibility and safety of emancipation. Very early, therefore, the abolitionists began humanitarian work with this group. . . .

Efforts of this kind produced a strong, hostile reaction in both North and South. When Theodore Dwight Weld and his fellow students at Lane Seminary in 1834 undertook to aid the colored people of Cincinnati, school authorities objected, apparently because they saw implications of racial equality in the close interracial relationships which Weld's projects involved. The consequent disciplinary measures imposed by the Lane trustees led some forty students to withdraw from the seminary. Two years later an anti-abolitionist mob in Cincinnati turned their wrath against the Negro section of the city, wrecking and burning as they went. Prudence Crandall's attempts to enroll Negro students in her school at Canterbury, Connecticut, caused so much popular opposition that she abandoned the project. In Jacksonville, Illinois, in 1844, a proposal to allow colored children from the local Sunday schools to participate in the Fourth of July celebration nearly rent the city's churches. . . .

Implicit in much of the opposition to educating free Negroes was the suspicion that racial equality would lead inevitably to racial amalgamation. The widespread fear of Negro social equality provided a powerful incentive to riot against abolitionists throughout the North and became a major factor in Northern opposition to them. Years of antislavery activity failed measurably to eliminate racial prejudice, especially in the states of the Old Northwest. "By nature, education, and association, it is believed that the [N]egro is inferior to the white man, physically, morally, and intellectually," asserted a legislative committee in Illinois after more than a decade of abolitionist agitation in that state; "whether this be true to the fullest extent, matters not, when we take into consideration the fact that such is the opinion of the vast majority of our citizens . . . ."

The abolitionists could not change Southern convictions of the Negro's anthropological inferiority, and they had been little more successful in the North. While it is true that in some limited areas, especially in New England, the abolitionists won local victories in altering views toward Negroes, these victories only dented and did not break the wall of prejudice, and the Civil War began with the bulwark essentially intact. The Union Army, which was to be the effective instrument in the destruction of slavery, contained many soldiers who exhibited extreme racial prejudice, and the three earliest settled states of the Northwest Territory—Ohio, Indiana, and Illinois—maintained legal discriminations against free people of color until the eve of the Civil War, and in some instances long after it.

The antislavery crusade gained numerous recruits in the North in the later 1830's. It may even be true, as some have thought, that as many as 200,000 Northerners belonged to antislavery societies at the height of the movement. But it is surely a mistake to suppose that this figure represents the number of Northerners who were anxious to free the slaves *and* grant them equality. The large accessions to antislavery society membership after 1835 did not, in fact, result solely from a disposition to aid and elevate the Negro. As Catherine Beecher observed at the time, a great many men either declared or implied that in joining the abolitionists "they were influenced, not by their arguments . . . but because the violence of opposers had identified that cause with the question of freedom of speech, freedom of the press, and civil liberty." . . . Each important mob incident brought accessions to the antislavery cause from among those . . . who believed that popular opposition to the abolitionists imperiled civil liberties. Many antislavery recruits, especially those in the West, entered the movement in order to preserve their own rights; they did not necessarily feel any considerable interest in Negro rights. . . . They were indeed eager to end slavery at once; yet they gave little attention to the corollary of emancipation—equal rights for the freedmen. The original abolitionists, therefore, soon found themselves and their aims submerged by the very success of their movement.

. . . Encountering failure at every turn, many of the antislavery leaders changed their methods in the late 1830's, frankly adopting political action, with its implied threat of coercion, as the only means offering a possibility of success for their campaign to end slavery. A shift in that direction had long been underway. James G. Birney, a leader in the political antislavery movement, had concluded as early as 1835, "that repentance is far off, if at all to be expected . . . ." Benjamin Lundy had early declared his belief that slavery could be ended only at the ballot box and by the national government. . . . As the issue became increasingly involved with politics, those who insisted on using only the old methods to achieve the old goals gradually found themselves thrust farther into the background. . . . Opposition to slavery and to the South continued as vigorously as ever in the 1840's, but it was henceforth to be expressed primarily in direct action, with decreasing emphasis upon moral suasion.

This was a momentous change. . . . [T]he change constituted a tacit admission by the antislavery group of the failure of the abolitionist program as a moral reform. . . . Other appeals, more practical and perhaps more selfish, were recognized to possess greater effectiveness than pleas for conformity to the moral law. Moreover, by failing to maintain its original position, the antislavery movement abandoned all hope of achieving its original goals of ending racial prejudice and persuading slaveholders to abandon their sin. For although force might end slavery, no coercion could possibly end prejudice, and repentance gained by force would not be repentance at all. Since public opinion toward Negroes had not been significantly changed, it became nearly certain that even if the slaves were freed, the freedmen would still be condemned to a long period of depressed status.

Most important at that time, however, was the fact that the refusal of the nation to accept the abolitionists' original program increased the chances for war. Slavery would not be ended voluntarily; yet abolitionists had succeeded in persuading Northerners that the South and its institutions were evil. Even if few Northerners believed in or wanted Negro equality, a great many of them had become convinced that slavery must somehow end. By succeeding to that extent, the antislavery crusade had moved the nation closer to war. . . .

. . . Although slavery was ended by the Civil War, racial prejudice was not; for abolition had come through the use of military power, without general willingness to relinquish the idea of racial inequality.

What was the relation between slavery and racial prejudice? Do you think abolitionists were wise in placing so much emphasis on eliminating prejudice? What was the relation between prejudice and plans for African American colonization?

The Politics
of Sectionalism,
1846–1861

The Compromise of 1850

Clay Proposes Compromise (January 29, 1850)

It is desirable for the peace and harmony of the Union that all existing controversies between the states, arising out of the institution of slavery, be settled amicably upon a fair, equitable, and just basis. Therefore,

Resolved, That California ought to be admitted as a state without Congress placing any restriction on the exclusion or introduction of slavery within the boundaries of that state.

Resolved, That since slavery does not exist by law, and is not likely to be introduced into any of the territory acquired by the United States from the Republic of Mexico, Congress ought not to provide by law either for its introduction into or exclusion from any part of that territory. Appropriate territorial governments ought to be established by Congress in all of the territory, outside the boundaries of the proposed State of California, without the adoption of any restriction or condition on slavery.

Resolved, That it is unwise to abolish slavery in the District of Columbia, while slavery continues to exist in Maryland, without the consent of that State, without the consent of the people of the District, and without just payment to the owners of the slaves within the District.

But resolved, That it is wise to prohibit within the District the slave trade of the slaves brought in from states or places outside the District. They should not be sold within the District nor sent to markets outside the District of Columbia.

Resolved, That a more effective law ought to be made, according to the requirement of the Constitution, for the return of slaves who may have escaped into any state or territory in the Union.

Congressional Globe, 31st. Congress, 1st. Sess., 1850, Appendix pp. 115–16

Resolved, That Congress has no power to promote or obstruct the slave trade between slave-holding states, but whether slaves may be admitted or excluded from a state to which they are brought depends entirely on that state's particular laws.

What is Clay's basis for compromise? What would the extremists of the North and South tend to think of this compromise?

Calhoun Replies (March 4, 1850)

A single section, governed by the will of a numerical majority, now controls the government and its entire powers. The North has absolute control over the government. It is clear, therefore, that on all questions between it and the South, where there are different interests, the interests of the South will be sacrificed to the North, no matter how oppressive the effects may be. The South possesses no political means by which it can resist.

Northern hostility towards the social organization of the South lay dormant a long time. The first organized movement against it began in 1835. Then, for the first time, antislavery societies were organized, presses established, lecturers sent forth to excite the people of the North, and incendiary publications were scattered over the whole South, through the mail. The South was thoroughly aroused. Meetings were held everywhere, and resolutions adopted, calling upon the North to arrest the threatened evil. But petitions poured into Congress from the North, calling upon it to abolish slavery in the District of Columbia, and to prohibit what they called the internal slave trade between the states, announcing at the same time that their ultimate object was to abolish slavery, not only in the District, but in the states and throughout the Union.

With the increase of their influence, the abolitionists extended the sphere of their action. In a short time, they had sufficient influence to get the legislatures of most of the northern states to pass acts which in effect repealed the provision of the Constitution that provides for the return of fugitive slaves. This was followed by petitions and resolutions of legislatures of the northern states and popular meetings, to exclude the southern states from all

Congressional Globe, 31st. Congress, 1st Sess., 1850, pp. 452–55

territories acquired or to be acquired, and to prevent the admission of any state into the Union which, by its constitution, does not prohibit slavery.

How can the Union be saved? There is but one way by which it can with any certainty; and that is, by a full and final settlement, on the principle of justice, of all the questions at issue between the two sections. The South asks for justice, simple justice, and less she ought not to take. She has no compromise to offer but the Constitution, and no concession or surrender to make. She has already surrendered so much that she has little left to surrender. Such a settlement would go to the root of the evil, and remove all cause of discontent, by satisfying the South, that she could remain honorably and safely in the Union. Nothing else can, with any certainty, finally and forever settle the question at issue, and agitation, and save the Union.

But can this be done? Yes, easily; not by the weaker party, for it can of itself do nothing—not even protect itself—but by the stronger. The North has only to do justice by conceding to the South an equal right in the acquired territory to do her duty by causing the constitutional provisions related to fugitive slaves to be faithfully fulfilled, to cease the agitation of the slave question, and to provide for an amendment to the Constitution. Such an amendment should restore to the South the power she possessed to protect herself, before the balance between the section was destroyed by this government.

But will the North agree to do this? It is for her to answer this question. But, I will say, she cannot refuse, if she has half the love of the Union which she professes to have, or without justly exposing herself to the charge that her love of power is far greater than her love of the Union. At all events, the responsibility of saving the Union rests on the North, and not the South.

What is Calhoun's main objection to the compromise?

The Election of Abraham Lincoln
and the Secession Crisis

South Carolina Justifies Secession (1860)

The Constitution imposed certain duties upon the several states, and restrained the exercise of certain of their powers, which necessarily implied their continued existence as sovereign states.

A compact between the states established a government with defined objects and powers, limited to the exact words of the grant.

We affirm that these ends for which this government was instituted have been defeated. The government itself has destroyed them by the action of the nonslaveholding states. Those states have assumed the right of deciding upon the propriety of our domestic institutions (slavery). They have denied the rights of property established in fifteen of the states and recognized by the Constitution. They have denounced as sinful the institution of slavery. They have permitted the open establishment among them of abolitionist societies, whose avowed object is to disturb the peace of and to take away the property of the citizens of other states. They have encouraged and assisted thousands of our slaves to leave their homes; and those who remain, have been incited by emissaries (representatives), books, and pictures, to servile insurrection.

For twenty-five years this agitation has been steadily increasing, until it has now secured to its aid the power of the national government. A geographical line has been drawn across the Union, and all the states north of that line have united in the election of a man to the high office of President of the United States whose opinions and purposes are hostile to slavery. He is to be intrusted with the administration of the national government, because he has declared that that "government cannot endure permanently half slave, half free," and that the public mind must rest in the belief that slavery is in the course of ultimate extinction.

Frank Moore (ed.),*The Rebellion Record* (1861), 1, pp 3–4

On the 4th of March, he will take possession of this government. He has announced that the South shall be excluded from the common territory of the nation. . . . and that a war must be waged against slavery until it shall cease throughout the United States.

We, therefore, the people of South Carolina, by our delegates in convention assembled, appealing to the Supreme Judge of the world for the rectitude (rightness) of our intentions, have solemnly declared that the Union heretofore existing between this state and the other states of North America is dissolved. The state of South Carolina has resumed her position among the nations of the world, as separate and independent state, with full power to levy war, conclude peace, contract alliances, establish commerce, and to do all other acts and things which independent states may of right do.

How does South Carolina use the United States Constitution in making its case for secession? Is this a legitimate use of the Constitution?

Abraham Lincoln, First Inaugural Address

Fellow citizens of the United States:

In compliance with a custom as old as the government itself, I appear before you to address you briefly, and to take, in your presence, the oath prescribed by the Constitution of the United States, to be taken by the President "before he enters on the execution of his office."

I do not consider it necessary, at present, for me to discuss those matters of administration about which there is no special anxiety, or excitement.

Apprehension seems to exist among the people of the Southern States, that by the accession of a Republican Administration, their property, and their peace, and personal security, are to be endangered. There has never been any reasonable cause for such apprehension. Indeed, the most ample evidence to the contrary has all the while existed, and been open to their inspection. It is found in nearly all the published speeches of him who now addresses you. I do but quote from one of those speeches when I declare that "I have no purpose, directly or indirectly, to interfere with the institution of slavery in the States where it exists. I believe I have no lawful right to do so, and I have no inclination to do so." Those who nominated and elected me did so with full knowledge that I had made this, and many similar declarations, and had never recanted them. And more than this, they placed in the platform, for my acceptance, and as a law to themselves, and to me, the clear and emphatic resolution which I now read:

"*Resolved*, That the maintenance inviolate of the rights of the States, and especially the right of each State to order and control its own domestic institutions according to its own judgment exclusively, is essential to that balance of power on which the perfection and endurance of our political fabric depend; and we denounce the lawless invasion by armed force of the soil of any State or Territory, no matter under what pretext, as among the gravest of crimes."

I now reiterate these sentiments: and in doing so, I only press upon the public attention the most conclusive evidence of which the case is susceptible, that the property, peace and security of no section are to be in anywise endangered by the now incoming Administration. I add too, that all the protection which, consistently with the Constitution and the laws, can be given, will be cheerfully given to all the States when lawfully demanded, for whatever cause—as cheerfully to one section, as to another.

There is much controversy about the delivering up of fugitives from service or labor. The clause I now read is as plainly written in the Constitution as any other of its provisions:

"No person held to service or labor in one State, under the laws thereof, escaping into another, shall, in consequence of any law or regulation therein, be discharged from such service or labor, but shall be delivered up on claim of the party to whom such service or labor may be due."

It is scarcely questioned that this provision was intended by those who made it, for the reclaiming of what we call fugitive slaves; and the intention of the law-giver is the law. All members of Congress swear their support to the whole Constitution—to this provision as much as to any other. To the proposition, then, that slaves whose cases come within the terms of this clause, "shall be delivered up," their oaths are unanimous. Now, if they would make the effort in good temper, could they not, with nearly equal unanimity, frame and pass a law, by means of which to keep good that unanimous oath?

There is some difference of opinion whether this clause should be enforced by national or by state authority; but surely that difference is not a very material one. If the slave is to be surrendered, it can be of but little consequence to him, or to others, by which authority it is done. And should any one, in any case, be content that his oath shall go unkept, on a merely unsubstantial controversy as to *how* it shall be kept?

Again, in any law upon this subject, ought not all the safeguards of liberty known in civilized and humane jurisprudence to be introduced, so that a free man be not, in any case, surrendered as a slave? And might it not be well, at the same time, to provide by law for the enforcement of that clause in the Constitution which guarranties that "The citizens of each State shall be entitled to all previleges and immunities of citizens in the several States?"

I take the official oath to-day, with no mental reservations, and with no purpose to construe the Constitution or laws, by any hypercritical rules. And while I do not choose now to specify particular acts of Congress as proper to be enforced, I do suggest, that it will be much safer for all, both in official and private stations, to conform to, and abide by, all those acts which stand unrepealed, than to violate any of them, trusting to find impunity in having them held to be unconstitutional.

It is seventy-two years since the first inauguration of a President under our national Constitution. During that period fifteen different and greatly distinguished citizens, have, in succession, administered the executive branch of the government. They have conducted it through many perils; and, generally, with great success. Yet, with all this scope for precedent, I now enter upon the same task for the brief constitutional term of four years, under great and peculiar difficulty. A disruption of the Federal Union heretofore only menaced, is now formidably attempted.

I hold, that in contemplation of universal law, and of the Constitution, the Union of these States is perpetual. Perpetuity is implied, if not expressed, in the fundamental law of all national governments. It is safe to assert that no government proper, ever had a provision in its organic law for its own termination. Continue to execute all the express provisions of our national Constitution, and the Union will endure forever—it being impossible to destroy it, except by some action not provided for in the instrument itself.

Again, if the United States be not a government proper, but an association of States in the nature of contract merely, can it, as a contract, be peaceably unmade, by less than all the parties who made it? One party to a contract may violate it—break it, so to speak; but does it not require all to lawfully rescind it?

Descending from these general principles, we find the proposition that, in legal contemplation, the Union is perpetual, confirmed by the history of the Union itself. The Union is much older than the Constitution. It was formed in fact, by the Articles of Association in 1774. It was matured and continued by the Declaration of Independence in 1776. It was further matured and the faith of all the then thirteen States expressly plighted and engaged that it should be perpetual, by the Articles of Confederation in 1778. And finally, in 1787, one of the declared objects for ordaining and establishing the Constitution, was *"to form a more perfect union."*

But if destruction of the Union, by one, or by a part only, of the States, be lawfully possible, the Union is *less* perfect than before the Constitution, having lost the vital element of perpetuity.

It follows from these views that no State, upon its own mere motion, can lawfully get out of the Union,—that *resolves* and *ordinances* to that effect are legally void; and that acts of violence, within any State or States, against the authority of the United States, are insurrectionary or revolutionary, according to circumstances.

I therefore consider that, in view of the Constitution and the laws, the Union is unbroken; and, to the extent of my ability, I shall take care, as the Constitution itself expressly enjoins upon me, that the laws of the Union be faithfully executed in all the States. Doing this I deem to be only a simple duty on my part; and I shall perform it, so far as practicable, unless my rightful masters, the American people, shall withhold the requisite means, or, in some authoritative manner, direct the contrary. I trust this will not be regarded as a menace, but only as the declared purpose of the Union that it *will* constitutionally defend, and maintain itself.

In doing this there needs to be no bloodshed or violence; and there shall be none, unless it be forced upon the national authority. The power confided to me, will be used to hold, occupy, and possess the property, and places belonging to the government, and to collect the duties and imposts; but beyond what may be necessary for these objects, there will be no invasion—no using of force against, or among the people anywhere. Where hostility to the United States, in any interior locality, shall be so great and so universal, as to prevent competent resident citizens from holding the Federal offices, there will be no attempt to force obnoxious strangers among the people for that object. While the strict legal right may exist in the government to enforce the exercise of these offices, the attempt to do so would be so irritating, and so nearly impracticable with all, that I deem it better to forego, for the time, the uses of such offices.

The mails, unless repelled, will continue to be furnished in all parts of the Union. So far as possible, the people everywhere shall have that sense of perfect security which is most favorable to calm thought and reflection. The course here indicated will be followed, unless current events, and experience, shall show a modification, or change, to be proper; and in every case and exigency, my best discretion will be exercised, according to circumstances actually existing, and with a view and a hope of a peaceful solution of the national troubles, and the restoration of fraternal sympathies and affections.

That there are persons in one section, or another who seek to destroy the Union at all events, and are glad of any pretext to do it, I will neither affirm or deny; but if there be such, I need address no word to them. To those, however, who really love the Union, may I not speak?

Before entering upon so grave a matter as the destruction of our national fabric, with all its benefits, its memories, and its hopes, would it not be wise to ascertain precisely why we do it? Will you hazard so desperate a step, while there is any possibility that any portion of the ills you fly from, have no real existence? Will you, while the certain ills you fly to, are greater than all the real ones you fly from? Will you risk the commission of so fearful a mistake?

All profess to be content in the Union, if all constitutional rights can be maintained. Is it true, then, that any right, plainly written in the Constitution, has been denied? I think not. Happily the human mind is so constituted, that no party can reach to the audacity of doing this. Think, if you can, of a single instance in which a plainly written provision of the Constitution has ever been denied. If, by the mere force of numbers, a majority should deprive a minority of any clearly written constitutional right, it might, in a moral point of view, justify revolution—certainly would, if such right were a vital one. But such is not our case. All the vital rights of minorities, and of individuals, are so plainly assured to them, by affirmations and negations, guarranties and prohibitions, in the Constitution, that controversies never arise concerning them. But no organic law can ever be framed with a provision specifically applicable to every question which may occur in practical administration. No foresight can anticipate, nor any document of reasonable length contain express provisions for all possible questions. Shall fugitives from labor be surrendered by national or by State authority? The Constitution does not expressly say. *May* Congress prohibit slavery in the territories? The Constitution does not expressly say. *Must* Congress protect slavery in the territories? The Constitution does not expressly say.

From questions of this class spring all our constitutional controversies, and we divide upon them into majorities and minorities. If the minority will not acquiesce, the majority must, or the government must cease. There is no other alternative; for continuing the government, is acquiescence on one side or the other. If a minority, in such case, will secede rather than acquiesce, they make a precedent which, in turn, will divide and ruin them; for a minority of their own will secede from them, whenever a majority refuses to be controlled by such minority. For instance, why may not any portion of a new confederacy, a year or two hence, arbitrarily secede again, precisely as portions of the present Union now claim to secede from it. All who cherish disunion sentiments, are now being educated to the exact temper of doing this. Is there such perfect identity of interests among the States to compose a new Union, as to produce harmony only, and prevent renewed secession?

Plainly, the central idea of secession, is the essence of anarchy. A majority, held in restraint by constitutional checks, and limitations, and always changing easily, with deliberate changes of popular opinions and sentiments, is the only true sovereign of a free people. Whoever rejects it, does, of necessity, fly to anarchy or to despotism. Unanimity is impossible; the rule of a minority, as a permanent arrangement, is wholly inadmissable; so that, rejecting the majority principle, anarchy, or despotism in some form, is all that is left.

I do not forget the position assumed by some, that constitutional questions are to be decided by the Supreme Court; nor do I deny that such decisions must be binding in any case, upon the parties to a suit, as to the object of that suit, while they are also entitled to very high respect and consideration, in all paralel cases, by all other departments of the government. And while it is obviously possible that such decision may be erroneous in any given case, still the evil effect following it, being limited to that particular case, with the chance that it may be over-ruled, and never become a precedent for other cases, can better be borne than could the evils of a different practice. At the same time the candid citizen must confess that if the policy of the government, upon vital questions, affecting the whole people, is to be irrevocably fixed by decisions of the Supreme Court, the instant they are made, in ordinary litigation between parties, in personal actions, the people will have ceased, to be their own rulers, having, to that extent, practically resigned their government, into the hands of that eminent tribunal. Nor is there, in this view, any assault upon the court, or the judges. It is a duty, from which they may not shrink, to decide cases properly brought before them; and it is no fault of theirs, if others seek to turn their decisions to political purposes.

One section of our country believes slavery is *right*, and ought to be extended, while the other believes it is *wrong*, and ought not to be extended. This is the only substantial dispute. The fugitive slave clause of the Constitution, and the law for the suppression of the foreign slave trade, are each as well enforced, perhaps, as any law can ever be in a community where the moral sense of the people imperfectly supports the law itself. The great body of the people abide by the dry legal obligation in both cases, and a few break over in each. This, I think, cannot be perfectly cured; and it would be worse in both cases *after* the separation of the sections, than before. The foreign slave trade, now imperfectly suppressed, would be ultimately revived without restriction, in one section; while fugitive slaves, now only partially surrendered, would not be surrendered at all, by the other.

Physically speaking, we cannot separate. We cannot remove our respective sections from each other, nor build an impassable wall between them. A husband and wife may be divorced, and go out of the presence, and beyond the reach of each other; but the different parts of our country cannot do this. They cannot but remain face to face; and intercourse, either amicable or hostile, must continue between them. Is it possible then to make that

311

intercourse more advantageous, or more satisfactory, *after* separation than *before*? Can aliens make treaties easier than friends can make laws? Can treaties be more faithfully enforced between aliens, than laws can among friends? Suppose you go to war, you cannot fight always; and when, after much loss on both sides, and no gain on either, you cease fighting, the identical old questions, as to terms of intercourse, are again upon you.

This country, with its institutions, belongs to the people who inhabit it. Whenever they shall grow weary of the existing government, they can exercise their *constitutional* right of amending it, or their *revolutionary* right to dismember, or overthrow it. I can not be ignorant of the fact that many worthy, and patriotic citizens are desirous of having the national constitution amended. While I make no recommendation of amendments, I fully recognize the rightful authority of the people over the whole subject, to be exercised in either of the modes prescribed in the instrument itself; and I should, under existing circumstances, favor, rather than oppose, a fair oppertunity being afforded the people to act upon it.

I will venture to add that, to me, the convention mode seems preferable, in that it allows amendments to originate with the people themselves, instead of only permitting them to take, or reject, propositions, originated by others, not especially chosen for the purpose, and which might not be precisely such, as they would wish to either accept or refuse. I understand a proposed amendment to the Constitution—which amendment, however, I have not seen, has passed Congress, to the effect that the federal government, shall never interfere with the domestic institutions of the States, including that of persons held to service. To avoid misconstruction of what I have said, I depart from my purpose not to speak of particular amendments, so far as to say that, holding such a provision to now be implied constitutional law, I have no objection to its being made express, and irrevocable.

The Chief Magistrate derives all his authority from the people, and they have conferred none upon him to fix terms for the separation of the States. The people themselves can do this also if they choose; but the executive, as such, has nothing to do with it. His duty is to administer the present government, as it came to his hands, and to transmit it, unimpaired by him, to his successor.

Why should there not be a patient confidence in the ultimate justice of the people? Is there any better, or equal hope, in the world? In our present differences, is either party without faith of being in the right? If the Almighty Ruler of nations, with his eternal truth and justice, be on your side of the North, or on yours of the South, that truth, and that justice, will surely prevail, by the judgment of this great tribunal, the American people.

By the frame of the government under which we live, this same people have wisely given their public servants but little power for mischief; and have, with equal wisdom, provided for the return of that little to their own hands at very short intervals.

While the people retain their virtue, and vigilence, no administration, by any extreme of wickedness or folly, can very seriously injure the government, in the short space of four years.

My countrymen, one and all, think calmly and *well*, upon this whole subject. Nothing valuable can be lost by taking time. If there be an object to *hurry* any of you, in hot haste, to a step which you would never take *deliberately*, that object will be frustrated by taking time: but no good object can be frustrated by it. Such of you as are now dissatisfied, still have the old Constitution unimpaired, and, on the sensitive point, the laws of your own framing under it; while the new administration will have no immediate power, if it would, to change either. If it were admitted that you who are dissatisfied, hold the right side in the dispute, there still is no single good reason for precipitate action. Intelligence, patriotism, Christianity, and a firm reliance on Him, who has never yet forsaken this favored land, are still competent to adjust, in the best way, all our present difficulty.

In *your* hands, my dissatisfied fellow countrymen, and not in *mine*, is the momentous issue of civil war. The government will not assail *you.* You can have no conflict, without being yourselves the aggressors. *You* have no oath registered in Heaven to destroy the government, while *I* shall have the most solemn one to "preserve, protect and defend" it.

I am loth to close. We are not enemies, but friends. We must not be enemies. Though passion may have strained, it must not break our bonds of affection. The mystic chords of memory, stretching from every battle-field, and patriot grave, to every living heart and hearthstone, all over this broad land, will yet swell the chorus of the Union, when again touched, as surely they will be, by the better angels of our nature.

March 4, 1861

How does Lincoln seek to pacify the South? What is the main issue for Lincoln?

Battle Cries and Freedom Songs: The Civil War, 1861–1863

INTRODUCTION

If the Civil War was the single most important episode in American history—and numerous historians have argued that it was—then the pivotal event of that conflict was President Abraham Lincoln's decision to free the 4.5 million enslaved African Americans living in the Confederate South. As many recognized at the time, the decision for emancipation had sweeping implications, not only for the Union war effort but also for the future development of the entire nation. It changed a limited war to quell rebellion into an all-out struggle to shatter the political, economic and social foundation of the South. It overthrew the fundamental basis on which American race relations had rested since colonial times. And it was an unprecedented extension of federal power—magnificent to some, alarming to others—that deeply undermined the American republic's original, sharply limited conception of national government.

"SLAVERY HAS FORFEITED ITS RIGHT TO THE LIFE OF ANY MAN": THE JOURNEY TO EMANCIPATION

It is common, but quite mistaken, to imagine that the Civil War began as a contest for human freedom. In fact the North began the war with a political commitment to defeat the South without touching slavery and maintained that commitment for well over a year. Most Northerners did not wish to vindicate Southern fears about an "Abolitionist" Republican administration and thus legitimize their decision to secede. They also wanted to hold the border states and hoped to tap latent Unionist sentiment in the South. An anti-slavery course would jeopardize all these aims.

Other considerations reinforced this basic contention. While Lincoln personally believed that slavery formed the heart of the rebellion and a substantial minority of other Northerners agreed, the majority did not. Most believed that the free and slave states might have coexisted indefinitely but for abolitionist agitation; others feared that emancipation would lead at once to an influx into the North of African Americans who would compete for jobs.

For all these reasons, the Lincoln administration began the war scrupulously avoiding the slave issue whenever possible. As time went on, however, Lincoln began to reconsider this basic policy. The documents that follow, drawn from Lincoln's private and official correspondence, reflect the president's evolving thoughts on the subject as he wrestled with this issue from the autumn of 1861 through the summer of 1862. Also included is a letter from a Union officer to his wife, reflecting the growing sentiment in favor of emancipation even from Northern soldiers who initially enlisted only to save the Union.

317

Lincoln Urges Congress to Accept Compensated Emancipation, March 1862

Troubled by both the constitutional obstacles to immediate emancipation and the opposition of the border states, Lincoln at first tried to float a program of compensated emancipation, whereby the U.S. government would reimburse slaveowners for the slaves they voluntarily freed. He explained his program to Congress in March 1862. Note how his proposal tried to deal with the constitutional issues; note too why he thought this proposal might help bring the war to an early end. From Basler, ed., The Collected Works of Abraham Lincoln, *5:144–46.*

Fellow-citizens of the Senate, and House of Representatives,

I recommend the adoption of a Joint Resolution by your honorable bodies which shall be substantially as follows:

"Resolved that the United States ought to co-operate with any state which may adopt gradual abolishment of slavery, giving to such state pecuniary aid, to be used by such state in it's [its] discretion, to compensate for the inconveniences public and private, produced by such change of system[.]"

If the proposition contained in the resolution does not meet the approval of Congress and the country, there is the end; but if it does command such approval, I deem it of importance that the states and people immediately interested, should be at once distinctly notified of the fact, so that they may begin to consider whether to accept or reject it. The federal government would find it's [its] highest interest in such a measure, as one of the most efficient means of self-preservation. The leaders of the existing insurrection entertain the hope that this government will ultimately be forced to acknowledge the independence of some part of the disaffected region, and that all the slave states North of such part will then say "the Union, for which we have struggled, being already gone, we now choose to go with the Southern section." To deprive them of this hope, substantially ends the rebellion; and the initiation of emancipation completely deprives them of it, as to all the states initiating it. . . . I say "initiation" because, in my judgment, gradual, and not sudden emancipation, is better for all. In the mere financial, or pecuniary view, any member of Congress, with the census-tables and Treasury-reports before him, can readily see for himself how very soon the current expenditures of this war would purchase, at fair valuation, all the slaves in any named State. Such a proposition, on the part of the general government, sets up no claim of a right, by federal authority, to interfere with slavery within state limits, referring, as it does, the absolute control of the subject, in each case, to the state and it's [its] people, immediately interested. It is proposed as a matter of perfectly free choice with them.

In the annual message last December, I thought fit to say "The Union must be preserved; and hence all indispensable means must be employed." I said this, not hastily, but deliberately. War has been made, and continues to be, an indispensable means to this end. A practical re-acknowledgement of the national authority would render the war unnecessary, and it would at once cease. If, however, resistance continues, the war must also continue; and it is impossible to foresee all the incidents, which may attend and all the ruin which may follow it. Such as may seem indispensable, or may obviously promise great efficiency towards ending the struggle, must and will come.

What does Lincoln hope to accomplish by supporting compensated emancipation? How are abolitionists in the North and slavery supporters in the South likely to react to his call?

Lincoln Betrays Growing Impatience, 28 July 1862

The border-state Congressmen continued their steadfast opposition to emancipation in any form. Meanwhile other Southern Unionists voiced concern with some of the military measures taken by the Lincoln administration. Reading one such complaint from a Louisiana Unionist, Lincoln penned this exasperated response. Abridged from Basler, ed., The Collected Works of Abraham Lincoln, *5:3 44–46.*

Sir: The copy of a letter addressed to yourself by Mr. Thomas J. Durant, has been shown to me. The writer appears to be an able, a dispassionate, and an entirely sincere man. The first part of the letter is devoted to an effort to show that the Secession Ordinance of Louisiana was adopted against the will of a majority of the people. This is probably true; and in that fact may be found some instruction. Why did they allow the Ordinance to go into effect? Why did they not assert themselves? Why stand passive and allow themselves to be trodden down by a minority? Why not hold popular meetings, and have a convention of their own, to express and enforce the true sentiment of the state? If preorganization was against them *then*, why not do this *now*, that the United States Army is present to protect them? The paralysis—the dead palsy—of the government in this whole struggle is, that this class of men will do nothing for the government, nothing for themselves, except demanding that the government shall not strike its open enemies, lest they be struck by accident!

Mr. Durant complains that in various ways the relation of master and slave is disturbed by the presence of our Army; and he considers it particularly vexatious that this, in part, is done under cover of an act of Congress, while constitutional guaranties are suspended on the plea of military necessity. The truth is, that what is done, and omitted, about slaves, is done and omitted on the same military necessity. It is a military necessity to have men and money; and we can get neither, in sufficient numbers, or amounts, if we keep from, or drive from, our lines, slaves coming to them. Mr. Durant cannot be ignorant of the pressure in this direction; nor of my efforts to hold it within bounds till he, and such as he shall have time to help themselves.

. . . [Mr. Durant] speaks of no duty—apparently thinks of none—resting upon Union men. He even thinks it injurious to the Union cause that they should be restrained in trade and passage without taking sides. They are to touch neither a sail nor a pump, but to be merely passengers,—dead-heads at that—to be carried snug and dry, throughout the storm, and safely landed right side up. Nay, more; even a mutineer is to go untouched lest these sacred passengers receive an accidental wound.

Of course the rebellion will never be suppressed in Louisiana, if the professed Union men there will neither help to do it, nor permit the government to do it without their help.

Now, I think the true remedy is very different from what is suggested by Mr. Durant. It does not lie in rounding the rough angles of the war, but in removing the necessity for war. The people of Louisiana who wish protection to person and property, have but to reach forth their hands and take it. Let them, in good faith, reinaugurate the national authority, and set up a State government conforming thereto under the constitution. They know how to do it, and can have the protection of the Army while doing it. The Army will be withdrawn so soon as such State government can dispense with its presence; and the people of the State can then upon the old Constitutional terms, govern themselves to their own liking. This is very simple and easy.

If they will not do this, if they prefer to hazard all for the sake of destroying the government, it is for them to consider whether it is probable I will surrender the government to save them from losing all. If they decline what I suggest, you scarcely need to ask what I will do. What would you do in my position? Would you drop the war where it is? Or, would you prosecute it in future, with elder-stalk squirts, charged with rose water? Would you deal lighter blows rather than heavier ones? Would you give up the contest, leaving any available means unapplied? . . .

I am in no boastful mood. I shall not do *more* than I can, and I shall do *all* I can to save the government, which is my sworn duty as well as my personal inclination. I shall do nothing in malice. What I deal with is too vast for malicious dealing.

What is the basis of Lincoln's "impatience"?

Lincoln Responds to Horace Greeley's "Prayer of Twenty Millions," 22 August 1862

On 20 August 1862, the New York Tribune printed an open letter to Lincoln from its publisher, Horace Greeley, one of the North's most influential opinionmakers. Greeley expressed disappointment with "the policy you seem to be pursuing with regard to the slaves of Rebels." Congress had recently passed the Second Confiscation Act, which provided for the emancipation of slaves belonging to known secessionists. Greeley chided Lincoln for not enforcing this provision as vigorously as possible. In effect, he was urging Lincoln to pursue a full-blooded emancipation policy as a way to defeat the rebellion. Any other course, Greeley maintained, was "preposterous and futile."

Lincoln, in fact, had already decided by this time to issue an Emancipation Proclamation but was not yet ready to do so. His response to Greeley, although it disappointed the publisher, was really an attempt to prepare the groundwork for the coming proclamation. From Basler, ed., The Collected Works of Abraham Lincoln, *5:388–89.*

Dear Sir:

I have just read your [open letter]. . . . As to the policy I "seem to be pursuing" as you say, I have not meant to leave any one in doubt.

I would save the Union. I would save it the shortest way under the Constitution. The sooner the national authority can be restored; the nearer the Union will be "the Union as it was." If there be those who would not save the Union, unless they could at the same time *save* slavery, I do not agree with them. If there be those who would not save the Union unless they could at the same time *destroy* slavery, I do not agree with them. My paramount object in this struggle *is* to save the Union, and is *not* either to save or to destroy slavery. If I could save the Union without freeing *any* slave I would do it, and if I could save it by freeing *all* the slaves I would do it; and if I could save it by freeing some and leaving others alone I would also do that. What I do about slavery, and the colored race, I do because I believe it helps to save the Union; and what I forbear, I forbear because I do *not* believe it would help to save the Union. I shall do *less* whenever I shall believe what I am doing hurts the cause, and I shall do *more* whenever I shall believe doing more will help the cause. . . .

I have here stated my purpose according to my view of *official* duty and I intend no modification of my oft-expressed *personal* wish that all men every where could be free.

Why do you think Lincoln still focuses on preserving the Union when he was already preparing the Emancipation Proclamation?

A Soldier's Views
on Emancipation, 10 August 1862

Meanwhile, a growing number of Union soldiers stationed in the South were becoming convinced that slavery lay at the bottom of the entire Southern rebellion. In early August 1862, Hugh B. Ewing, an Ohio colonel stationed in the mountains of western Virginia, received a letter from his wife in which she criticized the emerging sentiment in favor of making emancipation a Union war aim. His response is from the Hugh B. Ewing Papers, Ohio Historical Society, Columbus.

My Darling—

. . . I know that in society husbands & wives differ on religion and other vital questions and "get on" after a manner. I believe there is no true marriage, without a union of the mind & soul—and this belief was all that kept me from marrying a protestant, as they form our chief society & I was thrown chiefly among them—but believing this, I felt that no true *union* could exist between two who differed so essentially in thought and principle—and I early resolved never to marry a protestant: and steeled my heart against the attractions of protestant ladies, who otherwise pleased me.

Was I right?—

When we married, my opinions on slavery, were these—

I had been taught, by Church history, that the Catholic religion was anti-slavery; that it tolerated it as it did mixed marriages, when it could not help it: that it found slavery in existence in every country on earth; that as soon as it began Evangelizing a country it began its efforts at abolition, and never ceased until it attained its object. It thus abolished Slavery from every country where it had power on Earth. It abolished it in England, Ireland, Scotland, Norway, Sweden, Denmark, France, Spain, Portugal, Italy, Greece, Austria, Prussia, Poland, & all the German States, in parts of Asia & Africa, in Mexico, & all South America save Brazil, in all the Islands of Ocean save Cuba. Protestant historians, with a candor not common to them, learned me "That but for the heroic & untiring efforts of the Popes through the Middle Ages, one tenth of the human race in England Europe & America would be at this moment holding the other nine tenths in abject and unchristian bondage.["] Catholic historians all say the same, and point to it with exultation.

323

All history told me, that every country, without exception, that failed in due time to emancipate their slaves was through them brought to utter ruin by insurrections or external war—that the system was a disease—a social, moral, & political evil, and when no steps were taken for its case, it inevitably ended in terrible convulsions.

Knowing all this, I held the opinion, that the abolitionists, who wished to end it in a day, were wrong; as that would convulse—but that it should be left to the people who were affected by it, to effect the cure gradually. I never dreamed that they, with the light of the past before them, would hurry on the awful Judgment which had overtaken the persistant Slave holders of the past.

The time had come when the Southern people should have laid the foundation for gradual & future emancipation. They said—No, We will lay the foundation for its perpetuity & future extension—And we will lay it on the smoking ruins of the U S Government—that great gift of God to oppressed humanity, which Catholic Arch Bishops tell us is better for the progress & freedom of the Church than that of any other Country on the face of the earth. They have begun to clear away the ground for their new edifice. They have convulsed the entire Nation. The only reason why slavery was even allowed a days life by the Church, was to avoid convulsion. But Slavery has brought on a Convulsion & is shaking the whole Continant in its horrible Struggles. Now I say, in the name of Almighty God who abhors it, let it die; & disturb the world no more.

This convulsion, the child of Slavery, threatens, every day it lasts, to make you a widow and our children orphans. If emancipation would end it, would I be true to my wife & children to spare it? I think not. They are more dear to me than the System of Slavery, and if in my judgment, the choice is between abolition, & a widowed wife & orphaned children, I will choose Abolition. Who can ask me to offer up my life on the Altar of Slavery? No one. Slavery has forfeited its right, if it even had any, to the life of any man—especially to mine which it is laboring day & night to destroy—It has already spilt rivers of blood—it has spent enough.

I am willing to shed my blood, to preserve our Government to our children & grand children, but not to preserve the Slave System to them, nor make them orphans; to preserve that system for anybody else's children.

If any man is willing to die to perpetuate Slavery, let him do so. It is an ignoble cause to cast life away in. I am willing to die in the Cause of Freedom—but will risk life in no meaner cause.

We ought to communicate our thoughts & feelings. The master thought with me is how to end the war & return to my wife & children. I believe the only way to do it is to strike with vigor at the root of the Evil. It will otherwise linger for years. If we cannot communicate on this subject, it will be because we are not united in thought and feeling: because we have no unity of hope & purpose. Until recently I hoped we were as one person—hence the shock your letters caused me. I know well I cannot force your thoughts nor do I desire to. I would rather we differed on religion, than on that on which my life is staked; & which threatens to orphan our children & widow you. Still if we differ on the policy threatening & affecting my life, there is no help for it. One who carries his life in his hands, is apt to think more correctly on the best means of saving it, than a Lady safe at home in her parlor. The hourly presence of danger makes men keen sighted—and I believe the chances are great, that you will not at the end of the war see preserved both the Slave system & your husband. If Slavery is not broken, the war will last long supported & fed by it, and the loss of life on both sides will be frightful.

What is the influence of religion on Ewing's position on slavery? Why does he believe that the abolition of slavery must be a central aim of the war? Do you think he always felt that way?

The Preliminary Emancipation Proclamation

Lincoln had informed his cabinet that he intended to issue an emancipation proclamation as far back as 22 July 1862. But William Seward, his secretary of state, had pointed out that the federal armies had recently suffered several defeats, and that if the president issued an emancipation proclamation it would seem an act of sheer desperation. Better, thought Seward, to wait until a Union victory. Lincoln saw the logic of this and put away his proclamation for the time being. Finally, the Union success at the Battle of Antietam (17 September 1862), furnished the needed victory. Five days later, Lincoln issued his preliminary Emancipation

Proclamation. From Basler, ed., The Collected Works of Abraham Lincoln *5:433–36.*

September 22, 1862

I, Abraham Lincoln, President of the United States of America, and Commander-in-chief of the Army and Navy thereof, do hereby proclaim and declare that hereafter, as heretofore, the war will be prossecuted for the object of practically restoring the constitutional relation between the United States, and each of the states, and the people thereof, in which states that relation is, or may be suspended, or disturbed.

That it is my purpose, upon the next meeting of Congress to again recommend the adoption of a practical measure tendering pecuniary aid to the free acceptance or rejection of all slave-states, so called, the people whereof may not then be in rebellion against the United States, and which states, may then have voluntarily adopted, or thereafter may voluntarily adopt, immediate, or gradual abolishment of slavery within their respective limits; and that the effort to colonize persons of African descent, with their consent, upon this continent, or elsewhere, with the previously obtained consent of the Governments existing there, will be continued.

That on the first day of January in the year of our Lord, one thousand eight hundred and sixty-three, all persons held as slaves within any state, or designated part of a state, the people whereof shall then be in rebellion against the United States shall be then, thenceforward, and forever free; and the executive government of the United States, including the military and naval authority thereof, will recognize and maintain the freedom of such persons, and will do no act or acts to repress such persons, or any of them, in any efforts they may make for their actual freedom.

That the executive will, on the first day of January aforesaid, by proclamation, designate the States, and parts of states, if any, in which the people thereof respectively, shall then be in rebellion against the United States; and the fact that any state, or the people thereof shall, on that day be, in good faith represented in the Congress of the United States, by members chosen thereto, at elections wherein a majority of the qualified voters of such state shall have participated, shall, in the absence of strong countervailing testimony, be deemed conclusive evidence that such state and the people thereof, are not then in rebellion against the United States.

That attention is hereby called to an act of Congress entitled "An act to make an additional Article of War" approved March 13, 1862, and which act is in the words and figure following:

Be it enacted by the Senate and House of Representatives of the United States of America in Congress assembled, That hereafter the following shall be promulgated as an additional article of war for the government of the army of the United States, and shall be obeyed and observed as such:

Article—All officers or persons in the military or naval service of the United States are prohibited from employing any of the forces under their respective commands for the purpose of returning fugitives from service or labor, who may have escaped from any persons to whom such service or labor is claimed to be due, and any officer who shall be found guilty by a court-martial of violating this article shall be dismissed from the service.

SEC. 2. *And be it further enacted,* That this act shall take effect from and after its passage.

Also to the ninth and tenth sections of an act entitled "An Act to suppress Insurrection, to punish Treason and Rebellion, to seize and confiscate property of rebels, and for other purposes," approved July 17, 1862, and which sections are in the words and figures following:

SEC. 9. *And be it further enacted,* That all slaves of persons who shall hereafter be engaged in rebellion against the government of the United States, or who shall in any way give aid or comfort thereto, escaping from such persons and taking refuge within the lines of the army; and all slaves captured from such persons or deserted by them and coming under the control of the government of the United States; and all slaves of such persons found *on* (or) being within any place occupied by rebel forces and afterwards occupied by the forces of the United States, shall be deemed captives of war, and shall be forever free of their servitude and not again held as slaves.

SEC. 10. *And be it further enacted,* That no slave escaping into any State, Territory, or the District of Columbia, from any other State, shall be delivered up, or in any way impeded or hindered of his liberty, except for crime, or some offence against the laws, unless the person claiming said fugitive shall first make oath that the person to whom the labor or service of such fugitive is alleged to be due is his lawful owner, and has not borne arms against the United States in the present rebellion, nor in any way given aid and comfort thereto; and no person engaged in the military or naval service of the United States shall, under any pretence whatever, assume to decide on the validity of the claim of any person to the service or labor of any other person, or surrender up any such person to the claimant, on pain of being dismissed from the service.

And I do hereby enjoin upon and order all persons engaged in the military and naval service of the United States to observe, obey, and enforce, within their respective spheres of service, the act, and sections above recited.

And the executive will in due time recommend that all citizens of the United States who shall have remained loyal thereto throughout the rebellion, shall (upon the restoration of the constitutional relation between the United States, and their respective states, and people, if that relation shall have been suspended or disturbed) be compensated for all losses by acts of the United States, including the loss of slaves.

In witness whereof, I have hereunto set my hand, and caused the seal of the United States to be affixed.

Done at the City of Washington, this twenty second day of September, in the year of our Lord, one thousand eight hundred and sixty two, and of the Independence of the United States, the eighty seventh.

By the President: ABRAHAM LINCOLN
WILLIAM H. SEWARD, Secretary of State

How does the Emancipation Proclamation change the focus of the war? Why did it in itself free few slaves?

The Union Preserved:
The Civil War, 1863–1865

INTRODUCTION

When the Civil War broke out in 1861, few Americans, male or female, suspected that it would transform so many women's lives before it was over. For one reason, most people believed that the conflict would be a short one, with their respective side winning early on. For another, most women led highly restricted lives, and it was difficult for people in the North or South to imagine that the status quo would change. Women could not vote or hold public office, and the professions and most of the nation's universities were closed to them. Most married women could not own property in their own names, and only a small number worked for a wage. The typical white woman was a farmer's wife who was badly educated, bore many children, and worked very hard throughout her life. For slave women, of course, the picture was even more bleak. They worked extremely hard but could not enjoy the fruits of their labor. Denied access to education, they had to struggle in secret to learn to read and write. Their families were at risk, vulnerable to separation by sales and to sexual abuse by whites. And through it all they had to endure the daily indignities of bondage.

The war certainly changed much of this, as scholars have begun to discover. The restrictions on women's lives began to loosen at different times in different places. From the start, white Northern women had the opportunity, even the duty, to engage in charitable work on a massive scale to support the men in blue. The military permitted women to take up new occupations in nursing and teaching; several hundred women disguised themselves as men and fought in battle without official authorization. White Southern women also did charitable work, nursed the wounded, and fought in disguise, but most of them seem to have stayed home to run farms and plantations. As they gradually took up the decision-making power that had been in men's hands, they too faced distinctive challenges. For black Southern women, the war held out the promise of the ultimate transformation, that of bondage to freedom. Many women escaped during the war as the Union forces approached and immediately seized the opportunity to find family members, work for a wage, or assist the Union war effort. The war both initiated and accelerated profound social changes, and, by 1865, the lives of most American women—be they black or white, Southern or Northern—had been changed, many of them forever.

On the Home Front

Kate Poulton McLure was born in England in 1829 and came to South Carolina as a girl. In 1852 she married William McLure, a slaveowning merchant who was also a fire-breathing secessionist. Before the war the McLures had a very traditional marriage, but the war's relentless pressures forced Kate McLure to take on many untraditional responsibilities. As Joan E. Cashin demonstrates, they increasingly brought her into conflict with her husband, a quartermaster in the Confederate army, her overseers, and her male relatives. Excerpted from Joan Cashin, "'Since the War Broke Out': The Marriage of Kate and William McLure," Divided Houses: Gender and the Civil War, *ed.* Catherine Clinton and Nina Silber *(New York, 1992), 203–11.*

When South Carolina seceded in December 1860, William McLure did not hesitate to throw in his lot with his state. He enlisted in a local volunteer company in January 1861, and he was in Charleston when the shelling commenced at Fort Sumter in April. (He took a slave named Tom along with him as his personal servant). He expressed great contempt for "Yankees" and thought they would be easily beaten. In the only surviving letter she wrote during the secession crisis, Kate McLure agreed with her husband's views, calling the southern cause "our cause" and a "just" one, and she believed that it "must triumph," although she feared that southern independence would require a great loss of life. Her views were indistinguishable from those of thousands of white southern women. Although she might be perceived as a British or Northern figure, she had spent her formative years in the South; in the twenty-odd years since she had moved to South Carolina, she had accepted slaveowners' values, and she married a committed secessionist. Throughout the War she never wavered in her support for the Confederacy. Her racial views at this time were apparently just as conventional. She taught Bible classes to the McLure slaves and knew all of them by name, as her husband did not, but there is no hint in any of her antebellum letters that she ever questioned prevailing views of the racial inferiority of blacks.

During the first half of 1861, the McLure's Oakwood plantation operated much as it had before Fort Sumter. William McLure arranged for Elijah Dawkins, a relation of his brother-in-law Thomas Dawkins, to deliver extra food to the plantation if necessary, and he marketed his cotton crop himself when he was in Charleston in the spring of 1861. Then he left everything in the hands of a new overseer, B. F. Holmes. After McLure's unit was dispatched to Virginia, he corresponded directly with Holmes about the details of running the plantation. But McLure's absence inevitably began to alter his relationship with his overseer; in fact, several key relationships on the plantation shifted during the summer and fall of 1861. Whenever McLure forgot to tell Holmes something, he put it in his next letter to his wife, who either passed the instructions on to Holmes or carried them out herself. For instance, Kate McLure, not the overseer, purchased many of the plantation's supplies in September. William McLure was so surprised at her ingenuity at this task, which she had never done before, that he joked that he would leave this to her in the future—a prophecy that came true before the war was over.

William McLure sometimes confused the situation by sending contradictory directions. He once told his wife to instruct a slave named Jeff to look after the food crops, while simultaneously asking her to tell Holmes to sow a field of fall wheat. In another letter he urged her to "hurry" Holmes through the cotton harvest. By the end of 1861, Holmes's authority on the plantation was being divided in ad hoc manner between Kate McLure and the slave named Jeff. William McLure does not seem to have understood how he was dividing his authority, perhaps because he still saw himself as the ultimate authority. Holmes may have been uncomfortable with the situation; in November 1861 he still had not decided if he would stay on for the next year. He finally chose

---

"'Since the War Broke Out': The Marriage of Kate and William McLure," by Joan Cashin, reprinted from *Divided Houses: Gender and the Civil War*, Catherine Clinton and Nina Silber, editors. Copyright © 1992 by Catherine Clinton and Nina Silber. Published by Oxford University Press, 1992.

to stay, and the power triangle of overseer, mistress, and slave continued in uneasy balance.

It is frustrating that little can be discovered about Jeff, the slave who figures prominently in the McLure family's life during the war. The McLures had owned Jeff since 1856 at least, but their letters give no information on his age or marital status. He probably worked as a field laborer or stable hand rather than as a house servant, since in the past William McLure had put him in charge of caring for the horses. Kate McLure did not elaborate on her opinion of Jeff, but it is clear that she respected and trusted him. The overseer Holmes, the other actor in the triangle, was probably Benjamin "Homes," age twenty-five, listed in the county's 1860 census a few households away from the McLure residence. Married and the father of two children, he was the owner of almost a thousand dollars' worth of real estate, and he had been a farmer, not an overseer, before the war. His motives for taking the job, as well as anything else about his personality, remain obscure. . . .

. . . Kate McLure had to grapple with more immediate problems. The overseer Holmes did not plant enough food crops to feed everyone on the plantation, he raised too much cotton, and he did not care for the livestock properly. Although he was usually polite to her, Holmes took direction only from other white men, either William McLure or Doctor John A. Reidy, the husband of McLure's sister Frances who came over from neighboring Chester County to treat an outbreak of measles among the McLure slaves. Kate McLure was so worried about the general situation that she was plagued with chronic insomnia and tried to persuade her husband that Holmes had to go. By the summer of 1862, William McLure allowed that the plantation seemed to be in an "unsettled, unsatisfactory" condition. The fall harvests were paltry, and Kate McLure was finding it hard to obtain shoes for the slaves.

Subsequently, William McLure stopped writing directly to Holmes and instead conveyed his wishes through his wife, which no doubt increased the difficulties between overseer and mistress. She took to riding through the fields herself to see if Holmes was following instructions, something she had not done before the war, and only her strict economy with the food supply permitted everyone to get something to eat, as her husband now admitted. He finally agreed that Holmes was a "sorry fellow." William

McLure was genuinely concerned about his wife and children, but he seemed incapable of imagining that his wife could run the plantation unassisted. He promised to return to Oakwood at the first opportunity to straighten everything out, but he was able to come home only three times during the entire war—once in 1862 and twice in 1863. During his brief visits home he was preoccupied and did not seem to perceive how life on the plantation was being transformed.

At the end of 1862, William McLure fired Holmes, but he followed traditional lines of authority to do it. He told his brother-in-law Reidy, not his wife, that he decided to fire Holmes, and he asked Reidy, not his wife, to carry it out. Perhaps his method reflected the fact that Holmes would accept only these lines of authority, as William's mother implied that Holmes would not leave if Kate McLure alone tried to fire him. As a consequence, the other actors in the triangle, the slave Jeff and the mistress McLure, expanded their responsibilities. Jeff was now entirely in charge of the food crops and the livestock, and his mistress sent him out alone on errands across the countryside. Kate McLure set up a small, experimental salt works on the plantation to maintain her own salt supply. Her husband nonetheless directed her to ask her in-laws, Thomas Dawkins and John Reidy, for advice in order to relieve her of all "care and annoyance" regarding the plantation. He was glad to be able to "leave you in the care of such kind friends."

These impractical, not to say preposterous, suggestions reveal how badly William McLure misread the situation at home, or, perhaps, how much he wanted to have a white man in charge. Thomas Dawkins was a drunkard, and John Reidy resided in another county over twenty miles away, scarcely within handy reach of Oakwood plantation for daily consultation. By early January 1863, it was clear that Kate McLure did not want to ask either one of them for advice, especially Reidy. Her husband had given him "carte blanche," asking only that he "consult" Kate McLure, but Reidy irritated her by neglecting even to discuss arrangements with her. Elijah Dawkins, a wealthy bachelor, often forgot his earlier promise to send over food for Kate McLure and her four small children. But William still could not imagine his wife running the plantation alone, so in early 1863 another overseer arrived at Oakwood, a man named Mabery, hired by Thomas Dawkins. The overseer's first name does not appear in the correspondence, but his motives for taking the job were crystal-clear: he very much wanted to avoid service in the Confederate Army.

Another power triangle of mistress, overseer, and slave was set up on the plantation. This time, however, the mistress McLure and the slave Jeff had had two years of experience behind them, while the newcomer had taken the job as a last resort. His work was unsatisfactory almost from the beginning. By March 1863, William McLure was exhorting his wife to get Mabery to *"take care"* and "use every exertion to make enough [food] to live on," and he wanted frequent reports from her about Mabery's behavior. Kate McLure also became displeased with the overseer. That spring she returned from visiting her mother-in-law to say that "I find everything needing my attention here" and that the crop was "very much behind hand." Her responsibilities continued to increase: she began to work in the garden herself, and when two of the McLure slaves fell ill with pneumonia, she nursed them under the supervision of a local doctor (not Doctor Reidy). Her relationship with Mabery came to resemble her relationship with Holmes, but this one soured at an accelerated pace, quickened no doubt by her growing confidence in her own abilities and her personal dislike for Mabery. By the fall of 1863, mistress and overseer were on such bad terms that she communicated with him only in writing, leaving notes for him indicating her orders. Perhaps in retaliation, Mabery neglected to reply to William McLure's requests for information about the plantation. As the winter closed in, many of the slaves had inadequate clothing and shoes. Things were not working out.

Kate McLure wanted and expected Mabery to be fired at the end of 1863, and when her husband told her brother-in-law Dawkins to renew Mabery's contract anyway, she exploded in anger. The overseer did not carry out her instructions, she wrote to William, and she said it was "useless" to try to work with him. She reminded her husband that Mabery was a "low" and "profligate" man, the sort he should be protecting her from, not forcing her to work with, but, she observed with cutting sarcasm, "I suppose he suits you." Thomas Dawkins was unavailable to help her because he had suffered a bad fall and could not walk unassisted. The slave Jeff, she pointed out, gave her accurate information about the health of the other slaves. The implication was clear: Jeff alone could be relied on. Although it was in her interest to develop a good working relationship with Jeff, if only to keep the plantation operating, evidence of this kind of relationship between mistress and slave is rare. By the end of January 1864, she had deputized him to help her run the plantation so that "I am quite independent of Mabery." She announced that matters would run smoothly "if I can have Jeff when I want him." As if to underscore the point, she permitted Jeff to enter her house but not Mabery. By the spring of 1864, her husband began to agree with his wife on some points, at least in his letters; when a fence needed to be repaired he decided to "leave the matter to your judgment." Later that year, she decided to begin dyeing cloth herself, another task she had never done before. But, as she pointedly reminded her husband, "I am learning a good many things since the War broke out."

William McLure, however, had had a much less dramatic experience since the war began. He lived a comparatively tranquil life, one of the safest available to a soldier in uniform, and his duties as quartermaster were arguably less demanding than the responsibilities devolving on his wife at home. Yet he proved to have little imagination, and he could not seem to comprehend the new kinds of relationships developing on his plantation. Perhaps his seclusion in a virtually all-male community like the Confederate Army, in which a few elite white men still commanded everyone else, made it difficult for him to imagine anyone else exercising power. He still believed that only a white man could be in charge, as his surreptitious correspondence with one of his brothers-in-law in the summer of 1864 demonstrates. Unbeknownst to his wife, he wrote to John Reidy and asked him to help her run Oakwood, and if he could not, he asked James Dawkins, Thomas's unsavory younger brother, to do it. Any white man would do, it seems. . . .

In December 1864, the tension between Kate McLure, Mabery, and the McLure slaves reached its peak. She first reported a "disturbance" among the slaves regarding Mabery and a slave woman named Susan. She did not give the details, but it seems that the two had become involved in a sexual relationship. Mabery refused to explain the situation to Kate McLure, and she was not completely sure at first that the story was true, but she was inclined to believe the slaves, especially Susan's brothers and sisters who came to her about the matter. Mabery realized that he might lose his job at last, and he hoped that the master would come home for Christmas so he could make a last-ditch appeal to protest his innocence. (William McLure did not come home for Christmas.) Then one night in early December Kate McLure was awakened by the screams of a slave named Dane, Susan's husband. He had been the first to reveal the scandal, and now, in a moment of fury, Mabery "fell on him" and started whipping him. Dane broke away and ran toward the McLure's house, pursued by the overseer. When he found it locked up, he called out Kate McLure's name "like some one being murdered." In his terror, he broke a pane of glass in the door, and when she appeared and saw the two men through the jagged window, she immediately understood what had happened.

This was a turning point in the "civil war" on Oakwood plantation. Dane's appeal to his mistress suggests that he realized who had the power on the plantation; Mabery's resort to beating a slave in the middle of the night also indicates how much his authority had diminished. Furthermore, Kate McLure had made it clear that she took sides with the slaves against her overseer. Sometime in January 1865, Mabery disappeared. Thomas Dawkins, incredibly, wanted him to stay on as the McLure's overseer; it is not clear if Mabery quit or was fired, or if he was fired, who let him go. But Kate McLure ran the plantation with the assistance of Jeff for what remained of the war. Another white man, a disabled Confederate veteran, approached her several times about the job, but she would not hire him. In her letters she never discussed race, slavery, or emancipation, but on her own plantation she had broken the ranks of racial solidarity and allied herself with her slaves against her white overseers, her white male relatives, and, when necessary, against her husband.

To the very end of the war, however, William McLure proved unable to relate to his wife as a person who was in charge of a working plantation and several dozen slaves. He did not write about Susan, Dane's beating, or Mabery's behavior, but he sent his wife a patronizing letter in January 1865 about a horseback ride of several dozen miles she had taken alone to carry one of her daughters to visit her sister. He exclaimed that it was "quite a ride" for her and that she was returning to the vigorous "days of your girlhood." This was hardly an impressive feat, especially in light of the other problems with which she had dealt recently. And Kate McLure was no longer a girl; she was a mature and capable thirty-six-year-old. But her husband may have wished to see her as the passive young woman he had married in 1852, or the dependent wife he had left in 1861. The war had wrought substantial changes in Kate McLure's vision of herself but not in William McLure's perception of their roles.

How did the war change the marriage roles of the McLures? What was the greatest difficulty McLure faced in running the plantation?

INTO THE VORTEX

The Civil War is one of the best-documented periods in American history, and scholars are only beginning to delve into the rich manuscript sources on women. The documents presented here convey something of the vast scale of the conflict and its capacity to uproot millions of people's lives. They outline the multifarious, complex ways that women could experience the war, depending upon race, regional background, and the vagaries of individual personalities. They highlight as well the special circumstances of black women, who had to overcome the greatest obstacles to secure their dignity and reunite their relatives. Finally, these readings suggest that the war taught some whites new, more egalitarian ways of thinking about race, while others learned nothing, boding ill for race relations in the years to come.

A Secessionist in Carolina

Mary Boykin Chesnut, born in South Carolina in 1823, is one of the best-known diarists of the Civil War era and of the entire nineteenth century. A talented writer, Chesnut evokes the feverish excitement among secessionists as the Confederacy was organized in the winter of 1860-61. Despite the qualms about slavery she expressed occasionally in her diary, she stuck with the Confederate cause until the bitter end. Excerpted from Mary Chesnut's Civil War, *ed. C. Vann Woodward (New Haven, 1981), 3–4.*

February 18, 1861. . . . This Southern Confederacy must be supported now by calm determination and cool brains. We have risked all, and we must play our best, for the stake is life or death. I shall always regret that I had not kept a journal during the two past delightful and eventful years. The delights having exhausted themselves in the latter part of 1860 and the events crowding in so that it takes away one's breath to think about it all. I daresay I might have recorded with some distinctness the daily shocks— "Earthquakes as usual". . . . But now it is to me one nightmare from the time I left Charleston for Florida, where I remained two anxious weeks amid hammocks and everglades, oppressed and miserable, and heard on the [train] cars returning to the world that Lincoln was elected and our fate sealed. Saw at Fernandina a few men running up a wan Palmetto flag and crying, South Carolina has seceded. Overjoyed at the tribute to South Carolina, I said, "So Florida sympathizes." I inquired the names of our *few* but undismayed supporters in Florida. Heard Gadsden, Holmes, Porcher, &c&c—names as inevitably South Carolina's as Moses or Lazarus are Jews'. When we arrived in Charleston, my room was immediately over a supper given by the city to a delegation from Savannah, and Colonel Bartow, the mayor of Savannah, was speaking in the hot, fervid, after-supper Southern style. They contrived to speak all night and to cheer &c. I remember liking one speech so much—*voice*, tone, temper, sentiments, and all. I sent to ask the name of the orator, and the answer came: "Mr. Alfred Huger." He may not have been the wisest or wittiest man there—but certainly when on his legs he had the best of it that night. After such a night of impassioned Southern eloquence I traveled next day with (in the first place, a racking nervous headache and a morphine bottle, and also) Colonel Colcock, formerly member of Congress, and U.S. Judge Magrath, of whom likenesses were suspended, in the frightfullest signpost style of painting, across various thoroughfares in Charleston. The happy moment seized by the painter to depict him, while Magrath was in the act, most dramatically, of tearing off his robes of office in rage and disgust at Lincoln's election.

My father was a South Carolina nullifier, governor of the state at the time of the nullification row, and then U.S. senator. So I was of necessity a rebel born. My husband's family being equally pledged to the Union party rather exasperated my zeal, as I heard taunts and sneers so constantly thrown out against the faith I had imbibed before I understood anything at all about it. If I do yet.

I remember feeling a nervous dread and horror of this break with so great a power as U.S.A., but I was ready and willing. South Carolina had been so rampant for years. She was the torment of herself and everybody else. Nobody could live in this state unless he were a fire-eater [a dedicated secessionist]. Come what would, I wanted them to fight and stop talking. South Carolina—Bluffton, Rhetts, &c had exasperated and heated themselves into a fever that only bloodletting could ever cure—it was the inevitable remedy.

If Mary Chesnut was ambivalent about slavery, why did she stay so firmly with the Southern cause?

African American Women in the South

Of all of the women whose destinies were shaped by the war, black women's lives were transformed most completely, and those of slave women most of all, as they finally came to enjoy the blessings of freedom. Before slavery ended, however, these women had to contend with new heartbreaks, as their owners mistreated them and their families broke up, and fresh disappointments, as white Northerners proved to be unreliable allies. Yet black women continued to strive for freedom, some of them, such as Emma Bynum, traveling vast distances to reach Union lines. Harriet Tubman, probably the best-known black woman in America, served the cause as a nurse, cook, and scout, which she recalled with typical understatement years later. The following excerpts are taken from Dear Ones at Home: Letters from Contraband Camps, *ed. Henry L. Swint (Nashville, 1966), 252, 59–60, 132, 251;* The American Slave: A Composite Autobiography, *ed. George P. Rawick (Westport, Connecticut, 1972), 7:92, 95, 3:257–58; Adele Logan Alexander,* Ambiguous Lives: Free Women of Color in Rural Georgia, *1789–1879 (Little Rock, 1991), 134–35; and Gerda Lerner,* Black Women in White America: A Documentary History *(New York, 1972), 327–28.*

Charlotte Ann Jackson

When i was liveing whith White People i was tide down hand and foot and they tide me to the Post and whip me till i Could not stand up and they tide my Close over my head and whip me much as they want and they took my Brother and sent him to Richmond to stay one year And sent my Aunt my Sister my farther away too and said if he did not go away they would kill him they said they was Goin to Put me in Prisens But the light has come the Rebles is put down and Slavry is dead God Bless the union Forever more and they was puting people in tubs and they stead me to Death and i hope slavly shall be no more and they said that the yankees had horns and said that the yankees was Goin to kill us and somthing told me not to Believe them and somthing told me not to Be afraid and when they Come hare they would not let me Come out to see them and when i was out in the Street they was Stead i would go away from them and they said I Better stay whith them for the yankees would kill me I would Better stay

Lucy Chase

[1 April 1863, Craney's Island, near Norfolk]

Heart-broken too, some of them are! Husbands are with the army, they know not where. They are alone, with no one to comfort them. "All my children have died, since I came into the army," I hear lonely mothers say, every day. A good old, mother-soul came out into the darkness last evening, (while I stood waiting for Mr King to open the school-room for me) and said "Is that Miss Lucy? Wont you come in, and sit by the fire?" And she ushered me in right sweetly. Gave me a warm seat, stooped to the stature of her broom, fresh from the green-pine tree, made her hearth clean and attractive, lighted a new pine-knot, and held it, more gracefully than hand of stone can do. And told me of her husband with the rebels—her only remaining child of nine sold, she feared, "down South. My last child died two weeks ago. She was so high and she was amazing helpful. She could sew and knit. She could spin and weave, and mind the chickens, and tend the

343

children. Oh I should go wild, if I had not any children to look upon." A feeble cry from the bunk and she rose, and took in her arms a young infant, a motherless child, her charge. "My desire is mighty to hear from my husband," she said. Sad faces were around her, and each had her sad story to tell.

Sarah E. Chase to Fred May

[18 November 1864, Norfolk, Virginia]
A good man and his wife came in one day bringing a sweet faced granny with them—all enthusiastic, and eager for work, & full of cheer though the clothes they had on their back [and] in their hands were all they had in the World to start with. "Have you any children?"—said I to the old woman—"No honey—no I hasn't—and yet missus I has; fourteen children I'se raised and hugged in dese old arms; and sometimes I tinks I feels de little hands on my cheeks—but deys all gone;—I don't know whar dey air—and if I was lyn stark dead out yonder in de corner, dere wouldnt be one to bring me a cup of water."

Eliza Evans

[McAlester, Oklahoma]
One time some Yankee soldiers stopped and started talking to me—they asked me what my name was. "I say Liza, and they say, "Liza who?" I thought a minute and I shook my head, "Jest Liza, I ain't got no other name."

He say, "Who live up yonder in dat Big House?" I say, "Mr. John Nixon." He say, "You are Liza Nixon." He say, "Do anybody

Excerpt from *Dear Ones at Home: Letters from Contraband Camps*, Henry L. Swint, editor. Published by Vanderbilt University Press, 1966.

Excerpt from *The American Slave: A Composite Autobiography*, Vol. 7, George P. Rawick, editor. Published by Greenwood Publishing Co., 1973. Contribution of *Afro-American and African Studies*, No. 11, Vol. 7. Oklahoma and Mississippi narratives first published 1941.

Excerpt from *Black Women in White America: A Documentary History*, Gerda Lerner, editor. Published by Pantheon Books, 1972. Previously printed in Charles P. Wood Bill H.R. 4982, Papers of the House of Representatives 55th Congress, National Archives.

ever call you nigger?" And I say, "Yes Sir." He say, "Next time anybody call you nigger you tell 'em dat you is a Negro and your name is Miss Liza Nixon." The more I thought of that the more I liked it and I made up my mind to do jest what he told me to.

My job was minding the calves back while the cows was being milked. One evening I was minding the calves and old Master come along. He say, "What you doin' nigger?" I say real pert like, "I ain't no nigger, I'se a Negro and I'm Miss Liza Nixon." Old Master sho' was surprised and he picks up a switch and starts at me.

Mary Woodward

[Winnsboro, South Carolina]

"When de Yankees come, I was a settin' in de swing in de front yard. They ride right up and say: 'Where your mistress?' I say: 'I don't know.' They say: 'You is lyin'. Give her a few lashes and us'll find out.' Another say: 'No, us come to free niggers, not to whip them.' Then they ask me for to tell them where de best things was hid. I say: 'I don't know sir.' Then they ransack de house, bust open de smoke house, take de meat, hams, shoulders, 'lasses barrel, sugar, and meal, put them in a four-horse wagon, set de house, gin-house and barn afire and go on toward Rocky Mount.

Emma Bynum (Bryum)

I left North Carolina august be fore last and I had god by my side and he helped me a long. I traveled 65 miles and we had 52 in our number. before we crost the river we could whear the pickets soods [swords] strike the stirrup and we taught we wold be taken eny moment the babys cried and we could whear the sound of them on the wanter we lay all night in the woods and the next day we trabeled and we reached Suffolk that night and we lost twenty one of the Number

Excerpt from *Ambiguous Lives: Free Women of Color in Rural Georgia, 1789–1879*, by Adele Logan Alexander. Copyright © 1991 by Adele Logan Alexander. Reprinted by permission of University of Arkansas Press.

Excerpted from Alexander, *Ambiguous Lives*

One soldier watched awestruck as hundreds of African-Americans streamed out "from abandoned plantations or miserable hiding places, to join in the march with the Yankees." Throughout Middle Georgia black people wanted to follow along with the liberating armies, one Milledgeville woman vowing that "I walks till I drop in my tracks." The soldiers tried to turn them away, but the blacks formed wretched refugee caravans that trailed in the wake of the Union troops. Scrawny mules pulled wagons filled with meager belongings, and women trudged alongside leaning heavily on sturdy walking staffs, with large bundles of clothing balanced on their heads and small children clinging to their legs. Other more exuberant blacks "waved to the regiments as they marched by and called them 'de Lawd's deliverin' army.'" A group of youngsters in Baldwin County piled into a "big wagon" on their plantation and went down to see the Yankees marching by. "We did see 'bout 5,000 soldiers," one remembered from when she was only a girl of eight, "dey was tryin' to git back home . . . I had alluz been skeered o' soldiers, but after I seen dem I warn't skeered no mo'." Another local woman embraced one Yankee officer and greeted his men crying, "Bress de Lord! Tanks be to Almighty God, the Yanks is come! de day ob jubilee has arribed!"

Harriet Tubman's Petition, 1898

I am about 75 years of age. I was born and reared in Dorchester County, Md. My maiden name was Araminta Ross. [S]ometime prior to the late War of the Rebellion I married John Tubman who died in the State of Maryland on the 30th day of September, 1867. I married Nelson Davis, a soldier of the late war, on the 18th day of March, 1869, at Auburn, N.Y.

I furnished the original papers in my claim to one Charles P. Wood, then of Auburn, N.Y., who died several years ago. Said Wood made copies of said original papers which are hereunto annexed. I was informed by said Wood that he sent said original papers to one James Barrett, an attorney on 4 1/2 Street, Washington, D.C., and I was told by the wife of said Barrett that she handed the original papers to the Hon. C. D. MacDougall, then a member of the House of Representatives.

My claim against the U.S. is for three years' service as nurse and cook in hospitals, and as commander of Several men (eight or nine) as scouts during the late war of the Rebellion, under directions and orders of Edwin M. Stanton, Secretary of War, and of several Generals.

I claim for my services above named the sum of Eighteen hundred dollars. The annexed copies have recently been read over to me and are true to the best of my knowledge information and belief.

I further declare that I have interest in said case and am concerned in it's prosecution and allowance.

[Harriet Tubman Davis]

What impact did the war have on black women and their families?

Hard Lessons

Kate Stone's ancestors had owned slaves in the South for six generations, and when the war began, she was twenty years old. After her male relatives left for service in the Confederate Army, she had to work with slaves on her family's plantation for the first time. Her diary charts her increasing awareness of the humanity of slaves, especially slave women, and years later she remembered her growing horror of slavery and the burdens it imposed on black people. See Brokenburn: The Journal of Kate Stone, 1861–1868, *ed. John Q. Anderson (Baton Rouge, 1955), 7–8.*

[T]o toil six days out of seven, week after week, month after month, year after year, as long as life lasted; to be absolutely under the control of someone until the last breath was drawn; to win but the bare necessaries of life, no hope of more, no matter how hard the work, how long the toil; and to know that nothing could change your lot. Obedience, revolt, submission, prayers—all were in vain. Waking sometimes in the night as I grew older and thinking it all over, I would grow sick with the misery of it all.

Why did Kate change in her views of slavery?

White Women in the North

This song celebrates the contributions of Northern women to the Union effort. Women organized some ten thousand relief societies during the war—which were called "fraternal" societies—and, as the lyrics show, they engaged in many activities to care for soldiers and the survivors of the dead. The Grand Army Songster and Service Book, *comp. J. H. Foxworthy (1897), 63.*

Relief Song
Dedicated to the Fraternal Ladies.
J.H. Foxworthy. Arr. by J. H. F.

I saw a way-worn soldier,
In tattered garments clad,
His load of grief was heavy,
His strength was almost gone.
And struggling on his journey
He seemed so very sad.
But he met the Corps fraternal,
Relief to him had come.
Then sing their praises—
Cheer them onward—
Crowns of victory they shall wear.
A ladies band fraternal brings joy to earthly homes.
Ten thousand voices shouting,
Relief to them has come.
I saw a vet'ran's widow,
The sweat was on her brow,
But she kept pressing onward,
To reach her humble home.
Her garments worn and dusty,
Her feeble step was slow.
She had met the Corps fraternal,
Relief to her had come.
Then sing their praises—
Cheer them onward—
Crowns of victory they shall wear.
A ladies band fraternal brings joy to earthly homes

Ten thousand voices shouting,
Relief to them has come.
I saw the barefoot children,
They suffered grief and woe,
Their soldier Pa is yonder
Where angel's trumpet blow.
Fair ladies found them starving,
They'd lost their earthly home;
They shouted loud hozannas,
Relief to them had come.
Then sing their praises—
Cheer them onward—
Crowns of victory they shall wear.
A ladies band fraternal brings joy to earthly homes.
Ten thousand voices shouting,
Relief to them has come.
I saw a veteran dying,
Forsaken, sad and lone;
His prayer reached heaven eternal
For help that soon did come.
Fair, soft hands smoothed his pillow,
They cheered his lonely home,
The band fraternal saved him,
Relief to him had come.
Then sing their praises—
Cheer them onward—
Crowns of victory they shall wear.
A ladies band fraternal brings joy to earthly homes.
Ten thousand voices shouting,
Relief to them has come.

What were the roles of fraternal organizations in the North? How did the war experience differ for women in the North and the South? Why?

Reconstruction,
1865–1877

INTRODUCTION

Throughout the Civil War era the legal status of African Americans was, at best, ambiguous. In 1850, the Supreme Court, in Dred Scott v. Sandford, held that African Americans were not citizens of the United States. While this may have had little impact on the average slave, it stripped free blacks of all rights and protections due citizens of the federal government. At the same time, nearly all states deprived free blacks of some of the basic rights of state citizenship. In 1865, the northern victory opened the way for passage of the Thirteenth Amendment, which abolished slavery and freed over four million slaves. During the postwar reconstruction, Americans agonized over the problem of defining the rights of America's blacks.

President Andrew Johnson's plan of reconstruction reestablished Southern state governments that later passed "Black Codes." Often modeled after earlier slave codes, these restrictive black codes attempted to reestablish a familiar sense of order within Southern society by keeping blacks subservient to white economic, political, and social interests. The Republican majority in Congress, responding to black protests and afraid of a resurgence of the prewar Southern planter aristocracy, passed the Fourteenth and Fifteenth Amendments, in addition to the Civil Rights Act of 1866.

Since the early days of the Republic, political controversy divided the nation along sectional lines, both east/west and north/ south. The flood of new federal legislation during the Reconstruction era continued the debate over the boundaries between the federal government and the states. In the process of implementing reconstruction programs, power struggles between the legislative and executive branches culminated in an impeachment indictment against President Johnson. As political infighting became more and more enmeshed with the continuing struggle to secure black rights, many Americans tired of the seemingly insolvable problem. The First Reconstruction era died, mourned only by disenchanted African Americans. In 1896, the Supreme Court, in Plessy v. Ferguson, *held that the Fourteenth Amendment permitted state-enforced segregation, fostering a new era of "Jim Crow"—the forced separation of the races and the subordination of the black race to the white. Thus, the nineteenth century closed, leaving the task of securing basic rights for all Americans to future generations.*

The Black Codes

President Andrew Johnson's plan of reconstruction re-instituted Southern state governments. Due to Johnson's lenient policy of pardoning former Confederates, the white dominated state legislatures soon passed laws limiting the rights of the newly-freed people. These laws, known as Black Codes, were so severely restrictive that northern reaction caused some states to modify them. Taken from The Political History of the United States of America During the Period of Reconstruction . . ., *ed. Edward McPherson (New York, 1969) 31–32, 29, 33–36.*

Mississippi

An Act to confer Civil Rights on Freedmen, and for other Purposes, November 25, 1865.

. . . [A]ll freedmen, free negroes and mulattoes, who do now and have heretofore lived and cohabited together as husband and wife shall be taken and held in law as legally married, and the issue shall be taken and held as legitimate for all purposes. That it shall not be lawful for any freedman, free negro or mulatto to intermarry with any white person; nor for any white person to intermarry with any freedman, free negro or mulatto; and any person who shall so intermarry shall be deemed guilty of felony, and on conviction thereof, shall be confined in the State penitiary for life. . . .

[A]ll contracts for labor made with freedmen, free negroes, and mulattoes, for a longer period than one month, shall be in writing and in duplicate, attested and read to said freedman, free

Excerpts from *The Political History of the United States of America During the Period of Reconstruction, from April 15, 1865 to July 15, 1870,* Edward McPherson, LL.D., ed., published by Solomons & Chapman, 1875. Reprinted 1969 by Negro Universities Press, a division of Greenwood Publishing Corp.

negro, or mulatto by a beat, city, or county officer or two disinterested white persons of the county in which the labor is to be performed . . . and if the laborer shall quit the service of the employer before the expiration of his term of service without good cause, he shall forfeit his wages for that year up to the time of quitting.

. . . That all the penal and criminal laws now in force in this State, defining offences, and prescribing the mode of punishment for crimes and misdemeanors committed by slaves, free negroes or mulattoes, be and the same are hereby re-enacted, and declared to be in full force and effect, against freedmen, free negroes, and mulattoes, except so far as the mode and manner of trial and punishment have been changed or altered by law.

North Carolina

1866, March 10—The act "concerning negroes, and persons of color, or of mixed blood," passed by the Legislature, declares that "negroes and their issue, even where one ancestor in each succeeding generation to the fourth inclusive, is white, shall be deemed persons of color." It gives them all the privileges of white persons before the courts . . . in "all controversies at law and in equity where the rights of persons or property of persons of color shall be put in issue. . . . ["]

The criminal laws of the State are extended in their operation to embrace persons of color, and the same punishment is inflicted on them as on the whites, except for rape, which, if a white female is the victim, is a capital crime for a black.

Georgia

[1866,] March 12

. . . All persons wandering or strolling about in idleness, who are able to work, and who have no property to support them; all persons leading an idle, immoral, or profligate life, . . . all persons able to work having no visible and known means of a fair, honest, and reputable livelihood . . . shall be deemed and considered vagrants, and shall be indicted as such, . . . and upon conviction, they shall be fined and imprisoned or sentenced to work on the public works, for not longer than a year, or shall, in the discretion of the court, be bound out to some person for a time not longer than one year. . . .

That persons of color shall have the right to make and enforce contracts, to sue, be sued, to be parties and give evidence, to inherit, to purchase, lease, sell, hold, and convey real and personal property, and to have full and equal benefit of all laws and proceedings for the security of person and estate, and shall not be subjected to any other or different punishment, pain or penalty, for the commission of any act or offense, than such as are prescribed for white persons committing like acts or offenses.

Alabama

1866, February 16

. . . Whipping and branding are abolished, as legal punishments, and a new punishment is introduced, entitled "hard labor for the county."

South Carolina

An Act to Amend the Criminal Law, December 19, 1865

. . . [N]o person of color shall migrate into and reside in this State, unless, within twenty days after his arrival within the same, he shall enter into a bond, with two freeholders as sureties, to be approved by the judge of the district court or a magistrate, in a penalty of one thousand dollars, conditioned for his good behavior, and for his support, if he should become unable to support himself.

An Act to establish District Courts, December 19, 1865

. . . Colored children between 18 and 21, who have neither father nor mother *living in the district in which they are found,* or whose parents are paupers, or unable to afford them a comfortable maintenance, *or whose parents are not teaching them habits of industry and honesty,* or are persons of notoriously bad character, or are vagrants, or have been convicted of infamous offences, and colored children, *in all cases where they are in danger of moral contamination,* may be bound as apprentices by the district judge or one of the magistrates. . . .

When were Black Code provisions finally removed from the books? Does our legal system now demonstrate color blind justice?

Frederick Douglass Advocates Black Suffrage

Joined by radical Republicans, African American leaders, prior to the Civil War, demanded that suffrage be extended to blacks. Renowned black abolitionist, Frederick Douglass, endeavored to explain to the annual meeting of the Massachusetts Anti-Slavery Society "What the Black Man Wants." The agenda specified by Douglass in this 1865 speech was partially fulfilled by the Fifteenth Amendment, ratified in 1870, which eliminated race, creed, or previous condition of servitude as criteria for voting rights. Excerpted from The Frederick Douglass Papers, Series One: Speeches, Debates, and Interviews, *vol. 4: 1864–80, ed. John W. Blassingame and John R. McKivigan (New Haven, Connecticut, 1991), 62–64, 66–68.*

I have had but one idea for the last three years to present to the American people. . . . I am for the "immediate, unconditional and universal" enfranchisement of the black man, in every State of the Union. (Loud applause.) Without this, his liberty is a mockery; without this, you might as well almost retain the old name of slavery for his condition; for, in fact, if he is not the slave of the individual master, he is the slave of society, and holds his liberty as a privilege, not as a right. . . .

Some men have got along very well without it [enfranchisement]. Women have not this right. . . . Shall we justify one wrong by another? . . . But that question rests upon another basis than that on which our right rests. . . . We want it because it is our *right*, first of all. (Applause.) . . . We want it, again, as a means for educating our race. Men are so constituted that they derive their conviction of their own possibilities largely from the estimate formed of them by others. If nothing is expected of a people, that people will find it difficult to contradict that expectation. By depriving us of suffrage, you affirm our incapacity to form an intelligent judgment respecting public men and public measures; you declare before the world that we are unfit to exercise the elective franchise, and by this means lead us to undervalue ourselves, to put a low estimate upon ourselves, and to feel that we have no possibilities like other men. . . . [H]ere, where universal suffrage is the rule, where that is the fundamental idea of the government, to rule us out is to make us an exception, to brand us with the stigma of inferiority, and to invite to our heads the missiles of those about us. Therefore I want the franchise for the black man.

There are, however, other reasons. . . . [When those] who are leading in this rebellion shall have been blotted out, there will be this rank undergrowth of treason, . . . interfering with and thwarting the quiet operation of the Federal Government in those States. You will see those traitors handing down from sire to son the same malignant spirit which they have manifested and which they are now exhibiting, with malicious hearts, broad blades and bloody hands in the field, against our sons and brothers. . . . That enmity will not die out in a year, will not die out in an age. . . . They will endeavor to circumvent, they will endeavor to destroy the peaceful operation of this government. Now, where will you find the strength to counterbalance this spirit, if you do not find it in the negroes of the South! They are your friends, and have always been your friends. They were your friends even when the Government did not regard them as such. They comprehended the genius of this war before you did. It is a significant fact, it is a marvellous fact, it seems almost to imply a direct interposition of Providence, that this war, which began in the interest of slavery on both sides, bids fair to end in the interests of liberty on both sides. (Applause.) It was begun, I say, in the interest of slavery, on both sides. The South was fighting to take slavery out of the Union and the North fighting to keep it in the Union; the South fighting to get it beyond the limits of the United States Constitution, and the North fighting to retain it within those limits, the South fighting for new guarantees and the North fighting for the old guarantees;—both despising the negro, both insulting the negro. . . .

It is said that we are ignorant; I admit it. But if we know enough to be hung, we know enough to vote. If the negro knows enough to pay taxes to support the Government, he knows enough to vote—taxation and representation should go together. If he knows enough to shoulder a musket and fight for the flag, fight for the Government, he knows enough to vote. If he knows as much when he is sober as an Irishman knows when drunk, he knows enough to vote, on good American principles. (Laughter and applause.)

. . . You have called upon us to turn our backs upon our masters, to abandon their cause and espouse yours; to turn against the South and in favor of the North; to shoot down the Confederacy and uphold the flag—the American flag. . . . And now, what do you propose to do when you come to make peace? To reward your enemies, and trample in the dust your friends? . . . Do you mean to give your enemies the right to vote, and take it away from your friends? . . . When this nation was in trouble, in its early struggles, it looked upon the negro as a citizen. In 1776, he was a citizen. At the time of the formation of the Constitution, the negro had the right to vote in eleven States out of the old thirteen. In your trouble you have made us citizens. In 1812, Gen. Jackson addressed us as citizens, "fellow citizens." He wanted us to fight. We were citizens then! And now, when you come to frame a conscription bill, the negro is a citizen again. He has been a citizen just three times in the history of this government, and it has always been in time of trouble. In time of trouble we are citizens. Shall we be citizens in war, and aliens in peace? Would that be just?

. . . What I ask for the negro is not benevolence, not pity, not sympathy, but simply *justice*.

What is the effect of not having the vote? Ex-Confederates were regaining the right to vote. Why was this especially galling for many ex-slaves?

White Alabamians Respond to Black Suffrage

Agitated by feelings of loss of societal control during the reconstruction era, a number of white Alabamians sent the following petition to Congress. Like Frederick Douglass, these whites called upon the memory of the Founding Fathers, but these petitioners did so to urge protection from the feared consequences of the black vote—black dominion over whites. Selected from the Petition and Memorial File, Records of the House of Representatives, 40th Congress, Record Group 233, National Archives, Washington, D.C.

To The Honorable the Senate and House of Representatives of The United States in Congress assembled;

The White people of Alabama send this their humble petition.

We beseech your Honorable Bodies to withdraw yourselves from the influence of the passions and contests of the hour, and contemplate for a brief period, our miserable condition. . . .

According to the last census taken by the Federal Government, the white peoples of Alabama outnumber the negro or colored population more than eighty-eight thousand persons. . . . [N]early all of the education, intelligence and civilization of the State is to be found in our race. But poverty prevails throughout the land: We are beset by secret oath bound political societies; our character and conduct are systematically misrepresented and maligned to you, and in the newspapers of the North: the intelligent and impartial administration of just laws, is obstructed: property has become almost valueless: industry and enterprise are paralyzed, by the fears of the white men and the expectations of the black, that Alabama will soon be delivered over to the rule of the latter: And many of our best citizens are for these reasons leaving the homes they love for other and strange lands!

Before the late unhappy war, the white people of the South contributed their whole just proportion of the great and good men whose acts and characters constituted the chief renown of the Republic. Those of us who endeavored to withdraw the South from her partnership therein, did not do so in order to make war on the Northern States or their institutions, —but for the purpose (vain hope!) of establishing peacefully another and not unfriendly independent Confederacy, in which under almost identical constitutions, we might be more free from discord. And, however, criminal we may in your opinion, we may in this, have been, yet neither our sins nor our sufferings have reduced us to uncivilized barbarians.

On the other hand it is well known by all who have knowledge on the subject, —that while the negroes of the South may be more intelligent and of better morals than those of the same race in any other part of the world where they exist in equal density, — yet they are in the main, ignorant generally, wholly unacquainted with the principles of free Governments, improvident, disinclined to work, credulous yet suspicious, dishonest, untruthful, incapable of self-restraint, and easily impelled by want or incited by false and specious counsels, into folly and crime. Exceptions, of course, there are; chiefly among those who have been reared as servants in our domestic circles, and in our cities. But the general character of our colored population is such as we have described. . . .

Are these the people in whom should be vested the high governmental functions of establishing institutions and enacting and enforcing laws, to prevent crime, protect property, preserve peace and order in society, and promote industry, enterprise and civilization in Alabama, and the power and honor of the United States? Without property, without industry, without any regard for reputation, without controul over their own caprices and strong passions, and without fear of punishment under laws . . . — how can it be otherwise than that they will bring, to the great injury of themselves as well as of us and our children, —blight, crime, ruin and barbarism on this fair land?

. . . Of the negro population, whose numbers are many thousands less, the registered voters are over seventeen thousand more than those of the white race. And white men who hate us, and others, co from sordid motives, co-operating with them, —by their own procurement, or the procurement of others, and not by the intelligent choice of the negro voters, —have been elected as their delegates, and have framed and now presented to those registered voters for ratification, a Constitution; the best clauses of which are contained in the present one and in all other instruments of the same kind. But these are rendered delusive and useless by the diabolical ingenuity of other provisions, contrived to disfranchise us even beyond the enactments of Congress, and to insure over us and our children and all who shall come among us, the ascendancy of the negro race. And those same malignant and designing enemies stand prepared, so soon as their Constitution shall be ratified and accepted, —to organize, arm, and invest with power, under the forms of law, a militia to be composed chiefly of these same negro voters, —in order to perpetuate their lordship over us, with the aid of bullets and bayonets. We cannot believe that your Honor the majorities of your Honorable Bodies intended by your enactments to effect such a reconstruction as this.

Will you, nearly three years after the war has ended, . . . suffer a whole State full of your kindred civilized white inhabitants, not only those who had opposed the Government, but women, children, and loyal men who had adhered to it, —to be thus consigned over to the horrid rule of barbarian negroes!

Do not compel the honorable officers and brave men of the armies of the Republic, to hold us down, while such fetters are forged in our view and yours, and then ignominiously fastened upon us. We are compatriots of Washington, and Henry and Jefferson and Madison and Marshall and the Pinckneys and Marion and Jackson and Clay and Taylor. Are there no names among these potent enough to arouse any respect for us, in your legislative halls?

It is said, —and by frequent repetition you are made to believe it true, —that the negroes and self-styled loyalists, cannot have justice and are unsafe among us, —and that we are still in a state of rebellion. The charges are false. . . . [T]oward the negroes, (who aided the South as cheerfully while within the Confederate lines as they afterwards aided the northern armies when and where they had power,) we have been both from inclination and interest, humane and kind. . . .

When our people surrendered our their arms, they did so absolutely and without any purpose of ever again employing them against the Government. Upon its requirement, we also emancipated our slaves, and thus reduced ourselves from wealth to poverty. . . . Standing thus, stripped of arms, stripped of property, stripped even of credit and honor, —and with negroes at our doors to strike us down, at the command of your officers, —who can believe that the people of the South contemplate any thing else than submission to the United States? . . .

Continue over us, if you will do so, your own rule by the sword. Send down among us, honorable and upright men of your own people, of the race to which you and we belong: And ungracious, contrary to wise policy and the institutions of the country, and tyrannous as it will be; —no hand will be raised among us to resist by force their authority. But do not, we implore you, abdicate your own rule over us, by transferring us to the blighting, brutalizing and unnatural dominion of an alien and inferior race: A race which has never shown sufficient administrative capacity for the good government of even the tribes, into which it has always been broken up in its native seats; and which in all ages, has itself furnished slaves for all the other races of the earth.

January 1868—
[Signatures appended.]

How do these petitioners use the memory of the founding fathers? How does their view differ from that of Douglass?

Debate Over the Civil Rights Act of 1866

Motivated by the desire to extend the basic rights of citizenship to all Americans regardless of color, Republican Representative James F. Wilson managed the passage of the Civil Rights Act of 1866 in the House. Radical Republicans sought to guarantee to blacks equal rights that were often being curtailed in both the North and South. The proposed civil-rights act defined national citizenship and its subsequent rights. Selected from The Congressional Globe, *39th Congress, 1st Session (1 March 1866) 1115, 1117–18.*

Mr. Speaker, . . . [f]ew measures of graver import have ever commanded the attention of Congress. . . . Some of the questions presented by this bill are not entirely free from difficulties. . . .

The first section of the bill contains the following declaration concerning citizenship:

> That all persons born in the United States and not subject to any foreign Power, excluding Indians not taxed, are hereby declared to be citizens of the United States without distinction of color.

This provision, I maintain, is merely declaratory of what the law now is. This, I presume, would not be disputed if the language were qualified by the presence of the word "white." In the absence of this word, I am sure that my proposition will be disputed by every member of this House who believes that this Government is exclusively a "white man's Government." . . .

It is in vain we look into the Constitution of the United States for a definition of the term "citizen." It speaks of citizens, but in no express terms defines what it means by it. . . . [Some propose] that a negro is neither a citizen nor an alien, but a mere person with no definable national character. . . .

No nation, I believe, ever did recognize this absurd doctrine; and the only force it ever had in this country, was that given it by the Democratic party which used the negro as a football for partisan games. The growing importance of the colored race in the United States, now that the entire race is free, will soon cause even the Democratic party to abandon the indefensible position it occupies on this question. . . . By our law colored persons are citizens of the United States. . . .

We are reducing to statute form the spirit of the Constitution. We are establishing no new right, declaring no new principle. It is not the object of this bill to establish new rights, but to protect and enforce those which already belong to every citizen. I am aware, sir, that this doctrine is denied in many of the States; but this only proves the necessity for the enactment of the remedial and protective features of this bill. If the States would all observe the rights of our citizens, there would be no need of this bill. . . .

Mr. Speaker, if all our citizens were of one race and one color we would be relieved of most of the difficulties which surround us. This bill would be almost, if not entirely, unnecessary, and if the States, seeing that we have citizens of different races and colors, would but shut their eyes to these differences and legislate, so far at least as regards civil rights and immunities, as though all citizens were of one race and color, our troubles as a nation would be well-nigh over. But such is not the case, and we must do as best we can to protect our citizens, from the highest to the lowest, from the whitest to the blackest, in the enjoyment of the great fundamental rights which belong to all men.

Johnson's Veto Message

Worried over several issues, President Johnson vetoed the Civil Rights bill. This action inflamed the ongoing battle between Johnson and the Congressional leaders over who controlled the reconstruction process. Excerpted from The Congressional Globe, 39th Congress, 1st Session *(27 March 1866), 1679–81.*

To the Senate of the United States:

I regret that the bill which has passed both Houses of Congress . . . contains provisions which I cannot approve, consistently with my sense of duty to the whole people and my obligations to the Constitution of the United States. . . .

By the first section of the bill, all persons born in the United States, and not subject to any foreign Power, excluding Indians not taxed, are declared to be citizens of the United States. . . .

The right of federal citizenship thus to be conferred on the several excepted races before mentioned is now, for the first time, proposed to be given by law. If, as is claimed by many, all persons who are native-born already are, by virtue of the Constitution, citizens of the United States, the passage of the pending bill cannot be necessary to make them such. If, on the other hand, such persons are not citizens, as may be assumed from the proposed legislation to make them such, the grave question presents itself, whether when eleven of the thirty-six States are unrepresented in Congress at this time it is sound policy to make our entire colored population and all other excepted classes citizens of the United States? Four millions of them have just emerged from slavery into freedom. Can it be reasonably supposed that they possess the requisite qualifications to entitle them to all the privileges and immunities of citizens of the United States? . . .

Thus a perfect equality of the white and colored races is attempted to be fixed by federal law, in every State of the Union, over the vast field of State jurisdiction covered by these enumerated rights. . . . In the exercise of State policy over matters exclusively affecting the people of each State, it has frequently been thought expedient to discriminate between the two races. By the statutes of some of the States, northern as well as southern, it is enacted, for instance, that no white person shall intermarry with a negro or mulatto. . . .

Hitherto every subject embraced in the enumeration of rights contained in this bill has been considered as exclusively belonging to the States. They all relate to the internal policy and economy of the respective States. . . .

I do not propose to consider the policy of this bill. To me the details of the bill seem fraught with evil. The white race and the black race of the South have hitherto lived together under the relation of master and slave—capital owning labor. Now, suddenly, that relation is changed, and as to the ownership, capital and labor are divorced. They stand now each master of itself. In this new relation, one being necessary to the other, there will be a new adjustment, which both are deeply interested in making harmonious. Each has equal power in settling the terms, and if left to the laws that regulate capital and labor, it is confidently believed that they will satisfactorily work out the problem. Capital, it is true, has more intelligence; but labor is never so ignorant as not to understand its own interests, not to know its own value, and not to see that capital must pay that value. This bill frustrates this adjustment. It intervenes between capital and labor, and attempts to settle questions of political economy through the agency of numerous officials, whose interest it will be to foment discord between the two races. . . .

In all our history, in all our experience as a people living under Federal and State law, no such system as that contemplated by the details of this bill has ever before been proposed or adopted. They establish, for the security of the colored race, safeguards which go infinitely beyond any that the General Government has ever provided for the white race. In fact, the distinction of race and color is, by the bill, made to operate in favor of the colored and against the white race. They interfere with the municipal legislation of the States, with the relations existing exclusively between a State and its citizens, or between inhabitants of the same State—an absorption and assumption of power by the General Government which, if acquiesced in, must sap and destroy our federative system of limited powers, and break down the barriers which preserve the rights of the States. It is another step, or rather stride, towards centralization and the concentration of all legislative power in the national Government. The tendency of the bill must be to resuscitate the spirit of rebellion, and to arrest the progress of those influences which are more closely drawing around the States the bonds of union and peace. . . .

ANDREW JOHNSON.
Washington, D. C., *March* 27, 1866.

This argument centers on the idea of what a citizen is. How does this question manifest itself today?